THE NEW TESTAMENT WRITINGS:
History, Literature and Interpretation

THE
NEW TESTAMENT
WRITINGS:

History, Literature
and Interpretation

JAMES M. EFIRD

Fourth Printing

Acknowledgment is made for permission to quote from the following:

The Quest of the Historical Jesus by Albert Schweitzer, published in the United States by Macmillan Publishing Co., Inc., 1948. *Jesus* by Hugh Anderson, copyright © 1967 Prentice-Hall, Inc. *Jesus and the Word* by Rudolf Bultmann, trans. Louise P. Smith and Erminie Huntress, copyright © 1934 by Charles Scribner's Sons. *The Parables of the Kingdom* by C. H. Dodd, revised edition 1936 Nesbet & Co., Ltd., London; published in the U.S.A. by Charles Scribner's Sons.

The Scripture quotations in this publication are from the Revised Standard Version Bible, copyright 1946, 1952, and © 1971, 1973 by the Division of Christian Education, National Council of the Churches of Christ in the U.S.A. and used by permission.

Library of Congress Cataloging in Publication Data

Efird, James M
    The New Testament writings.

    Bibliography: p.
    1. Bible. N. T.–Introductions. I. Title.
BS2330.2.E33   225.6   79-87750
ISBN 0-8042-0246-X

For
VIVIAN
MICHELLE
TONY
With Much Love

Preface

The task of writing a New Testament introduction is not an easy undertaking. Not only is this true because of the vast amount of material to be examined, sifted, and selected, but also because no two teachers or scholars agree exactly on what to include or emphasize, or in the conclusions reached. It appears then that any attempt to satisfy those who already are knowledgeable in the field will find varying degrees of success, usually less rather than more!

Any attempt, therefore, to write an introduction to the study of the New Testament must first begin by deciding exactly what kind of audience one wishes to reach through the finished product. Many New Testament introductions now exist, some of which are very good, but as yet there does not seem to be one that *really* seeks to introduce the books of the New Testament, the historical background, and the critical methodologies, to persons who had never had any formal training in the often complex and confusing world of biblical scholarship. The book presented here is, therefore, designed with the uninitiated student in mind.

Another problem encountered after determining the audience to be addressed lies in deciding how to present the material. There are some introductions that attempt to view the New Testament against the basic historical development of the early church; there are some that use a book-by-book approach in an order of their own selection; others attempt to survey and present all (or nearly all) of the theories and complexities of New Testament scholarship; some of more recent vintage have begun to approach the New Testament as literature and to view the writings (or some of them) from that perspective; there are still others which appear to be little more than "scholars addressing other scholars." Each of these approaches has its own peculiar strengths and weaknesses.

There is, however, one dimension which is all too often missing in these presentations. Overlooked is the fact that these writings are documents of a religious faith, and to be understood and interpreted correctly the investigator (no matter what kind of approach is being utilized) must attempt to view these writings from the perspective of the people for whom the writings were designed. The literature of the New Testament originated in a *faith setting* and was directed to a *faith setting* for the purpose of ministering to the needs of that *faith setting!* Because of this the writings, then, are basically to be understood as documents of faith; and, because they were written to minister to the needs of that faith community, practical and pragmatic considerations were by necessity involved. As these people encountered particular problems and obstacles in the development and understanding of their own religious convictions, church leaders wrote to them in an effort to clarify (and sometimes to purify) the problems encountered by the newly founded religious community. Therefore, one of the most important elements in any study of the New Testament writings is that of wrestling with and understanding both the background and the content of the text of each document. This is, therefore, the basic emphasis of the approach pursued in this presentation of the New Testament literature. And this seems to be what is needed and wanted today by those who wish to study these books—an involvement and encounter with the text and content of the writings.

This book is designed with the uninitiated student in mind. The approach will attempt to involve the student with the content of the text as much as possible. Each of the other types of viewpoints and methodologies such as the historical approach, emphasis upon critical scholarship, analytical examination of the data, the investigation of various viewpoints and theories relating to the problems involved, the emphasis upon the books as literature, and others as well will be used in this study to support and illuminate the main theme, that of the meaning of the text itself. By such an approach the student will learn to appreciate how these other emphases and approaches such as the historical or the critical shed light on the meaning and interpretation of the text.

The basic format in the investigation of the New Testament literature will be to present certain historical and critical material as introductory to an examination of each book. There will then be presented a working outline of the book under consideration. This will be followed by a brief summary of the contents of the writing. At that point the student should read the text. This method will give some direction for the study of the text itself, for it is the opinion of this writer that students today want more involvement in the reading of and wrestling with the biblical writings *per se*. This book is designed to encourage just that.

The student should be aware at the very beginning that it is very important to examine and interpret the various New Testament books as wholistic entities by themselves. Far too often biblical material has been studied piecemeal, as if each passage or even each short sentence was of equal value and significance. For example, some persons believe that one can take a saying from one book, a story from another, a short passage from yet another and feel that the meaning of the New Testament is being comprehended. It is interesting that other literature is not studied in this manner. Who could lay claim to understanding Shakespeare, for example, by reading a line from *King Lear,* a soliloquy from *Hamlet,* a scene from *Macbeth,* and a few dialogues from *Romeo and Juliet?* When one approaches literature, one attempts to determine the kind of writing one is dealing with and then proceeds to read the work *in its entirety* following the development of the plot, the characters, etc. When this process is completed, a person can lay some claim to understanding the message of the book.

The same method should be used when one approaches the biblical books. Each one should be examined to determine the type of literary genre it is, what the plot is and how it is developed, what kinds of characters are involved, and how they fit into the overall pattern of the writing. When one concludes such a study, a great deal more depth and understanding can be gleaned from the book. To assist in understanding the content of the New Testament writings, this method of approach will be followed in this presentation when dealing with the individual books.

For those who wish to do more detailed work on the problems and issues of New Testament study, there will be at the conclusion of each chapter a rather lengthy and diverse annotated bibliography which will point the way for further study. The writer hopes that this work will stimulate the student to investigate more deeply and with additional emphases other facets of New Testament study, for this presentation simply opens the way for more serious investigation. The field is indeed large and complex but very fascinating and rewarding.

Finally, my personal debt to so many persons who have contributed and continue to contribute to my own understanding of the New Testament must be acknowledged. To my teachers and to my students I owe more than I can ever repay. I wish to thank them all. Also I am grateful to the fine people at the John Knox Press, Dr. Richard A. Ray, Director, Mr. R. Donald Hardy, Associate Editor, and to others for their encouragement and assistance in seeing this work to its completion. And last, but certainly not least, my heartfelt thanks to my family for their patience during the writing process; and a special thanks to my dear wife, Vivian, for typing the manuscript not once but twice! It is to them that this book is lovingly dedicated.

Durham, N. C.
November 1978   James M. Efird

Contents

CHAPTER I

Palestinian Background for the Ministry of Jesus

Historical Survey

One knows by experience that nothing really happens in a vacuum. The New Testament writings did not suddenly appear from nowhere but are the products of the faith of the early church. The church itself came into existence as a result of certain events which took place in Palestine basically in the early years of the current era, ca. 25–30 A.D. Those events revolved around the life and ministry of a man from Galilee, Jesus from Nazareth. As a result of what happened to Jesus and the subsequent development of the movement led by his followers, the "church" was formed. The New Testament documents then were produced by the church and basically revolved around this Person and the interpretation of this Person as the early church remembered him and interpreted his importance and significance. But to understand something about Jesus and the early New Testament church one must know something about the cultural and political history of Palestine during this particular era, for it was in this setting that the man appeared and the movement began.

The most appropriate point to begin a review of that period would be with the figure of Alexander the Great. The short-lived but highly successful career of this remarkable man (332–323 B.C.) marked the beginning of a new era in the history of the world, in general, and Palestine, in particular. Alexander made his lightning fast conquests of the nations he conquered by military might and skillful military tactics. He was wise enough, however, to know that an empire based on military might alone would not long hold together. He dreamed of a unified world empire based upon a single culture, basically Greek, but that culture would be the product of a blending of the Greek culture with the cultures of the "conquered" peoples. This resultant new blended culture usually is referred to as "Hellenistic."

After his untimely death in 323 B.C., Alexander's generals fought among themselves over the empire he had accumulated. These wars are known as the Wars of the "Diadochi" (i.e., successors). When the smoke of those battles had cleared ca. 301 B.C., the empire had been divided into four divisions. Two of them were concerned with the area of Palestine: Ptolemy had gained control of Egypt and southern Palestine; Seleucus held Babylonia and Syria (cf. the map on p. 3). The Jewish people, therefore, at this time were under the control of the Ptolemies of Egypt. The Ptolemies were very lenient in their policy of "Hellenization," i.e., the enforcement of Greek culture and thought upon the peoples over whom they ruled. Thus under their rule the Jewish people were left alone as far as customs and religion were concerned.

The Ptolemies and the Seleucids, however, continued to fight sporadically over who would control southern Palestine. This situation continued until 198 B.C. when the Egyptians were defeated at Banias (or Panium) by Seleucus III. At this point all of Palestine basically passed under the rule of the Seleucids. Their policy had been and continued to be to enforce the process of Hellenization where possible and to their advantage.

This turn of events meant that the Jewish people became vassals of the Seleucid Kingdom. Off the beaten track, the Jewish community was suffering hard times. Politically weak, culturally different, and economically poor, these people had experienced some very difficult years. They were so hard pressed, in fact, that the Egyptians did not even collect taxes from them every year; and when the Seleucids took over they decreed that for three years the area of Judea would not have to pay any taxes!

In spite of this gesture of good will, trouble was almost inevitable, however, for the Jewish people were not about to accept Greek culture easily. And the Seleucids were determined to push that process

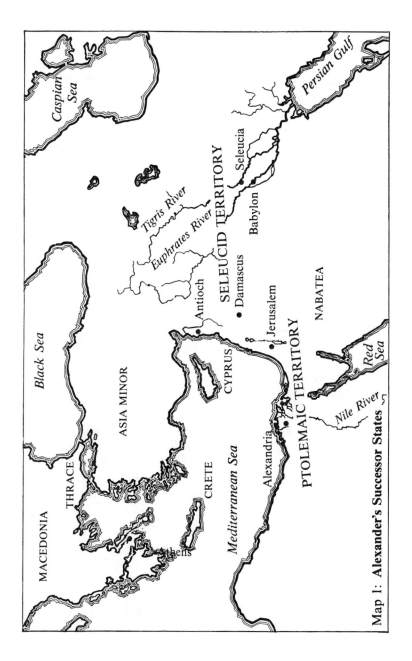

Map 1: Alexander's Successor States

even though the Egyptians had not. The crucial events began in 175 B.C. when Antiochus IV, called Epiphanes ("God Manifest"), sold the position of the High Priest in Jerusalem to the brother of the current office holder, Onias III. The High Priest under the arrangement and organization current then not only exercised religious authority but also political authority as well. Therefore, when Joshua (Onias' brother) was awarded the office of High Priest, Antiochus felt that the process of Hellenization would be speeded up (in addition to lining his pockets further!).

This chain of events infuriated the Jews, but little came of the situation immediately. After all, Joshua was a member of the high priestly family. Upon taking office Joshua changed his name to Jason (the Greek equivalent of the Aramaic Joshua) and supported the policy of Hellenization among the Jewish people. Greek culture was introduced, gymnasiums were built (an abomination to the Jews since the Greek games were performed in the nude), Greek clothing was worn, and young men even submitted to painful operations to conceal the mark of circumcision. There was, of course, a great deal of opposition both in leadership circles and among the people to these policies and events.

In 171 B.C. the situation became much worse when another person, named Menelaus (or Menahem), outbid Jason for the office of High Priest and was awarded the position by Antiochus. This infuriated the Jews. Jason had been, if not the rightful heir to the High Priesthood, a member of the priestly family, but Menelaus was not. And he pushed harder the policy of Hellenization, even allowing Antiochus to strip the gold from the facade of the Temple. Many events were occurring, far too numerous to mention here, but opposition to him and his policies continued to mount until it became obvious to Antiochus that the reason for Jewish opposition lay in their religious faith and convictions. Therefore the simplest solution to the problem seemed to be to cut off the opposition at its source; so in 168/167 B.C. an edict was issued proscribing Judaism. It became a capital offense to be in possession of a copy of the Torah or even to have one's child circumcised, or to keep the Sabbath. A statue of Zeus was placed in the Temple; and to add insult to injury a pig was sacrificed on the altar of Yahweh, the God of Israel. The situation was ripe for an explosion.

The explosion came when a Syrian officer attempting to enforce the edict gathered a group of Jews at Modin, a place northwest of Jerusalem, and prepared them to sacrifice to Zeus. When one Jewish person stepped forward to do this, an old priest named Mattathias killed the apostate Jew and the Syrian officer. Along with his sons Mattathias fled to the hills to lead a group of guerrilla fighters against the Syrians. During this crisis, as with any nation, some were more zealous than others in feeling the necessity to fight. There was a group of persons known as the *Hasidim* or "pious ones" who believed in and wanted religious freedom. Being religious zealots and not really politically active, they refused to enter wholeheartedly into the fracas until about 1,000 of them were slaughtered by the Syrians when they refused to fight or even to defend themselves on the Sabbath. This tended to unify the effort and in 165/164 Judas Maccabaeus, Mattathias' son, won a victory whereby the proscription against Judaism was lifted. The temple was rededicated in December 165/164 and this event is still observed in Judaism even today (the feast of Hanukkah).

At this point the Hasidim had won their victory; but the sons of Mattathias continued the fight for political freedom and power. In 141 Simon, the last remaining son, won political freedom and the succession of "priest-kings" began in Judea. This particular dynasty lasted for over one hundred years and was known as the Hasmonean line, but it is interesting to note that the first one to call himself "king" was Aristobulus I (105–104).

Much interesting and intriguing history has to be omitted because of space, but suffice it to say here that a great deal was going on in this period. One interesting aspect is that a division existed between the Pharisees (possibly the successors of the Hasidim) and the Hasmonean "priest-kings" until the first century B.C. when "peace" finally was made between the two groups.

Our historical survey is joined again with John Hyrcanus II who was appointed High Priest after the death of Alexander Jannaeus in 76 B.C. Alexander's widow, Alexandra, really held the power but because she was a woman could not be high priest. Thus she ruled through the weak Hyrcanus II. Another of her sons, Aristobulus II, was much more able and ambitious than his brother, however, and when Alexandra died in 67 B.C. he deposed Hyrcanus II. At this juncture Antipater, who was military governor of Idumea (old Edom), became alarmed because of the ability and ambition of Aristobulus. He then championed the cause of Hyrcanus and persuaded the Nabateans (a large Arab nation east of the Jordan) to join in the struggle to return Hyrcanus to office.

About this time Rome was expanding its influence into this area of the world. The Romans had been waging wars with Mithradates of Pontus (in Asia Minor) for some time, but in 63 B.C. the Roman armies under the command of Pompey finally completed the task of defeating these enemies. Therefore Rome was in the area when the conflict between Hyrcanus and Aristobulus was being waged. Pompey then proceeded to capture the area for Rome. He drove out the Nabateans, took Aristobulus to Rome, and placed Hyrcanus II in office, but with the title of ethnarch (ruler of a people). For all practical purposes Jewish independence had ended. The real power in this area was Antipater who ruled as a vassal king for Rome.

Most students are aware of the internal problems which then affected the Roman government and of the civil wars which did not conclude until Augustus had won power and became the first Roman Emperor. All of these occurrences were bound to affect the situation in Palestine. The situation there, however, continued about as it was as far as the Jews were concerned until 40 B.C., when Antigonus (son of Aristobulus II) overthrew Hyrcanus II and allied himself with the Parthians (the successors of the old Persian Empire) when they invaded the area. Hyrcanus was mutilated (his ears were cut off or even perhaps chewed or bitten off!) so that he could never be high priest again. The fighting continued until 37 B.C., at which time Rome helped to restore order to the area. Herod, Antipater's son, consolidated his hold on the territory and was appointed king by the Romans. He exercised authority here until his death in 4 B.C.

Herod's reign has been praised by some and damned by others. Ruthless and cruel he indeed was, as one can immediately learn by reading of the events which occurred during his reign. But it must

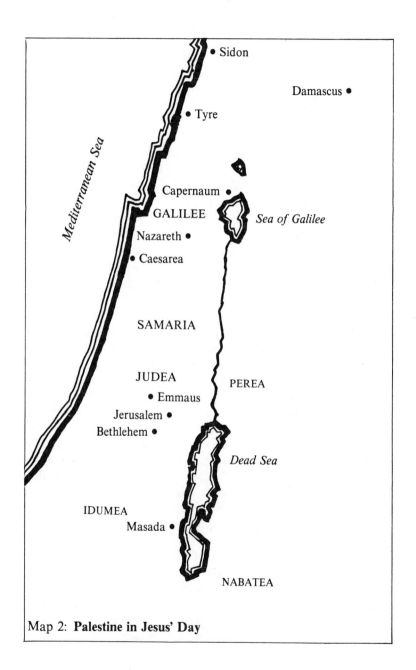

Map 2: **Palestine in Jesus' Day**

also be pointed out that his political and economic contribution to the area was immense. One of his major contributions was the construction of the temple in Jerusalem. This project was begun in 20/19 B.C. and was not completed until ca. 62–64 A.D. Even the rabbis commented upon the beauty of this structure being built by the hated Herod.

Upon the death of Herod the Great the land, at his request in his will, was divided among his three sons. Herod Antipas was to govern Galilee and Perea; Philip was to govern Trachonitis, Batanea, and Gaulanitis; Achelaus was to govern Judea and Samaria with the title of king. Rome approved this arrangement with the exception of Archelaus' title, which was changed to ethnarch. Archelaus, however, proved to be so unpopular that a delegation from Judea went to Rome to protest his rule. In 6 A.D. he was deposed and the area became a Roman province ruled by a Roman governor called a procurator.

The situation continued to be "explosive" because the relationship between the Romans and the Jews was exceedingly tenuous. It must be understood that from the Roman viewpoint it was essential that peace and tranquility prevail. Rome felt it had to keep order—after all, this was the frontier of its empire. Such a situation of constant unrest and turmoil could not be tolerated. The Jews, however, looked upon the Romans as intruders, not simply upon their land but upon the land of their God. They looked forward, therefore, to the time when God would vindicate himself and his people. Many hopes of varying degrees and intensity were present among the people. Some extremists even advocated open war with Rome with the conviction that in such an event God himself would intervene directly on their behalf. Into such a setting Jesus came and was crucified ultimately as a potential (or real?) threat to the peace of the area.

To complete the picture, a word needs to be added about the continuing relationship between Rome and the Jews. In 66 A.D. open war broke out between the two which was concluded in 70 A.D. with the fall of Jerusalem and the destruction of the temple there. (This is an important point in attempting to date certain books of the New Testament.) Further, a final confrontation came in the area in 132

A.D. when the Roman emperor, Hadrian, ordered that no physical mutilation would be allowed. This was not aimed at the Jewish practice of circumcision but definitely affected and included it. Add to this the plan to put a pagan temple on the site of the old temple of Yahweh and the situation was ripe for another confrontation. Thus another rebellion broke out led by Simon bar Kosibah (also called bar Cocheba). The Jews lost (naturally) and were banned from entering the city except for one day a year to weep at the site of the temple (the famous "wailing wall" of Jerusalem).

Literary Survey

To assist one in understanding the religious developments of the time, there is an abundance of literature which was written during this period and much of which is still available to aid in this study. Perhaps these documents are not exactly the kind one would like as scientific researchers, but they do give significant insights into the period. There are numerous ways to present this mass of literature, but the basic approach here will be to group the material by basic type rather than by chronology or theology since the dating and even the interpretation of many are highly speculative matters.

It should be noted, however, that these works about to be cited are not by any means a complete listing of the intertestamental literature. Apart from the Rabbinic literature and the writings found at the Dead Sea, the works which we know about are basically divided into two groupings, the Apocrypha and the Pseudepigrapha. *Apocrypha* is a technical term referring to those books found in the Greek version of the Old Testament but *not* included in the Jewish canon. The term *Pseudepigrapha* usually includes those works not included in the Apocrypha but which were nonetheless popular in various parts of the Eastern world. (The best place to study these works is still R. H. Charles, *The Apocrypha and Pseudepigrapha of the Old Testament,* 2 vols.)

There was a large body of various types of literature which were popular and important during the years ca. 200 B.C.–100 A.D. The diversity of the materials and their viewpoints assist one in the attempt to understand the religious setting of that time.

Rabbinic Literature

One of the basic groups is that material known as the *Rabbinic literature*. This literature to a certain degree reflects the interpretation of the Jewish Torah prevalent during the period of history with which we are dealing. This material was not collected and written down until much later (ca. 200–500 A.D.), but many scholars believe that it can be a genuine guide to the teaching of the Rabbis in the time of Jesus and the early church and that it reflects the type of interpretative methodology in use at the time. This material was later collected and codified. The following units of material are most frequently cited and studied.

(1) *The Mishnah:* This collection contains oral exposition and interpretation of the Torah. The material contained here was probably collected and written down ca. 200 A.D. by Rabbi Judah ha-Nasi. It is arranged topically in six orders with 63 tractates. This material tries to make clear the intended meaning of the scriptural texts. For example, what exactly is "work" and what is included in "keeping the Sabbath holy"?

(2) *The Gemara:* If the Torah needed exposition and interpretation, so did the Mishnah. Thus there arose a group of teachings called the Gemara which was a commentary on the Mishnah. In ca. 500 A.D. the Gemara and the Mishnah were collected together; this collection is called the *Talmud,* the "learning" of the Jewish people.

To illustrate the interpretative methodology of the Rabbinic thinkers and to acquaint oneself with the kinds of issues which were at that point in history considered important, here are some excerpts from a portion of the Talmud. These indicate something about the plethora of minute laws applicable to keeping the Sabbath holy, and something about the Jewish attitude toward the Gentiles as well.

In this section the general subject is what constitutes "work" on the Sabbath. But what about specific situations one often faces where necessity and need are involved? For example, one was not allowed to carry an item on the Sabbath for more than four cubits. What happens, however, when one is caught out as the Sabbath begins (Jewish days were counted from 6 P.M. to 6 P.M.) and has one's money pouch along? The person could continue home, but what about the money pouch? Here is what one section of the Talmud has to say about that situation.

MISHNAH 153a: If darkness falls upon a person on a road, he entrusts his purse to a Gentile; but if there is no Gentile with him, he places it on the ass. When he reaches the outermost courtyard he removes the objects which may be handled on the Sabbath, whilst as for those which may not be handled on the Sabbath, he unties the cords and the sacks fall off automatically.

GEMARA: Why did the Rabbis permit him to entrust his purse to a Gentile?—The Rabbis knew for certain that no man will restrain himself where his money is concerned; if you do not permit it to him, he will come to carry it four cubits in public ground.

Raba said: *His* purse only, but not something found. . . .

IF THERE IS NO GENTILE WITH HIM, etc. The reason is that there is no Gentile with him, but if there is a Gentile with him he must give it to him: what is the reason?—As for an ass, you are under an obligation that it should rest; but as for a Gentile, you are under no obligation [to ensure] that he should rest. . . .

What if neither a Gentile, an ass, a deaf-mute, an imbecile nor a minor is there?—R. Isaac said: There was yet another [expedient], but the Sages did not wish to reveal it. What was the other [expedient]?—One may carry it in stretches of less than four cubits at a time. . . . (Shabbath 153a, 153b. *The Babylonian Talmud: Seder Mo'ed,* Shabbath II. Trans. and edited by I. Epstein. London: The Soncino Press, 1938. Pp. 783–84.)

(3) *Midrash:* The Midrash is a verse by verse commentary on the books of the Torah. To illustrate the Midrash here is a portion of the commentary on the story of Jacob and his dream of the "ladder" at Beth-el (Genesis 28:10–17).

What precedes this text? *And, behold, the angels of God ascending and descending on it.* R. Abbahu said: It may be compared to an infant prince sleeping in his cot on whom flies were settling; when his nurse came she bent over and suckled him, and they flew away. Similarly, at first, *'And, behold the angels of God ascending and descending on it';* but when the Holy One, blessed be He, revealed Himself to him, they fled from him. This is the meaning of AND, BEHOLD, THE LORD STOOD BY HIM.

AND, BEHOLD, THE LORD STOOD 'ALAW ['ALAW is the Hebrew word]. R. Hiyya and R. Hannai disagree. One maintains that 'ALAW means on the ladder; while the other says that 'ALAW means on [or, over] Jacob. The view that 'ALAW means on the ladder presents no difficulty; on the view that it refers to Jacob, it means that He stood [protectingly] over him. R. Johanan said: The wicked stand over their gods, as it says, *And Pharaoh dreamed and, behold, he stood over the river* (Gen. XLI, 1); but the God of the righteous stands over them, as it says, AND, BEHOLD, THE LORD STOOD OVER HIM, etc. R. Simeon b. Lakish said: The Patriarchs are the Chariot [of God], as it says, *And God went up from upon Abraham . . . ; And God went up from upon him . . . ; And God went up from upon him . . . ;* AND, BEHOLD, THE LORD STOOD UPON HIM. *(Midrash Rabbah: Genesis.* Translated by H. Freedman. London: The Soncino Press, 1939. II, 630–631. [LXIX–3].)

(4) *Septuagint:* Perhaps it is unwise to catalog the Septuagint along with the other Rabbinic writings, for it is not technically a "writing." It is the Greek translation of the Hebrew Scriptures (i.e., the Old Testament), a process which probably began in Alexandria in Egypt in the third or second century B.C. The first section to be translated was the Torah. This version of the Old Testament was used by the Jews of the Graeco-Roman world and by some New Testament writers. The Septuagint is usually designated LXX since tradition has it that seventy (or seventy-two) persons collaborated in the translation project.

"Historical"

A second type of literature is that usually known as "historical." This is not history writing in the modern twentieth century style or method, but is as close to history as the people of the ancient world usually got (which is not to depreciate their contribution or genius at all). What we know of the period already recounted comes basically from the two works, I Maccabees and II Maccabees. These are written from a particular bias but are valuable in aiding our understanding of the political and religious climate of the area.

Further, the great Jewish historian, Josephus, aids in understanding the period especially around the time of Jesus and through the time of the destruction of the temple in 70 A.D. His works include *The Antiquities of the Jews* and *The Jewish War*. Many of his countrymen considered him a traitor because he was a "pro-Roman sympathizer." He felt that opposition to Rome was folly and would simply bring more harm to the people than good. Through these "apologetic" writings he attempted to create in the Roman world an appreciation for the Jewish people.

"Religious Fiction"

A third category, and probably the most interesting, we can label "religious fiction" or, as some others call it, "Historico-Romantic" writing. These literary creations are to a greater or lesser degree based on "history" but the manner of their presentation is such that the history is subordinated to the purpose of the story and many times obscured altogether. These are delightful to read. They usually point out the virtues of Jewish people and their laws, the rewards for keeping the faith pure, and the general superiority of the Jewish faith. Included in this category are the Books of Judith, Tobit, III Maccabees and the Letter of Aristeas (an account of how the Septuagint came into being).

Poetry

Poetry is almost always to be found among the writings of any people and no less the Jewish people of this period. There are a number of Psalms contained within the Psalter of the Old Testament which many scholars feel come from the Maccabaean period (cf. 44, 74, 79, 83, and perhaps 110 and 149). A collection apart from the Old Testament Psalter is found in a work called the Psalms of Solomon. Of these Psalm 17 is the most important because it speaks about a "Messiah" in a manner quite reminiscent of Isaiah 9 and 11.

Apocalyptic

One of the most important categories, if not *the* most important category, is that body of literature known as "apocalyptic." This type of literature has many peculiar characteristics. The style of writing developed basically from Persian influence and was adopted by the Jews into their own situation. It is highly symbolic and figurative with sometimes weird images. This literature usually flourished in a time of persecution, urging faithfulness on the part of those being persecuted, and was usually written in the name of some ancient worthy. Religiously speaking it was characterized by theological dualism; the apocalyptic writers believed that there was being waged a gigantic life and death struggle between the forces of good and evil on a cosmic scale. This battle manifested itself in the world of human affairs and human history. The war must be fought and many will be made to suffer, but those who are to be saved have already been determined as well as the final outcome of the struggle. Good would eventually triumph and the forces of the present evil age would be overthrown. History was thus divided into two periods, a present evil age which becomes progressively worse until God or his agent intervenes and establishes the coming good age, variously called the Messianic Age or the Kingdom of God. It is the time when the persecution has been removed.

Because of its nature, this literature enjoyed wide popularity and distribution especially among the "common people." Their hopes were essentially apocalyptic hopes—the idea of God's dramatic and direct intervention with the cataclysmic destruction of the forces of evil and its manifestations in their lives and the life of their nation.

The more important of these works are: (1) I Enoch, which is probably a collection of apocalyptic writings. This work is important because in it a "Son of Man," perhaps a pre-existent being, is an important character. (2) II Baruch and IV Ezra (or II Esdras)—these works were written to describe the reasons for the fall of Jerusalem in 70 A.D.

It must be noted that many works which were not apocalyptic *per se* were influenced by apocalyptic motifs and ideas. Therefore, it is not too much to say that the theological and religious teaching of this period was permeated by apocalypticism.

Wisdom Literature

As the student of the Old Testament knows, wisdom literature developed in Judaism in the post-exilic period and continued to exert influence on the thinking of the times under consideration here. One recalls that there was a practical kind of wisdom (exemplified in the Book of Proverbs) and a speculative type (illustrated by the Books of Job and Ecclesiastes). This literature deals with life and its meaning. One of the most significant aspects of it was the development of the idea of "Wisdom" as a kind of separate entity utilized by God in the creative and sustaining aspects of one's existence.

In the inter-testamental period three examples stand out most clearly: (1) the Wisdom of Ben Sirach (or Ecclesiasticus), (2) the Wisdom of Solomon, and (3) IV Maccabees. There are some scholars who think that the work known as the Testaments of the Twelve Patriarchs is basically a wisdom writing while others list this work under apocalyptic.

During this period of time there were "schools" led by wise men who dispensed wisdom. Some of this type were found in the famous Rabbinic schools of the period led by two of the most famous rabbis, Hillel and Shammai. These wise people usually taught by means of parables, riddles, short pithy sayings, proverbs, stories and the like. In many respects Jesus and his disciples appear to have constituted something like one of these wisdom "schools."

Philo

One final writer needs to be mentioned here because of his genius and his supposed influence on parts of the New Testament, especially certain interpretations of the Old Testament. Philo, a Jew of Alexandria, attempted to interpret the Jewish Scriptures with reference to Greek philosophy by the "allegorical" method, that is, by finding the "hidden" meaning beneath the words of the text itself. He found by this method that the great teachings of the Greeks had been anticipated by Moses. It has even been suggested that Philo attempted to make Judaism into a Greek mystery religion!

Dead Sea Scrolls

Our survey would not be complete if mention were not made of the finds at Qumran popularly known as the Dead Sea Scrolls. The community there which produced these documents consisted of a group of people separated from the "ordinary" world with rules and regulations for orderly conduct within their society. One can find these rules in the famous *Manual of Discipline*. These people were hoping for God's intervention to establish truth and justice, and they evidently looked for the Messiah to arise from their own ranks. Their basic theology, naturally, was based on the Old Testament but their thought exhibited Pharisaic theology tempered by a healthy dose of apocalyptic ideas.

Religious Development Between the Testaments

Anyone who has studied the books of the Old Testament and then turns to those of the New Testament is shocked to find that much development, religiously speaking, had occurred during the years following the last book of the one, Daniel ca. 165 B.C., and the first book of the other, 1 Thessalonians ca. 50 A.D. A person should read and study the books of the Apocrypha and Pseudepigrapha (including the Dead Sea literature) in order to study this development of religious thinking and ideas during the so-called intertestamental period—and in addition the Jewish literature described above.

It would take a good sized volume to do justice to this topic (and space does not allow that here), but an attempt will be made to point out the areas where the most significant changes took place in religious ideology in those years. By learning about these developments the differences will not seem so abrupt or sudden.

The first area of development was in the thinking about God. In the writings of the Old Testament God dealt directly with his chosen people, speaking to them, chastising them, rewarding them, protecting them, and the like. Yahweh, the God of Israel, was always, however, viewed as an awesome Being. He was to be feared (in the best sense of that word), and his name was not to be used lightly. As the Old Testament understanding of Yahweh grew ever larger, the idea began to develop that Yahweh was too pure, powerful, and exalted to deal with the human race directly.

Therefore, with the development of the Wisdom movement and Apocalyptic movement, it was thought that God dealt with the created order through intermediaries. The Wisdom thinkers developed the idea that wisdom was a "person" and was used as the agent in God's creative activity. Under the influence of the apocalyptic ideology there developed the concept of angels and demons; therefore God communicated with people through angels and sometimes rewarded or punished people by the same agents.

God basically was viewed as removed from the world, far-off, transcendent. This can be seen in some ways in which the rabbis talked about God. Often, when they would mention God, they would add doxologies or brief expressions such as "The Holy One, Blessed be He!" They did not like to use the name of God at all; this reverence for the name, Yahweh, began in the Old Testament period but developed even further by this time. Often rather than refer to God, the people would use the word "Power" to designate him. Or they would use the term "heaven" metonymously to mean God, since God was in "heaven." (This phenomenon is reflected in the Gospel of Matthew which was written in a Jewish environment. The term "Kingdom of God" was used by Mark and Luke, but Matthew used the term "Kingdom of Heaven." The meaning is, of course, the same, but Matthew's terminology reflects the culture of the time and area.)

A second area of considerable development is that related to the ideas about the afterlife. Throughout the Old Testament the basic concept was that of Sheol, the place of the dead where everyone went upon physical death. It was not a place of reward or punishment, only the weakest kind of existence one could imagine. There is really only one real deviation from this idea in the Old Testament writings, that being in the book of Daniel (cf. Daniel 12:1-2). In that apocalyptic work there is a doctrine of resurrection, but it is not a general resurrection only a resurrection of some to life in a new age and some to shame and punishment in a new age. The meaning there seems to be that those who were not rewarded or punished properly in the period of the persecution during the time of Antiochus IV would be raised to receive their just deserts. After the scales had been balanced, the persons would return to Sheol.

During the intertestamental period much thinking was being done in this area dealing with the afterlife, so much so that there were numerous ideas which were current. Some people still held to the concept of Sheol. Others believed in a life-after-death with rewards and punishments. Exactly how one received these good or bad deserts or when was a matter of considerable diversity of opinion. Some argued that the rewards and punishments began immediately upon death; others held that there was an intermediate state where all remained until the final judgment at the conclusion of all history; still others believed that there would be a resurrection at the appointed moment when the old body would be rejoined with the spirit; others believed that there would be a new physical body and still others a body but not a material body. Some even believed in "soul" sleep, and others were believers in the Greek idea of immortality. No one set of ideas really held the day, but most people seem to have believed in some form of resurrection. Whether it was physical or spiritual, future or present, to be accomplished in this historical continuum or in a supra-historical sphere—none of these was really *the* theory. Each theory had its own advocates and in some instances the ideas were rearranged in such ways as to present "new" hypotheses.

A third area in which speculation occurred centered in the ideas connected with the origin of sin. Several ideas recurred frequently: the idea of sin originating with Eve; the idea that corporately all human beings fell with Adam; the idea that sin was intrinsic to human beings as human beings; the concept that sin was an intruder brought in by evil forces from without; and others. The Rabbis developed a concept of two forces within each human being that fought to control the person's life. This was the "yetzer" idea, the idea of two "inclinations." One was the inclination toward good, the *yetzer ha-tob;* the other was the inclination toward evil, the *yetzer ha-ra'.*

Another religious motif that grew during the period under consideration was the movement which continually exalted the Law, the *Torah.* In some circles the Law had become so important, and the keeping of the Law so important, that all else was secondary—even God. The Law was God's greatest gift to the human race; it had to be preserved, protected, and upheld. As can be readily surmised this emphasis came primarily from the Rabbinic schools. There were supposedly over 600 precepts of the Law which were to be kept by the people. And one stream of interpretation held that if the people of Israel could keep the precepts of the Law on one day or on one Sabbath, the Kingdom of God would have to come!

One further development needs to be mentioned. In connection with apocalyptic literature and its Persian origins there developed a very structured hierarchy of angels and demons. Out of this latter there emerged a leader for the forces of evil at the cosmic level. In several of the writings this figure was called by various names, Beelzebul, the devil, but more usually Satan. Satan who was the adversary or accuser of the human race in Job, Zechariah, and Chronicles had now become the full-fledged leader of the enemies of God against the people of God.

Another development which received impetus from this thinking was that of demon possession. In the Old Testament there was little, if any, of this type of phenomenon. In the New Testament, however, especially in the Synoptic gospels, there are abundant cases of demon possession, so many that exorcisms are the most common type of Jesus' mighty works.

Another area of thought was related to the ideas concerning how God was going to deliver his people. Some argued for a Messiah who would be the instrument of God's power to exalt his people and destroy his enemies. What kind of Messiah this would be was not agreed upon. Several theories were held: the old Davidic type of political leader; a quasi-divine being who would come to earth at the proper time; a priestly Messiah; or even a prophetic Messiah. There were those who believed that God would intervene directly without any intermediary and would establish his Kingdom— whether here or elsewhere was not agreed upon.

There were other types of development also, but these are the most important areas to be considered. It is clearly the case that religious thinking at the time of Jesus was definitely in a state of almost constant change.

Jewish Structure and Organization

The last area which reflects the background of the time leads to a consideration of Jewish structure and organization during the period under study. It may be helpful to consider first of all what are usually referred to as "parties" in the Judaism of that time. One should not leap to the conclusion that these were highly organized, closely knit factions, but rather should be considered as loosely connected groups of persons who generally held similar beliefs.

Pharisees

The most influential were the Pharisees. This group probably evolved from the old Hasidim of the Maccabaean era. They did not attempt to dabble in politics any more than was absolutely necessary and were more concerned about religious matters, especially interpreting the Law. Certain beliefs were attributed to them. Basically, they held that all things were directed by Providence, but it was not held that this in any way infringed on the freedom and responsibility of people in relationship to their own actions. They held the belief in a life after death, specifically the hope of a resurrection to reward or punishment. Belief in angels and demons even to the point of hierarchies of good and evil spirits also characterized their theology. They upheld the authority of the Torah but also accepted the oral tradition relating to the interpretation of the Torah. This group was not primarily drawn from the priestly class and thus had an element of the "laity" about it.

Sadducees

A second group was the Sadducees. This group consisted of the priestly and relatively "powerful" who were very active in political affairs. Basically their beliefs centered in the Torah (apart from the oral tradition) and the temple. They rejected the idea of the resurrection, any doctrine of the Messiah, and the belief in angels and demons. They felt that human beings have the freedom to choose to do good or to do evil and that each is responsible for these decisions. Naturally enought they were connected with the temple cultus, and it is not surprising that after 70 A.D. they disappeared from Jewish history.

Essenes

A third group is known as Essenes. Believing that the world and society was hopelessly corrupt, these people separated themselves into communities apart from the ordinary life of the time. Some were completely separatists while others lived apart but did "mission" work among the people of the world. These communities had rules and regulations to govern their people. It is not definitely known whether the Qumran community was Essene or not, but that group does seem to fit the general pattern for this category.

Zealots

Josephus calls the next group the "Fourth Philosophy." Here were persons spurred on by zeal for Jewish purity, independence, and power which had characterized the Maccabaean era. These people were usually saturated with apocalyptic hopes and advocated open war with Rome believing that by so doing the Lord would be "forced" to intervene on their behalf.

One group in this "party" was known as the *Sicarii.* These were the "assassins" whose practice it was to stab Romans or Roman sympathizers in the marketplace or otherwise and melt back into the crowd. The word comes from the Latin for "dagger" and may be the ancient equivalent to the "switchblade" set of today.

People of the Land

A fifth segment of the population is often discussed by New Testament scholars, the *amme ha-arets* or "people of the land." These constituted the vast majority of the Jewish community and probably were simply the ordinary people who worked hard to survive. They did not know the Torah and all the minute details concerning its practice but were probably sincere in their own way. It was primarily among this group that Jesus worked and preached. These people above all others were most likely to be thoroughly saturated with extreme apocalyptic hopes and expectations.

Characteristic Institutions

Three great institutions characterized Judaism at this time. These were the Temple, the Sanhedrin, and the Synagogue. Since the time of Josiah's reform in 621 B.C. "true" worship could not be carried out except in the Jersulem Temple. Daily sacrifices were offered there as well as special services on the occasion of the great feasts. By this period of history many Jews were scattered throughout the known world of that time but were expected to return to Jerusalem for at least one of the special feasts each year if possible. Further, each person was expected to pay a special "temple tax" of $\frac{1}{2}$ shekel per year for contributions toward the expenses of the operation of the Temple.

The Sanhedrin was the governing body of the Jews which exercised both legislative and judicial power. It consisted of seventy members and was presided over by the High Priest (making seventy-one in all). This body ruled, of course, with the approval of Rome, and many believe that it did *not* have the power to pronounce the death sentence. The Sanhedrin in Jerusalem was the most important and powerful but there were others as well.

The synagogue probably characterized the Jewish people as much as any other single institution. Services were held in the synagogue, which *may* have originated during the exile, on Sabbaths and weekdays as well. The basic service involved the reading and interpretation of the Torah. There were perhaps "schools" which were connected directly and indirectly with the synagogue which enabled young Jewish male children to learn how to read and write; adult education naturally centered in the synagogue also. The synagogue is important because of two factors: (1) it was the base for proclamation of the Christian gospel when Paul (or others) went into a new city or population center; and (2) its service became the pattern for the service of the early Christian worship.

Summary

The Jewish people when Jesus came onto the scene entertained all kinds of hopes and dreams for a better time. To say that there was *one* consistent idea as to what form and manner the hope might take would be totally erroneous. Some thought that the kingdom would be basically political and would be given to Israel as "Queen of the Nations." Others looked for a great cataclysmic event which would destroy the forces of evil and inaugurate a "supra-historical" kingdom perhaps on this earth, perhaps not.

These things, whatever may be the mode of their happening, would be accomplished by God's power and intervention. But again there was no consistent picture of how this would take place. God may intervene directly or indirectly through his agent. The idea of God's agent was closely related to the belief in a Messiah. Some looked for a prophetic Messiah; others for a political Messiah from the line of David; others for a Messianic priest (perhaps from the Hasmoneans or at least from the tribe of Levi); while still others looked for a kind of supernatural Messiah, a spiritual type of pre-existent being.

One can see the complexity of the situation in the period under consideration. No single clear-cut picture emerges from the material, and the more discoveries which are made only reaffirm how complex the times were. About all that can be said with certainty is that the people were looking forward to some kind of deliverance and that *soon.*

Suggestions for Further Study

The period just described very briefly is rich and full of interesting and intriguing history and religious development. The sources cited here will give some direction to the student who is interested in pursuing certain aspects of that era.

History

F. F. Bruce. *Israel and the Nations: From the Exodus to the Fall of the Second Temple.* Grand Rapids, Mich.: Wm. B. Eerdmans Publishing Co., 1963. Pp. 120–225.

M. S. Enslin. *Christian Beginnings.* New York: Harper & Row, 1938. Published now in two papercover editions. Cf. especially volume I.

W. Forster. *From the Exile to Christ: A Historical Introduction to Palestinian Judaism.* Translated by Gordon E. Harris. Philadelphia: Fortress Press, 1964.

S. H. Perowne. *The Life and Times of Herod the Great.* London: Hodder and Stoughton, 1956.

———. *The Later Herods: The Political Background of the New Testament.* London: Hodder and Stoughton, 1958.

R. H. Pfeiffer. *History of New Testament Times With an Introduction to the Apocrypha.* New York; Harper & Bros., 1949.

B. Reicke. *The New Testament Era: The World of the Bible From 400 B.C. to 100 A.D.* Translated by David E. Green. Philadelphia: Fortress Press, 1968.

D. M. Rhoads. *Israel in Revolution 6–74 CE: A Political History Based on the Writings of Josephus.* Philadelphia: Fortress Press, 1976.

D. S. Russell. *The Jews From Alexander to Herod.* London: Oxford University Press, 1967.

E. Stauffer. *Christ and the Caesars: Historical Sketches.* Translated by K. and R. Gregor Smith. London: SCM Press, 1955.

The Jewish and Intertestamental Background
C. K. Barrett, editor. *The New Testament Background: Selected Documents.* London: SPCK, 1956.

S. W. Baron and J. C. Blau, editors. *Judaism: Postbiblical and Talmudic Period.* New York: Liberal Arts Press, 1954.

R. H. Charles. *The Apocrypha and Pseudepigrapha of the Old Testament.* London: Oxford University Press, 1913. 2 vols.

David Daube. *The New Testament and Rabbinic Judaism.* New York: Arno Press, 1956.

Martin Hengel. *Judaism and Hellenism.* Philadelphia: Fortress Press, 1974.

J. Jeremias. *Jerusalem in the Time of Jesus: An Investigation into Economic and Social Conditions During the New Testament Times.* Translated by F. H. and C. H. Cone. Philadelphia: Fortress Press, 1969.

H. C. Kee. *The Origins of Christianity: Sources and Documents.* Englewood Cliffs, N. J.: Prentice-Hall, Inc., 1973.

Eduard Lohse. *The New Testament Environment.* Translated by John E. Steely, Nashville: Abingdon Press, 1976.

G. F. Moore. *Judaism in the First Centuries of the Christian Era.* 3 vols. Cambridge, Mass.: Harvard University Press, 1927–30. The "classic" statement on Judaism during this period.

Leonhard Rost. *Judaism Outside the Hebrew Canon: An Introduction to the Documents.* Translated by David E. Green. Nashville: Abingdon Press, 1976.

Lawrence E. Toombs. *The Threshold of Christianity.* Philadelphia: Westminster Press, 1960.

Apocalyptic Thought

James M. Efird. *Daniel and Revelation: A Study of Two Extraordinary Visions.* Valley Forge, Pa.: Judson Press, 1978.

Leon Morris. *Apocalyptic.* Grand Rapids, Mich.: Wm. B. Eerdmans Publishing Co., 1977.

H. H. Rowley. *The Relevance of Apocalyptic.* 3rd edition. New York: Association Press, 1964.

D. S. Russell. *The Method and Message of Jewish Apocalyptic.* Philadelphia: Westminster Press, 1964.

Walther Schmithals. *The Apocalyptic Movement: Introduction and Interpretation.* Translation by John E. Steely. Nashville: Abingdon Press, 1975.

The Dead Sea Scrolls

Matthew Black. *The Scrolls and Christian Origins: Studies in the Jewish Background of the New Testament.* London: Thomas Nelson, 1961.

F. M. Cross. *The Ancient Library of Qumran and Modern Biblical Studies.* Garden City, N. Y.: Doubleday, 1958.

G. R. Driver. *The Judean Scrolls.* Oxford: Basil Blackwell, 1965.

Helmer Ringgren. *The Faith of Qumran.* Philadelphia: Fortress Press, 1961.

Geza Vermes. *The Dead Sea Scrolls in English.* Baltimore: Penguin Books, 1962.

CHAPTER II

The Ministry of Jesus: The Synoptic Gospels

The Kerygma

Before examining the individual writings of the New Testament and their content, it is of significant value to understand that these documents were products of the early church. Therefore, they reflect the thoughts, beliefs, and concerns of those groups of people in various and sundry parts of the world who were wrestling with the meaning of their newly accepted faith and the implications of that faith in their lives. This means that the New Testament writings are primarily "occasional" in nature, i.e., each one was written for a specific occasion, a particular need of the community at that moment. In other words, they were not written primarily as theological treatises or to expand or expound doctrines and dogmas.

The early Christian community believed it had something to proclaim to the world. It was, they felt, the "good news" concerning what God had done and would continue to do for his people. This "good news" centered in the Person of Jesus of Nazareth. It was in and through this Person that God had acted, had even revealed himself to the world in a unique and special way. Their basic orientation, therefore, was to proclaim to the world this newly revealed faith and exhort others to share with them in its glory.

Exactly what the basic content of this proclamation was can be determined by a close examination of the New Testament writings, especially the speeches of the leaders and the "confessions" found in certain writers. From such sources one can find certain recurring themes which seem to have formed the basis of the proclamation.

Together these specific points form the skeleton of the New Testament teachings and are designated the *kerygma*.[1] There are basically six points in this scheme:

(1) The age of fulfillment which was announced in the Scriptures (i.e., the Old Testament) had now dawned. To support this affirmation some scriptural quotation was generally cited as an illustration.

(2) This new age had been brought near through the life-death-resurrection of Jesus of Nazareth. It is important to note that these people considered all the events connected with Jesus as necessary parts of the development. They emphasized that Jesus was of Davidic descent, exercised a ministry of healing and care for those in need, taught about the new age, was unjustly condemned and executed, and was finally raised from the dead by the power of God. While the resurrection validated all that Jesus was and had done, that occurrence *by itself* did not convince these people of Jesus' Messiahship.

(3) Jesus has now been exalted to the right hand of God as head of the new Israel.

(4) The presence of the Holy Spirit active in the church is the sign that Jesus is still present with them in power and glory.

(5) Jesus will return *soon* to consummate the Kingdom. This belief was the reason, at least in part, for the extreme zeal which the early Christians exhibited in proclaiming the marvelous power of God. The technical term for the belief in Jesus' *early* return, i.e., within their lifetime and soon, is *Parousia* (Greek for presence, coming).

(6) Repent and believe in the good news. Accept the new life given to all who respond to the gift of God.

There are some who distinguish between a Palestinian kergyma (that outlined above) and the Pauline kerygma. Essentially they are the same except that Paul adds several features: (1) he designated Jesus as "Son of God"; (2) he included the idea that Jesus died "for our sins"; and (3) he believed that the exalted Christ intercedes for His people. Even with these added aspects, however, the basic ideas remain the same.

The importance of this scheme cannot be overemphasized because these motifs recur over and over in the New Testament writings. And it is interesting to see how each of the writers utilize and, even at times, modify the basic points of this proclamation. The gospels, for example, may even be considered expanded versions of the second point!

It is to the first three gospels that one first turns for the purpose of studying the beginnings of this movement. Even though the Synoptic gospels were not written as we have them now until after the writings of Paul, nevertheless they contain traditions that originated with the life and ministry of Jesus. It was out of that ministry that the church evolved; therefore it seems best to begin with an examination of these portraits of the one who started it all.

The Synoptic Gospels

Since the New Testament revolves around the significance of Jesus (as the Old Testament revolves around the Exodus and its meaning), it is quite understandable that the collection contains four documents which attempt to interpret Jesus' life and ministry. Even though these books are not the earliest written of the New Testament documents, they do deserve "pride of place" and rightfully stand at the beginning of the New Testament collection.

These writings are called "gospels," the word in the Greek meaning "good news." There is nothing quite like these documents in the literature of the ancient world. They are not biographies yet contain biographical material. They are not histories yet contain historical data. They are not mythological yet contain some elements that a few scholars call mythology. These are primarily documents of faith, the presentation and interpretation of Jesus, his life and significance. Three of these writings will be examined at this point; the fourth will be considered later along with other writings closely related to its style and content.

The three gospels which share basically a common tradition in presenting a portrait of Jesus are called the "Synoptic" gospels. The reason for this is because these three gospels "see together" the life and ministry of Jesus. This is true in spite of the fact that each gospel writer has his own particular understandings and emphases in painting his portrait of Jesus.

To assist in the understanding of these writings and to assist in the task of attempting to unravel the mysteries involved in the transmission of the material, New Testament scholars have utilized three basic disciplines. These are called *form-criticism, source criticism,* and *redaction criticism.* All of these must be utilized when one attempts to understand the material included in the gospels because there is unmistakable evidence that the material contained in the traditions about Jesus had been selected, transmitted, and even modified by the theological needs and ideas of the early Christian community.

Form-Criticism

The first of these disciplines is known as form-criticism. The term comes from the German, *Formgeschichte,* which means "form-history." This discipline basically attempts to study the tradition before it was written down, i.e., while it still existed in oral form. This methodology arose in Germany ca. 1919–1922 and was associated with the work of several scholars who pioneered in this field, Martin Dibelius, K. L. Schmidt, and Rudolf Bultmann.

There are several assumptions that proponents of this methodology emphasize: that the traditions about Jesus at first circulated orally; that these traditions circulated basically in single self-contained units; that these units have no real chronological value; that the units were preserved by the churches in the light of their own needs; that these units can be classified according to form.

In the classification process there is general agreement among the critics about two of the forms. The first is called a "Pronouncement Story," i.e., a story about Jesus which centers around a saying of Jesus. (This is also called an "apothegm" or a "paradigm.") Generally speaking there are four basic parts to such a story: (1) the scene is set (i.e., he was going through the grainfields on the Sabbath); (2) an incident occurs (the disciples plucked ears of corn which was disputed by the Pharisees) which leads to; (3) the saying of Jesus

("... the son of man is lord of the sabbath"); and (usually) (4) a response from the bystanders.

The second form is that of the miracle story (also called "wonder stories" or "Novellen," "tales"). There are three basic steps in this type: (1) the illness (danger, need) is described (i.e., Simon's mother-in-law was sick with a fever); (2) the "cure" is effected (Jesus took her by the hand and lifted her up, and the fever left her); and (3) the effect of the deed is related (including the effect on the bystanders), ("she served them"). In some instances it appears that the two forms may have been merged together, for example where a miracle story has as an important part of its structure a saying of Jesus (cf. Mark 2:1–12; 3:1–6).

In addition to these two categories there are others as well such as myths, legends, and various sayings groups, but these are named according to content primarily and not according to form. The study of these forms has greatly enhanced our understanding of how these traditions were passed along and, if used properly, can be very useful at points in the interpretation of certain gospel stories.

The passing along of the tradition in single, self-contained units has only one exception–the Passion narrative (the events related to the death of Jesus, especially the events of the last week). This appears to have been transmitted as a larger unit almost from the beginning. In all probability the single units began to be attached together by catchword, similarity of content, etc., and were circulated as groups (cf. Mark 2:1–3:6, stories of Jesus in conflict with the religious authorities; or perhaps parables about the Kingdom of God, Mark 4 or Matthew 13). Later these larger and shorter collections were probably written down and were utilized in the composition of the gospels as they now exist.

Form-criticism, therefore, is a very useful resource in dealing with the gospel material. Some of the more extreme form-critics have made extravagant claims for the discipline and have reached some very negative conclusions about the historical value of the material contained in the gospels. Such negativity is neither necessary nor even likely. But this should not be an excuse for failure to acknowledge and use the very useful aspects of the discipline. If nothing else, it has called attention to the fact that this tradition was preserved and transmitted through the early church and was used by the early church to speak to its own needs in that time.

Source Criticism

The second discipline which assists in one's study of the gospels, especially the Synoptic gospels, is called source criticism. As the name implies, this discipline attempts to find sources used by the gospel writers in the composition of their works to ascertain how they were used, what kind of sources they were, and what kinds of emphases the sources made. This type of study is especially helpful in dealing with the relationship between the three Synoptic gospels, Matthew, Mark, and Luke. Upon close examination of these three it can be clearly seen that they are very similar in many ways and yet different. The question becomes one of attempting to explain the similarities and differences of these gospels to and from each other. To put it simply, this investigation is known in scholarly circles as the attempt to solve the "Synoptic Problem."

For many centuries in the history of the church the Gospel of Matthew was regarded as the earliest written. Mark was viewed as a "condensation" of Matthew. With the detailed research that began on the biblical books in the eighteenth century, careful attention was given to these matters, and a rather startling discovery was made. Mark, far from being a later abbreviation of Matthew, was found to be the earliest of all the gospels. And further, the evidence pointed in the direction that Mark had been used as a major source in the composition of both Matthew and Luke.

This conclusion is supported by the following reasons.

(1) Most of Mark (over 600 of Mark's 661 verses) is found in either Matthew or Luke (or both).

(2) The arrangement of the material seems to follow Mark's order, and when Matthew or Luke deviates from Mark the other usually remains in sequence with that writing. In other words, Matthew and Luke do not agree together against Mark in the material that is common to all three.

(3) Similarly, the chronological order of Mark is usually followed by both Matthew and Luke. Again, these two never agree against Mark. (Some of these arguments can be seen clearly where the gospels are placed side by side. A good *gospel parallels* can be used for such an examination.)

Therefore, it is the opinion of most reputable New Testament scholars that Mark has been used by both Matthew and Luke *as a source* in the composition of their gospels. This conclusion that Mark is the earliest gospel and was foundational for the others is often referred to as "the priority of Mark."

Upon close examination of the three in parallel columns, it becomes obvious that when Mark is removed from both Matthew and Luke there is a considerable amount of material yet left to both. And upon further examination it is also obvious that a large amount of the remainder is found in *both* Matthew and Luke. Most of this common material consists of sayings of Jesus. Many scholars, therefore, have argued that Matthew and Luke had access to a written source containing sayings of Jesus, and they have designated this source Q (from the German, *Quelle*, source). Even though this document is not available to us and does not seem to have been directly alluded to by the early traditions of the fathers, the theory seems logical. Most interpreters accept the validity of a Q tradition though not all would now want to accept the existence of a specific written source.

If one then removed the Q material from Matthew and Luke (minus Mark), there still remains a substantial amount of material unique to each writing. Where this material originated, when, whether it was written or oral, are questions that scholars do not agree upon. But they do agree that the material special to Matthew can be designated as M, and the material special to Luke as L.

These insights using basically source materials give us some clues as to the "solution" of the Synoptic Problem. Mark's gospel was the first written and was used as a source by both Matthew and Luke in the composition of their gospels. But each of these authors also used a common source, Q, plus material "special" to him. This can be graphically depicted in the following diagram.

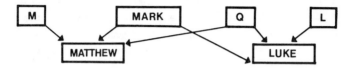

This explanation leaves many problems unanswered, but it does give some insight into the complex of problems involved in understanding about these three gospels which "see together" the ministry of Jesus of Nazareth.

Redaction Criticism

A third and more recent approach to the gospels is called redaction criticism (in German *Redactiongeschichte*). This approach basically views the individual gospel as a unit and seeks to determine the author's ideas, purposes, and theological motifs in writing the work as he did. The exponents of this discipline argue that the transmission process of handing down the traditions about Jesus led to fragmentation of the material, but the gospel writers counteracted that trend. In other words the author of the gospel is to be considered as a person who writes and tells the story with specific purposes in mind. No matter what the history of the form or the written source, the selection, writing, editing and arrangement of each gospel is a product of its author. The book should be interpreted, therefore, as a unity not in fragmented fashion.

In approaching the gospels, therefore, one needs to bear in mind each of these three disciplines. The principles, insights, and cautions of these approaches can greatly enhance one's understanding of these writings.

The Gospel of Mark

When examining a book of the New Testament, there are several matters of "critical" concern that face the interpreter. Who wrote the book? Where? When? Why? To whom? Once these issues are settled one can then turn to the text itself with a far greater likelihood of understanding what the book actually said and meant to the people of that time. There are two types of evidence which one may utilize in this process. One is called *external* evidence, i.e., what the early traditions about these books had to say about their origins. The second is called *internal* evidence, i.e., what the writing itself says about its own origins.

Upon turning to the New Testament gospels, one learns rather quickly that all of the gospels are anonymous writings. And beyond that they do little explicitly to speak to the further questions of origin. Therefore, most of what can be known about the gospels must come from tradition and from clues gleaned from a careful examination of the book itself.

The Gospel of Mark has strong traditions relating it to the person of John Mark, the same person whose mother's house was used as a meeting place for the early church in Jerusalem (cf. Acts12:12) and who accompanied Paul and Barnabas for a short while on the first missionary journey recorded in Acts. It is also a part of the tradition that later Mark had accompanied Peter on his travels through the Graeco-Roman world, a trip that ultimately culminated at Rome. Mark served as the "interpreter" (translator?) for Peter on these journeys. The various traditions point to Mark as the writer of this gospel, but there is some disagreement as to the time of the writing. One tradition says that it was written after Peter's (and Paul's) martyrdom in the Neronian persecution which took place against Christians in Rome ca. 64–66 A.D. Another tradition has it that the gospel was written before Peter's death. But as far as the tradition goes, Mark is looked upon as the author, and the date of his writing is somewhere ca. 65–68 A.D. The internal evidence from the gospel itself points very strongly in the direction of a date prior to the destruction of Jerusalem and the Temple in 70 A.D.

The place of writing is also strongly attested as somewhere in Italy, in all probability, Rome. Since Mark was the shortest and least popular of the gospels, it seems logical to assume that an attachment of that document with a powerful church would have been necessary for it to survive and become one of the selected four. There are a few scholars, however, who find in the gospel itself enough strong references to Galilee that they argue for an origin in that area. It is possible but not probable that they are right.

The purpose of the writing and the audience for which it was intended are very closely interrelated. According to the tradition Mark wrote down the words Peter had spoken about Jesus but *not in order.* Therefore one reason for writing would have been the desire to preserve an eyewitness' account of the things which Jesus said and did, especially if this person were Simon Peter. A second reason would have been to bolster the faith of persons who had just experienced a period of intense persecution. That this may have been one of the primary reasons can be detected in the emphasis in Mark's gospel on the suffering of Jesus and his continued calls for suffering on the part of his disciples. A third, and closely related emphasis, is the decidedly pointed challenge in Mark's gospel to discipleship, not simply in the face of persecution but in every aspect of one's life. A church that had lived through the kinds of experiences which this church had experienced probably needed a challenge to be active in proclaiming the good news about God's Messiah and the new Kingdom which the Messiah had made available. In reality all the specific reasons for Mark's writing may not be available to us, but these appear to be valid ones if the external and internal evidence has been correctly interpreted.

As for the audience to which the gospel was addressed, it seems logical to assume that the Christian community in Italy, most probably at Rome, was the intended recipient. The people there had just undergone a period of persecution, losing two of the early church's greatest leaders. They needed to be reminded that the great leader of the church had already faced the worst that the world had to offer, yet God had vindicated his life and his teachings. The gospel was then a vehicle for transmitting hope to the people of that area when hope was really needed.

With the advent of scholarly study on the gospels, when it became an accepted premise that Mark was the earliest of the gospels, there was awakened a deep interest in the Gospel of Mark. It was argued that the other gospels because they were later and because they had some obvious theological "overlay" in the interpretation of Jesus' life and ministry were of little value in attempting to reconstruct the "real" Jesus, called the "Jesus of History." In the search to discover Jesus as He really was, scholars turned to Mark because they felt that his presentation of Jesus was closest to the "Historical Jesus." During the nineteenth and twentieth centuries scholars argued and struggled attempting to reconstruct the life and ministry of Jesus, exactly as it happened. This struggle is usually referred to as the "Quest for the Historical Jesus." Mark's gospel was at the center of this study.

About the turn of the century two works appeared which cast serious doubt on the entire project, however. Albert Schweitzer in his book, *The Quest of the Historical Jesus,* argued that all the previous attempts had been in vain and would be in such a search to find a historical portrait of Jesus. But Schweitzer, after having reviewed and criticized the attempts that had been made up to that point, proceeded to espouse his own viewpoint on this matter! But the question had been raised. Can one really discover the "Jesus of History" from the documents as they now exist?

Another work which appeared in 1901 raised a serious question about the Gospel of Mark. W. W. Wrede, a German scholar, questioned whether Mark's gospel was in fact a "historical" account. He examined Mark's gospel and found that one of Mark's emphases (a secrecy motif) was theologically motivated. From this point on it was gradually recognized that Mark's entire gospel was highly theological. This recognition did not deny that there was much historical data contained in Mark's gospel, but it was recognized that the interest of Mark (as well as the other gospel writers) lay above and beyond a simple recitation of history. To attempt, therefore, to interpret Jesus only historically was counter to the aims and purposes of the gospel writers. The search for the "Historical Jesus" is a fascinating study, but the gospels present to faith a Jesus that is historical but beyond mere historicality.

What, therefore, are the religious emphases of Mark's gospel? First of all, it is clear that Mark means to present Jesus as uniquely Son of God. In that society and in the Old Testament background numbers of unique people could be given the title, "son of God." But Mark uses the term somewhat differently because Mark presents a Person who has a unique relationship with God and who has a unique mission to perform and, therefore, has unique power and authority. Even so, there is a realism about Jesus in this gospel that does begin to be diminished in other gospels.

The mission of Jesus was to inaugurate the Kingdom of God. This is demonstrated by reference to Jesus' constant conflict with the powers of the demon world, the Kingdom of Satan. At the time of Jesus the Jewish people were looking for a Messiah, a deliverer, who would come and establish God's Kingdom. Even though there was no real unanimity about what kind of being the Messiah might be, there was a concensus as to what the Messiah would do. He would destroy the enemies of God's people and establish a new Kingdom where God's people would be freed from political and religious oppression. When Jesus appeared, then, he did not exactly fit the patterns of Messiah which were expected; and he certainly did not interpret the Kingdom of God as it was expected at that time. That, however, is beside the point, for Mark's view was that Jesus was indeed the one who would establish the new Kingdom, and Jesus' entire life and ministry were given over to that work.

A third emphasis in Mark's gospel has to do with the continuing injunctions to secrecy with regard to Jesus and his works. Over and over in the gospel Jesus commands that the people or his disciples or a person healed or the demons tell no one about him or his actions. This is often referred to in New Testament studies as the "Messianic Secret." Scholars have argued since the time of Wrede to attempt to understand exactly what Mark meant by this strange and unusual motif. That it in some way goes back to Jesus is probably without question, but it is also without question that Mark has made use of this idea in ways that suited his telling of the story. (Matthew, for example, uses the same episodes as Mark with far fewer injunctions to remain quiet! In fact in some the opposite interpretation from Mark has been given. Cf. Mark 4:10–12 with Matthew 13:10–17.) The fact is that Mark's use of the secrecy motif has not, as yet, been given a fully satisfactory interpretation in New Testament circles. No one theory seems to fit all the instances given.

Another closely related idea is that of the spiritual blindness of Jesus' disciples. It is emphasized over and over again in Mark's gospel that the disciples do not understand fully the nature of Jesus and his mission. He repeats his message to them, especially about his having to suffer, but they do not comprehend the essential meaning of what he says. This may well reflect the truth in Jesus' relationship with his disciples and be the basis for Mark's expanded ideas about secrecy.

Another emphasis of this gospel is that depicting Jesus as a man of action. Jesus is in constant conflict with the forces of evil, and in this portrait he is much more a "doer" than a teacher. It is a curious fact that Mark calls Jesus "Teacher" more than any other gospel but has less emphasis on the teaching of Jesus *per se* than any other gospel.

The Gospel of Mark: Outline

   I.   Introduction and Background 1:1–13
  II.   The Ministry in Galilee 1:14–8:21
 III.   The Recognition and Cost of Discipleship 8:22 –10:52
 IV.   The Road to Jerusalem 11:1–12:44
  V.   Saying on the Destruction of Jerusalem 13:1–37
 VI.   The Passion Narrative 14:1–16:8

From the very beginning of Mark's gospel it is clear that Mark's intention is to portray Jesus as Son of God. The superscription makes that point very clear. After a brief introduction depicting the work of John the Baptizer, the author introduces Jesus and his baptism by John. By the use of the two Old Testament texts (1:11) joined together the tone and structure of Jesus' ministry is set. The two passages reflect Messiahship and Suffering Servant. Mark's portrait of Jesus is that of a suffering Messiah. In keeping with his secrecy motif, Mark shows that this was a private experience between Jesus and God. (In Matthew the voice makes the announcement to the crowd!)

This is followed "immediately" by the temptation narrative. The short choppy style of Mark is already apparent here, for everything in this gospel happens "immediately" (the term is used 41 times in this gospel). There is little in Mark to give a clue as to what the temptation was all about. Most commentators fill this in from the larger accounts of Matthew and Luke (probably from the Q tradition). The usual explanation is that the temptation set the stage for what kind of Messiah Jesus was to be. He rejects the "easy" way of compromise, spectacular display of power, or special protection. His ministry is to be a ministry of humility and suffering.

Having settled this crucial issue, Jesus then comes to public ministry after John has been arrested proclaiming the good news that the Kingdom of God had drawn near. Mark sets the tone of the ministry almost immediately by having Jesus cast out a demon (a sign that the Kingdom of God was already in the process of conquering the Kingdom of evil) and showing that Jesus could heal leprosy which was considered a religious malady which caused the person to be religiously unclean and separated from the community of God's people.

During the course of his ministry Jesus on numerous occasions comes into conflict with the religious authorities. Mark demonstrates this by including a series of such incidents (2:1–3:6). Later these authorities accuse Jesus of being in partnership with the Devil (3:22).

Chapter four is a collection of parables about the nature of the Kingdom. There is in this chapter, perhaps, the center of the Secrecy motif. The disciples ask Jesus about the parables, and Jesus replies: "To you has been given the secret of the Kingdom of God, but for those outside everything is in parables; so that they may indeed see but not perceive, and may indeed hear but not understand; lest they should turn again and be forgiven" (4:10–12). This is a very curious statement since teaching by means of parables in those days was supposed to be the most effective method of making oneself clear and thus being understood.

Efforts have been made to find underneath the Greek of this passage a misunderstanding of an Aramaic original. For example, the word parable can be translated "riddle." If this is done the translation could very well mean that parables for "those outside" seem to be riddles because they are not part of the select group chosen to understand the new mysteries of the Kingdom. Another possibility is the mistranslation of an Aramaic particle *di* which can mean

either "in order that" or "who." If so, the translation could read
" . . . for those outside everything is in parables *who* see but do not
perceive. . . ." This relieves the problem by making the statement a
simple comment on the fact that those who remain outside do not
understand. Still another possibility is a mistranslation of the Aramaic word translated into the Greek as "lest." The same word in
Aramaic does double duty for "lest" and "unless." Some speculate
that the original saying then had the people who saw but did not
see, etc., as doomed to that state, ". . . unless they repented and were
forgiven."

All of the above conjectures could be possible in terms of the
original saying in Aramic. The fact is, however, that the statement
as it is translated (RSV) is true to the Greek, and, further, that
meaning fits into the context of Mark's emphasis on secrecy. As it
stands, it is a harsh saying. The key to understanding the saying as
Mark uses it here seems to lie in the term "those outside." The disciples themselves do not understand either, so how do they differ
from those others? The implication seems to be that those who are
committed to the Kingdom will ultimately understand, but for those
outside all this will remain an unsolved mystery.

As Jesus' Galilean ministry progresses, he continues to heal and
to act in order to demonstrate the presence of the Kingdom. John is
beheaded, and this section speeds toward its conclusion. Jesus is on
the way to Caesarea Philippi, and on the way he asks his disciples
who they think he is. With the confession of Peter, "You are the
Messiah," the Gospel of Mark takes a new turn. Most scholars feel
that this confession marks a watershed in the account of Jesus' ministry. Up till this point Jesus' ministry has been basically directed
toward the crowds, preaching about the nature of the Kingdom.
After this Jesus seems to be more concerned with teaching the disciples the nature of discipleship and trying to get across to them the
necessity of the cross. His teaching about the nature of the Kingdom seems to focus now more on how one participates as a member
of that Kingdom. From this point on the necessity of the cross is
reiterated many times.

Jesus comes then to Jerusalem. While he is there, most everything
which he does seems to revolve around the Temple. He drives out

the commercial personnel from the court of the Gentiles, lashes out at hypocrisy, and dodges the ensnaring questions of the religious leaders.

A very interesting discourse is placed at this point in Mark's account, chapter 13, which is known as the "Little Apocalypse." The chapter contains numerous eschatological sayings of Jesus couched in apocalyptic terminology. Some scholars argue that this chapter is a later collection of Jesus' sayings on eschatological matters which Mark has inserted at this point. Whether this is the correct interpretation of this passage is irrelevant, for the interpretative question is not about the origin of the sayings but rather what do the sayings mean in this context.

If one reads the chapter carefully, it is very clear that Mark understands this discourse to refer to the destruction of the Temple in Jerusalem (cf. 13:1–4). At that point there are two possible interpretations. The first, and the most usually accepted, is that Mark expected the Parousia to occur at the time of the destruction of Jerusalem. The second interpretation, and the simplest, is that Mark was relating the account of Jesus' actual prediction of the fall of Jerusalem and the destruction of the Temple. Many scholars hold that this prediction is not really a prediction at all but a *vaticinium ex eventu* or a *vaticinium post eventu,* i.e., a prophecy from the event or after the event. This seems highly unlikely since there is no sign in Mark's gospel that this event has already occurred and since Mark is usually dated ca. 65–68. This passage then is a genuine prediction by Jesus of Jerusalem's being captured and the Temple destroyed. Given the intense nature of the times, such a prediction is not all that remarkable. Anyone who was sensitive to the situation could see if the Jewish Zealots ever began a war with Rome what the outcome would be. Whether Mark believed that the Parousia would indeed occur at that same time is an open question, however.

The Passion narrative now begins in some detail and moves inextricably to its conclusion—the death of Jesus on the cross. The religious authorities have determined that Jesus is a threat to them and their way of life; therefore, he must die. They are aided in their plot by one of Jesus' own disciples, Judas. Exactly why Judas was so disillusioned with his Master so as to betray him to the authorities is not told. What it was, exactly, that Judas "betrayed" is not related either. It could have been where Jesus was to be at the time they wished to arrest him, or that Jesus had claimed to be the Messiah, or some other matter. Mark simply does not tell his readers.

Jesus eats the Passover meal with his disciples on Thursday evening. He is then arrested, tried before the Jewish council, delivered to Pilate, and finally condemned as a threat to Rome. He is scourged, taken to the place of execution, and crucified. On Friday afternoon he dies. The disciples have scattered; only a few women remain close to him until the very end (15:40–41; 15:47). Even his most ardent follower has denied any acquaintance with him! It is a scene of ignominy and death.

But in the midst of all this, even the darkest hours, Mark shows that the light will ultimately shine. Even hanging on the cross, the unique nature of Jesus is recognized by the Roman centurion. "Truly this man was the Son of God!" (15:39) At the time of his death the curtain of the Temple was ripped in two. This curtain was the veil separating the Holy of Holies from the world. The Holy of Holies was the place where God dwelt and could only be approached once a year and only by the High Priest. Now the curtain was torn; God's Presence was unleashed to all people, everywhere without limit.

Because of the Jewish custom concerning the burial of the dead before the sun set, Jesus was placed in a tomb near the crucifixion site. The women (again) see where it is and made plans to return to anoint the body properly at their first opportunity. This would not be until Sunday morning after the Sabbath had passed. They came to the tomb as early as they dared travel, and upon arrival found the tomb empty. A young man tells them that Jesus is not there, that he had risen. They do not really understand, and they leave, frightened.

At this point, 16:8, the original text of Mark's gospel ends. The verses, 16:9–20, are a later composition that at some time was copied into the text by the old scribes. But these verses are not found in the earliest and most reliable copies of the Greek text. The question then becomes: did the original text of Mark end with 16:8? Obviously the old scribes thought that something was lacking, for other endings were also written in addition to the one familiar to people today (16:9–20). Many scholars feel that the references in 14:28 and 16:7 to at least one resurrection appearance in Galilee surely pointed the way to additional material at the conclusion of Mark's gospel. Because of the way books were made in those days (scrolls) and the type of writing material (papyrus), somehow, they argue, the original conclusion to this gospel had been lost.

There are some other scholars of late who have begun to question whether the gospel had lost a larger ending or whether the gospel concluded where Mark wanted to stop his story. There is no real evidence for a lost ending, and Mark is a writer with an abrupt style. Therefore, they conclude that the Gospel of Mark is intact in the form in which we have it, concluding with 16:8.

It appears very strange, however, that with so much emphasis on an appearance in Galilee, there would be none. In all probability there was some additional data which somehow very early was lost. Included in such a portion of material would surely have been a resurrection appearance in Galilee. But the ending is lost. Mark as we have it concludes with 16:8.

The Gospel of Matthew

The Gospel of Matthew has been for many years one of the most popular, if not the most popular, of the portraits of Jesus. It is a curious phenomenon that so little is known about the critical details of this writing. The only early evidence tells us that Matthew wrote down the "oracles" (Greek, *logia*) of Jesus in Aramaic and that each person then translated them as one could. The problem with this statement is that it seems to be describing something other than the present Gospel of Matthew!

There are several problems with this tradition. One concerns the exact meaning of the word "oracles." Some have interpreted this to refer to the Old Testament passages cited by Matthew to bolster his arguments; and others (most, in fact) interpret that word to designate sayings of Jesus, of which there are numerous ones in this gospel. But the clear evidence is that Matthew's gospel is not simply a collection of Old Testament texts or sayings of Jesus. Further, there is no evidence that this document in the Greek was translated from another source. It is a matter of concensus among New Testament scholars, then, that this bit of tradition originally described something else which either was totally lost or which in some way may have become a part of the present Gospel of Matthew. There are even those who have held that the tradition originally was describing Q. The answers to these questions are highly speculative, and the evidence is exceedingly sketchy. Therefore, most of the critical questions must be answered by an examination of the internal evidence.

As for the authorship, absolutely nothing can be said definitely. The author seems to have been a Palestinian Jewish-Christian who knew his Greek rather well (since he polishes some of the material he takes from Mark). The orientation of the gospel appears to be that of a community which is in direct contact with a Jewish community and society. This would indicate an origin somewhere in Palestine, probably Syria; some have specifically argued for Antioch. The date must be after 65–68 A.D. since Matthew used Mark, but it must also be before ca. 110 A.D. since Ignatius of Antioch seems to have known this gospel. Suggestions range usually from 75 to 100 A.D., generally about 80–90. That the date may be somewhat later in this time span is illustrated by the fact that the church seems to have a type of structural development not found earlier (cf. 18: 16ff.), by the fact that there is now concern in the church about the "bad" who are included in it (cf. 13:24ff.; 13:36ff.; 13:47ff.), and by the fact that there are several comments such as "to this day" (28:15) which indicate a considerable passage of time. Others argue that the emphasis on the coming Parousia tends to push the date earlier. Certainty cannot be reached, but a date of ca. 85–90 A.D. would probably not be far from wrong.

The most crucial point seems to be the purpose for writing. Again various hypotheses have been proposed: that the book was written as a manual of instruction for use with new church members; that it was intended for a Jewish-Christian community to bolster their faith; that it was a manual to assist in "evangelizing" Jews. Again certainty cannot be assured, but it appears from the internal emphases of the document that the book was written to a group of people composed primarily of former Jews and who lived in the midst of a highly Jewish population to present Jesus as the fulfillment of the true Judaism. This was their primary concern in that particular setting. Such an aim serves both the internal needs and the external needs of the church for which Matthew wrote.

To emphasize his point the author used texts from the Old Testament. These texts are cited frequently, thereby demonstrating that this Jesus really did fulfill the best hopes of their Scripture. At this point it is wise to discuss briefly the manner in which the early Christians interpreted their Scriptures (i.e., the Old Testament). Generally speaking they used the passages in much the same way as the Rabbis of that time. There are two basic ways in which Scripture was approached to ascertain if it spoke to their situations and to determine if fulfillment of the Scripture had indeed taken place.

First of all, there was the procedure where a historical event (there is almost always a historical event included) was being examined. For example, one may take the story of the slaughter of the innocent children under Herod (2:16ff.). That was a historical event (or the author thought it was a historical event); from this event one read the Scriptures to determine if there was there any passage that spoke to what had happened. In this case they found a passage from Jeremiah which depicted Rachel (mother of the Northern tribes) weeping over her children who had been carried away into exile. The context was similar so therefore this passage from Jeremiah could be viewed as speaking to or fulfilling the present situation. (For a similar illustration of this type cf. Acts 1:15–26.)

A second type of approach seems to emphasize not so much the literal correspondence but more importantly the underlying meaning of the Old Testament text and the situation to which it is applied. This is especially noticeable in the use of the "Emmanuel" passage by Matthew. In Isaiah 7:10–17 there is the famous passage (7:14) which talks about a "young woman who is already pregnant and about to bear a child" (literal translation from the Hebrew). The birth of the child in Isaiah was a sign that God would destroy the two enemies of Judah that were then menacing her. Before the child was, at most, twelve years old, those two nations would be destroyed. As a sign of this, the child was named Emmanuel, which means in Hebrew, "God is with us." The basic meaning of the passage has to do with God's activity to deliver his people. This passage was then taken up by Matthew and used in his narrative to depict a deliverance of a more important kind. Instead of God's action delivering from enemies from without, God's action now delivers the human race from the power of sin. "... You will call his name Jesus, for he will save the people from their sins." (1:21, paraphrase) The central issue here lies in the deeper meaning of the text not in the surface connection about a "virgin." That Matthew had received the tradition about the virgin birth is clear, but that particular issue was secondary to the deliverance from sin. It is this kind of interpretation that Jesus emphasized himself in the teaching of the Sermon on the Mount. "You have heard it said, 'Do not kill.' But I say to not even be angry at your neighbor" (5:21–22, paraphrase). One needs to look beneath the literal words to ascertain the real meaning.

Having discussed briefly Matthew's use of the Old Testament it should be made clear that Matthew presents Jesus as the new Messianic King of Israel, the fulfillment of true Judaism. There are a large number of interpreters who see in Matthew a deliberate attempt to depict Jesus as the new Moses, bringer and dispenser of a new Law (Torah) for the new Israel. One can point to many similarities: escaping from almost certain death as a child, being kept safe in Egypt, but most especially dispensing the new Law on the Mountain (cf. chapters 5–7). Since Matthew has a decided tendency to group the sayings of Jesus together into "sermons," these scholars find five such collections which, they argue, point to the five books of the Law that Moses gave.

It is true that Matthew depicts Jesus as the fulfillment of the true Judaism and that he collects the sayings of Jesus into "sermons," but it is a bit strained to find in the gospel such a conscious effort on the part of the author to portray him as a new Moses. Jesus to Matthew is the fulfillment not only of Moses and the law but also the prophets. He is a Messiah-King who gives a new teaching, but that he is Moses redivivus is more uncertain. The five blocks of teaching are usually designated as chapters 5–7, 10, 13, 18, 24–25. It is interesting that there is at least one other collection of sayings (chapter 23) and perhaps two (chapter 11 also). If this is true, it would destroy the theory of the five "books." Therefore it seems best to acknowledge the strong emphasis of Matthew on Jesus as the fulfillment of the true Messiah-King with the church viewed as the new Israel, the new people of God, and leave open the question of the gospel as depicting a new Moses and a new law.

Jesus is portrayed in this gospel as a great teacher and as a regal figure. Whereas in Luke humble shepherds come to Jesus at birth, in Matthew Magi, men of wisdom and means, come to bring gifts worthy of a king—and to worship. In fact, one of Matthew's emphases not found in Mark or Luke is the emphasis upon the worship of Jesus (cf. especially 2:11; 14:33; 20:20; 28:9, 17).

In studying Mark's gospel one found the strong emphasis upon the secrecy motif. Very little of that is retained in Matthew's gospel. Most of the Markan references to secrecy are either omitted or changed, some to complete openness. This is probably most evident in the discussion about the purpose of the parables. In Mark 4: 10–12 the purpose of the parables was to obscure the meaning of the Kingdom. In Matthew's account of this (13:10–17) the purpose of the parables is to make *clear* the meaning of the Kingdom, so that when the people do not respond positively to its challenge they will have no excuse for not accepting. In Mark's gospel when Jesus is baptized, only Jesus hears the voice; in Matthew's gospel the voice addresses itself to the bystanders in a public announcement!

There is one other aspect of Matthew's gospel that deserves special mention, not simply because these matters are peculiar to Matthew but because they are characteristic of Jesus' teaching in all of the Synoptic gospels. This concerns the manner in which Jesus taught.

All of the gospels depict Jesus as a teacher, and a teacher with authority. As with numerous "wise men" of that time, Jesus gathered around himself a number of devoted "learners" (the basic meaning of the Greek word for "disciples"). The "wisdom" movement in the history of the Hebrew people began in very ancient times but was given a status and place in the history of Israelite religion by Solomon. After the exile (ca. 587–539 B.C.) the movement grew and branched into two segments, a practical wisdom and a more speculative or philosophical type. Both of these attempted to deal with the basic questions of how to cope with this world. The method of teaching by a wise man to his disciples was basically that of the *mashal* (the Hebrew word for parable). Included under the *mashal* were such types of teachings as parables, fables, proverbs, riddles, and similar types of sayings used to compare certain concepts or ideas. Usually these types of sayings were designed to assist people in living in this world and understanding the ways of the world better.

Another characteristic typical of this kind of teaching and also of the Semitic mind was that of expressing ideas and points in *hyperbole,* i.e., by exaggeration. It is obvious that teaching by such a method should not be interpreted literally. If one reads an extreme statement (such as cutting off one's hand), it must be remembered that a point is being emphasized by the use of hyperbole.

This leads to a last point to be made in dealing with Jesus' teaching. Quite a large amount of it is done specifically in parables, a comparison type of teaching technique that basically makes only one point. Therefore, when interpreting a parable, the reader should be very careful to look for the point that is being made. Many persons are led astray by misinterpreting the parables. One error commonly found is that of interpreting the parable as an allegory. An allegory is a story in which the teller intends a hidden esoteric meaning behind every detail presented. The parables of Jesus are not allegories. There are a few allegorical interpretations given in the gospels, but the interpreter of the gospel texts must be careful to interpret as allegories only those stories which the gospel writers interpret in that fashion.

Another common error in interpreting the parables comes at the point of attempting to understand each part of the parable as an absolute teaching of Jesus. This can lead into serious difficulty! For example, in Jesus' parable of the treasure hidden in a field (Matthew 13:44) the man finds a treasure, covers it up, and buys the land. This should not be interpreted as an ethical precept taught in the parable which depicts Jesus as condoning cheating in business dealings! The parable simply is a story which makes use of current happenings in life to illustrate a point. It is the point which is important and to be emphasized. The other parts of the parable are support- ive material, and no attempt should be made to absolutize these supports.

Matthew's portrait of Jesus is then a more "intellectual" one than Mark's. To Mark Jesus was a man of action in conflict with the powers of evil in all its forms, whereas Matthew depicts a more "re- gal" figure, the King of Israel, the teacher of the new people of God.

The Gospel of Matthew: Outline

- I. Birth Narratives 1–2
- II. Beginning of the Ministry 3–4
- III. Sermon on the Mount 5–7
- IV. Public Ministry and Teaching 8:1–16:12
- V. Recognition and Confession 16:13–23
- VI. Cost of Discipleship and the Road to Jerusalem 16:24–20:34
- VII. Jesus in Jerusalem 21–25
- VIII. Passion Narrative 26–28

The Gospel of Matthew (and Luke) is much fuller than Mark's gospel. Whereas Mark began with the preaching of John the Bap- tizer and Jesus' public ministry, Matthew introduces all that plus some background material basically relating to the birth of Jesus. In the ancient world it was quite common for a great king to have stories told connected with the events surrounding his birth. In Matthew's gospel the same is done for Jesus. Wise powerful persons come to pay honor to the new king; the child is saved from almost certain death; the family has to flee the land and the king-designate is preserved in a foreign land—all these stories are similar to others dealing with the lives of truly significant persons. Matthew, how- ever, sets all of this into a broader context; he emphasized that these things happened to fulfill the Scriptures and cited biblical texts to demonstrate his understanding of these events and their signif- icance.

To strengthen this emphasis upon Jesus as the fulfillment of the true Judaism, Matthew placed all of these stories within the context of a genealogy which traced Jesus' lineage back to Abraham, the father of the Jewish people and religion (cf. 1:1–17). In the arrangement of the "family tree" there are three groups of fourteen persons each. It is interesting to note several things in connection with this genealogy. First, the number 14 is the number of the name, *David* (i.e., adding up the numerical value of the letters of the name); and secondly, one notes that each section concludes with a person who really does inaugurate a new age in the history of the Jewish people. David inaugurated the great period of the United Kingdoms; Jechoniah (or Jehoiachin) was the ruler at the time of the exile (the conclusion of the Kingdom period); and finally Jesus, who is the one who would bring in the new and better Kingdom for the people of God. One can see, therefore, that Matthew depicts Jesus not simply as the new Moses, but as the new Abraham and the new David as well.

The stories that follow the genealogy are selected to present Jesus as a unique and special person, and in each episode Matthew connects the event with a passage from the Scriptures to demonstrate the connection between Jesus and Israel.

At this point Matthew joins Mark by introducing John the Baptizer. One pointer to the idea that Matthew's gospel is late can be seen in the baptismal scene where John argues that Jesus does not really need to be baptized! This kind of tradition obviously arose later to attempt to explain why Jesus was baptized if indeed he was without sin (cf. 3:13–17). Matthew also depicts the voice at the baptismal scene as speaking to the crowds, not simply to Jesus as in Mark.

Matthew includes what appears to be a Q tradition into the Markan account of the temptation. This fuller account makes it clear that the temptation centered in the point of what kind of a Messiah Jesus was going to be. He rejects using his power selfishly; he rejects doing foolish acts to "test" God (as the Zealots advocated); and he refused to take the "easy" way by compromising with the world and its patterns of values.

Since Jesus is depicted as the great Teacher of the new Israel, Matthew now presents the first of his collections of Jesus' teachings.

Most of this material originated in the Q and M traditions, but some of it is from Mark also. The primary point to keep in mind in reading this great collection of Jesus' teaching is to remember that Jesus is teaching here basically as a wisdom teacher, not primarily as a theologian or ethicist. For many years interpreters of Matthew's gospel have missed this simple point. They have taken these teachings as *absolutes* when in reality they should be seen as guidelines or as pointers toward certain principles for life in this world as a member of the new Kingdom.

To illustrate how far afield some can go in this matter, no less a person than Albert Schweitzer argued that the teachings presented were impossible for a human being to keep. Therefore, he argued, Jesus did not really intend persons to keep these new commandments over a long period of time; that would be impossible. What Jesus meant was that his followers could keep them for a short period of time, i.e., the time between the present and the soon-to-come Parousia. The system of ethics taught here, then, was called an "interim-ethic," to be kept in the interim between the present and the coming of Jesus which would be very soon.

The fact is that there is no evidence that Matthew interpreted these teachings of Jesus to be "interim." And further, there is definite evidence in the teachings themselves that these were not intended as a new system of laws; the entire tone is antithetical to that kind of interpretation. Jesus is not advocating here a new legalism. He is arguing against legalism and attempting to go beneath the letter of the law to the spirit of the law. This point is especially emphasized in the series of "antitheses" ("You have heard it said ... but I say ..." 5:17ff.). The ethics of Jesus as they are presented here (and if this is what Matthew really intended) can be categorized as attitudinal but not propositional. The new life of the Kingdom is to be characterized by fulfilling the law at its deepest level in terms of commitment to God and real care and concern about one's neighbors. The "Sermon on the Mount," then, appears to be a fuller commentary on Jesus' teaching about the commandments: "You shall love the Lord your God ... and your neighbor as yourself" (cf. Mark 12:30).

One other comment is perhaps in order before leaving this collection of Jesus' teachings. In the section 5:38ff. many have attempted to make of Jesus' teaching a proof text for pacifism. To be sure, pacifism has many points to commend itself to the human race, and a number of Christians do hold to that position, but this particular text cannot bear the weight of such an interpretation. The words here do seem to be an advancement on the principle of "an eye for an eye," (which was in its own time an advancement, for it curtailed the principle of vengeance which often went beyond the bounds of reason even for the ancient world), but in this context the teaching is more appropriately understood as wisdom-type instruction on how best to get along in this world, especially with cantankerous people!

From chapter 8 through chapter 13 Matthew at points follows Mark and at points presents his own chronology. The material is quite similar to Mark's account except that Matthew edits the stories and teachings in such a way as to emphasize his own interests, such as the deletion of the secrecy motif, Jesus as the Leader of the new Kingdom, and the idea that all of this is a fulfillment of the finest hopes and aspirations of the Old Testament. Beginning with chapter 14, however, Matthew usually follows Mark through the remainder of the chronology, editing the material at points to suit his concerns and adding additional materials for the same purpose. (The easiest and best way to see how these two compare is by the use of a gospel parallels.)

Matthew does include an account of a resurrection appearance in Galilee. Whether this was part of Mark's "lost" conclusion cannot be known.

Before leaving this all too brief summary of Matthew's presentation of Jesus, it needs to be pointed out that the eschatological teaching in Matthew's gospel has been altered somewhat from Mark's presentation. Whereas Mark emphasized the importance of the destruction of the Temple (cf. Mark 13) and looked forward to a new age following that event, Matthew stands after the event (cf. 23:38). The question as to whether Mark understood the destruction of the Temple to be a part of, or even identical with, the Parousia is not really relevant here. The destruction of the Temple had come and there had been neither new age and/nor Parousia. Therefore Matthew was forced to reinterpret. Instead of asking about the destruction of the Temple (cf. Mark 13:1-4), the disciples in Matthew's eschatological discourse (chapters 24-25) ask, "Tell us, when will this be [i.e., the destruction of the Temple], and what will be the sign of your coming and of the close of the age?" (24:3) This passage then seems to be Matthew's answer to the question that began to plague the members of the early church in the years after 70 A.D., namely, when will the Parousia come?

The answer to that is, no one knows (cf. 24:36)! The important point for the Christian is to continue to live in such a way that it will not matter when the time arrives. If one is always prepared, there will be no problem. One should continue to do those tasks that persons who are living under the new Kingdom already are obligated to do. This teaching is clearly emphasized in 24:36-51; and to support the point even further Matthew attached three parables, each of which makes the same emphasis (cf. chapter 25)!

The gospel concludes with a command to make disciples of all the nations and to teach them what Jesus had taught his disciples. And the promise is that he would be with them until "the close of the age," whenever that might occur. It is a challenge for the future, a long-range future at that. It seems that Matthew has given up any hope of an early return of Jesus. But that should not in any way deter his followers from being what the Master commanded them to be. The Kingdom is present, and one can begin to participate in it already.

It is easy to see how the Gospel of Matthew has retained its popularity among Christians of all ages. The strong emphasis on ethical values, the delightful parables, and the imposing figure of the King-Teacher make this a most impressive writing for people of faith.

The Gospel of Luke

In turning to study the Gospel of Luke, one must be aware that this book is only the first of a two-volume work (the second volume being Acts). Therefore the critical problems of the one will affect the decisions made about the other, and the religious emphases will be much the same throughout both volumes.

As for the external evidence, the tradition is very strong that Luke, who was a physician and sometime companion of Paul, wrote these books. Internally the gospel yields no clues as to the author except that he was a person of some education and knowledge of the Greek language. The Book of Acts, however, does yield some evidence. In the second half of that book there are several points at which the narrative changes from the third person (i.e., "they did,") to the first person (i.e., "we did,"). These passages are scattered throughout chapters 16–28 (cf. 16:9–18; 20:5–15[16–38]; 21:1–18; 27:1–28:16). Many have thought that this indicates that the writer was a companion of Paul at these points and wrote a diary which he used in the writing of Acts. If one takes the Acts accounts and compares them with the letters of Paul (especially Colossians 4:10–17), by the process of elimination the name of Luke is left as the probable author of the diary. Since the style and language of these portions seems to be the same as that of the remainder of Acts, many feel that the case for Lukan authorship is established.

There are some very reputable New Testament scholars who disagree with this conclusion, however. They argue that the traditions asserting Lukan authorship are relatively late, that there are seeming contradictions between Paul's letters and the Acts account, and that the utilization of the "we" sections could have been done by someone other than the author of the diary. Efforts to demonstrate that the language of Luke is filled with "medical" terminology (thus substantiating the claim for Luke the physician) have failed to be convincing.

In this instance, as in some others, various people interpret the data differently. While it is possible that the tradition may be incorrect, the internal evidence is overall quite supportive of the tradition. And since the tradition is so strong and so uniform, there seems to be no reason to doubt it in this case. Luke, therefore, is assumed to be the author of these two works.

The place of writing is, in the scholarly theories, widely ranged. Some have argued for Caesarea, some Greece, some Palestine, some

Asia Minor, and some Rome! Here is a place where one can muster some very good arguments for each of the theories. The probability, perhaps, causes one to lean toward Greece or Asia Minor, but one cannot be dogmatic at this point. As for the date of the writing, it must be later than 65–68 A.D. since Luke used Mark's gospel. Dates ranging then from 70–100+ have been defended, but the probability points to a date not long after 70 A.D. Some have even interpreted Luke 19:43f. as a description of what happened to Jerusalem in the 70 A.D. war related shortly after the event. True or no, this cannot be substantiated, but the internal evidence of the gospel and the traditions that were used in the composition of the writing lead one in the direction of an earlier rather than a later date. Somewhere ca. 75 A.D. would probably not be far from wrong.

There were several sources used by the author in the composition of the gospel. Mark again seems to stand as the basis for the overall structure with ample material added from the Q and L traditions. One of the characteristics of Luke's use of sources is his decided tendency to follow one rather closely before turning to another. His inclination to do this has raised a question concerning the manner in which this gospel was composed. If one removes the Markan material, what is left (minus the birth narratives) seems to form a connected story by itself. This phenomenon has caused some to argue that Luke wrote a shorter preliminary gospel using the Q and L traditions (this gospel is labeled "Proto-Luke"). When Luke then came into contact with Mark's gospel, so the theory goes, he expanded this shorter version by the addition of Markan material plus the birth narratives to produce the gospel which now bears his name. This theory is fascinating but very few New Testament scholars have accepted it. Some such procedure may very well have been the way the gospel came to its present form, however.

Luke's purpose in writing such a lengthy account which comprises two volumes is not as clear as one would like. Both documents are addressed to a "most excellent Theophilus." Who this is, however, is simply not known. The title may be a clue that he was a Roman official of some sort, or perhaps even a "patron" who helped finance Luke's literary project.

Several theories have been espoused concerning the purpose of

Luke's writing. One is that Luke wrote simply to record a history of Jesus and the early church. He says that he wants to present an "orderly account" of the events that have happened. But it is not necessarily true that an "orderly account" and a chronological history are the same. We are already aware that these writings are basically "faith" oriented and therefore more than simple history. That becomes even more apparent when one reads through these two volumes.

Another popular and current interpretation of Luke's purpose is that he wrote to explain the delay in the Parousia. Therefore, Luke wrote to present the events depicted in the gospel and the history of the church as a kind of "salvation history" scheme which is part of the larger plan of God for his people and his world. The most popular of the ideas has Luke divide history into three periods: (1) up to John the Baptizer; (2) the life of Jesus; (3) the period of the church. As popular as such schemes are, there really seems to be little evidence for them from the biblical texts themselves. And they certainly do not fit into any theory that holds that the reason for such a schematic division of history is based on the delay of the Parousia. Luke not only keeps the Mark apocalypse (Mark 13) but adds another (chapter 17)! This certainly does not seem to be the work of someone who is trying to explain away the delay in the Parousia's appearance.

A few have even argued that Luke-Acts was written to be used as a defense for Paul at his trial in Rome. Others have argued that the purpose in writing was to keep the people in the church where Luke was away from "heretical" teachings such as were espoused by the gnostics (for a fuller description of this type of thinking, cf. pp. 87ff.). Still others have argued that the main purpose was to explain the relationship between Judaism and Christianity and why the Jews had rejected the Messiah and now were rejected themselves. Certainty and unanimity at the point of purpose of writing simply cannot be attained.

To summarize the critical matters briefly it can be said that the evidence points to Luke as the author of this gospel (and Acts). The volumes were addressed to a "most-excellent Theophilus" who was probably a member of the church but was also a Roman official, perhaps for the purpose of his relating to his superiors that Christians were not and were not going to be dangerous or subversive citizens. Such a time would be soon after the Neronian persecution and the destruction of Jerusalem in 70 A.D. Until this time the Roman government and the world at large simply viewed the Christians as, in a sense, a sect within Judaism. The church audience for which Luke wrote seems to have been composed of ordinary people who needed encouragement and hope. For the Jesus presented in this gospel is a friend of all, especially those who have little to hope for.

Exactly what are the religious emphases of Luke's work? There are several themes which are strongly emphasized throughout both of the volumes. One of the major themes is that of "universalism," i.e., that Jesus as Messiah was proclaiming the gifts and graces of God to all people, Jew and Gentile, male and female, slave and free. This new gospel is not limited; it is for all.

A second emphasis of Luke's writing highlights true piety and the importance of being a truly pious person. The term "pious" has too often in our culture come to have very negative connotations. A "pious" person is one who is hypocritical or makes a continuous public display of long-faced religion. The basic meaning of the word underlies, however, the way Luke depicts his characters. The people in Luke are truly aware of God's Presence in their lives, and they live in the light of that understanding. These are people for whom God makes a difference in the manner of their lives. This is what true piety means. Prayer, therefore, also finds a central place at crucial points in the narrative, for truly pious people want and need to pray.

Further, Luke fills his gospel and Acts with the idea of the Holy Spirit and the activity of the Holy Spirit. In no other gospel does the Holy Spirit find such a significant and important place. And in the Book of Acts the emphasis is even more pointedly made.

Also, Luke emphasizes the political innocence of Jesus and the Christian leaders, especially as they may come into contact with Roman authorities. Scholars are divided over exactly what historical cause called for such a strong emphasis in this area. Whatever the reason, there is no question about its prominent place in the writings, however.

Perhaps the most well-known of the emphases of these books, and the one which makes the gospel especially human and loved, is that of the great concern shown for the "outcasts" of the world: the poor, the sick, the despised, the powerless, and even women who would fall under this category in that time. These are the people Jesus works with and who gladly hear him. This motif is so emphatically stressed in the gospel that some have even labeled it "The Gospel of the Outcasts."

The Gospel of Luke: Outline

I.   Birth Narratives 1–2
II.   Background for Jesus' Ministry 3:1–4:13
III. The Galilean Ministry 4:14–9:50
IV.   The Perean Ministry 9:51–19:27
V.   The Events in Jerusalem 19 :28–21:38
VI.   The Passion Narrative 22–24

Luke's gospel, as does Matthew's, begins with a number of incidents relating to the birth of the Messiah. Whereas Matthew emphasized Jesus as a King-Messiah, the fulfillment of true Judaism, Luke emphasizes Jesus as a friend of all people. True to his usual emphases these first chapters are filled with truly pious people— John the Baptizer's mother and father, Mary, Simeon, Anna, and others. These people are so filled with the understanding of the importance of God in their lives that the chapters are filled with hymns of poetic praise (cf. 1:14ff.; 1:31ff.; 1:46ff.; 1:67ff.; 2:14; 2:29ff.). In addition the emphasis upon the "outcasts" of the world is made very plain. Instead of Joseph being the central character as in Matthew, Luke has Mary at the center of the events. Whereas in Matthew rich and knowledgeable persons come to do homage, in Luke's gospel the announcement of Jesus' birth is made to common ordinary shepherds (a group not too highly respected in those days!).

The background for Jesus' ministry is again found in the events surrounding the person of John the Baptizer. As part of the background section, Luke includes a genealogy of Jesus. It is a different genealogy (not exactly the same as Matthew's), but the most important change is that Luke traces Jesus' descent not from Abraham but back to Adam, the prototype of the entire human race. The temptation episode is essentially like that of Matthew's gospel with the exception of the arrangement of the "trials."

The initial incident which begins Jesus' ministry in Luke again reflects one of his major emphases. Whereas in Mark Jesus came proclaiming that the Kingdom was at hand and "immediately" went to work demonstrating that the power of God was already triumphing over the Kingdom of Satan; and whereas in Matthew's gospel he began with a long "sermon," in Luke's gospel Jesus goes to the synagogue and proclaims the "acceptable year of the Lord," meaning that *all* people, the poor, the needy, even the Gentiles, are to be included in God's Kingdom. For this he receives the wrath of the hearers who attempt in a mob-type scene to kill him.

Throughout this section (down to 9:50) Luke basically follows Mark's outline even though he does add material that reflects his own special emphases. In addition he omits a large portion of Mark (Mark 6:45–8:26) undoubtedly in order that he can include material that is important to his own presentation. At 9:51 Luke begins a section that almost totally departs from Markan material, a section that comprises what some commentators on Luke call the "Great Interpolation" (9:51–18:14). This material is a combination of Q traditions plus L traditions, and this section includes some of the more well-known and beloved of Luke's stories. Included here are the parables of the Rich Fool, the Good Samaritan, the Prodigal Son, the Rich Man and Lazarus, and the Pharisee and the Publican, among others. As one can readily see, these stories reflect Luke's particular emphases.

The last week in Jerusalem follows much the same pattern as Mark, but Luke has included some of his own material to support his peculiar themes. For example there is added another trial, this one before Herod Antipas (23:6–12), and neither Pilate nor Herod find any evidence against Jesus deserving of death. To emphasize this point even further, the centurion, who in Mark's gospel declared that Jesus was "Son of God" (Mark 15:39), declares, "Certainly this man was innocent!" (Luke 23:47).

According to Mark, Jesus was to appear to the disciples in Galilee (even though no appearances are preserved), and Matthew's resurrection appearance takes place there. But in Luke the resurrection appearances take place in and around Jerusalem. The gospel concludes with a look toward the second volume: "... but stay in the city, until you are clothed with power from on high" (24:49). The connecting link between the two specifically seems to be the account of Jesus' leaving the disciples, for the last verses of the gospel records that incident and the first verses of Acts also gives an account (though somewhat different).

Of all the gospels Luke's seems to be the most "religious," if by religious one understands that every aspect of life is under the care of God, that religion is for all people, that religion focuses on one's duty to and relationship with God, and that religion touches people where they live in everyday existence. The Jesus of Luke is a friend of the poor and outcast and lonely. He speaks to people whose lives are not exciting or full of wealth and power. True humility is an important aspect for the people who are to belong to this Jesus.

The Titles of Jesus

Throughout these three gospels one finds several "titles" which are given to Jesus by the gospel writers. Three such titles are worthy of mention: Messiah, Son of God, and Son of Man.

Messiah

The first of these titles is Messiah. The term comes from the Old Testament background where the word means "anointed." Special persons were *anointed* during that period, usually to perform a particular duty for Yahweh. Three groups of people could lay claim to being "anointed"—the priests, some prophets, and the king. The basic concept of and hope for a Messiah grew out of the general understanding of being anointed to perform a special task for Yahweh, but more specifically focused upon, in the hope for a ruler, a king like David, who would lead the people of God under the guidance of Yahweh himself! Such hope began to arise in the pre-exilic period (reflected in the pre-exilic prophets Micah 5:2ff. and Isaiah 9:2ff. and 11:1ff.) that Yahweh would send a good king to restore the people to the proper relationship with God and to a position of political and economic strength.

Strangely enough (and contrary to much popular belief) there was not really that much emphasis in the Old Testament literature about a Messiah. Jeremiah (23:5ff.) spoke about a "righteous Branch" from the lineage of David who would reign as a king wisely and justly. And Ezekiel (34:23–24; 37:24f.) looked for a shepherd like David who would rule over the people in accordance with the rules of Yahweh. After the exile both Haggai (2:20ff.) and Zechariah (4:6–10a) thought that Zerubbabel was the promised Messiah (ca. 520 B.C.), but Zerubbabel suddenly vanished from the scene and was heard from no more. From this point on there is no more mention of a Messiah.

The idea of such a person arising to assist the people did not regain impetus until after the time of the Hasmonean rulers. As already mentioned this led to the idea of a priestly Messiah (since these rulers were priest-kings). But in reality no settled idea of what the Messiah would be ever emerged as *the* picture of God's anointed.

Because Jesus was of the lineage of David the early church naturally interpreted that as a fulfillment of the Scriptures. But Davidic descent was not considered to be a prerequisite for being Messiah. The tradition included in Mark 12:35ff. (and parallels Matthew 22:41ff., Luke 20:41ff.) definitely downplays the relationship of the Messiah to David. It was much more important to be properly related to God than to David.

Another pointer to the Messiahship of Jesus is found in the stories of the miraculous feedings (Mark 6:30–44 and parallels; Mark 8:1–9 and parallel). It was a common thought of that time that when the Messiah established the Kingdom of God, he would be the host at a great banquet. When Jesus fed the multitude on these occasions, the usual interpretation of these incidents is that he was fulfilling the ideas connected with the Messianic banquet. And this point is also reflected at another setting, Matthew 8 : 11ff., where Jesus talks about others who will come to eat at table with Abraham, Isaac, and Jacob in the Kingdom.

Some interpreters of the gospels make a great deal of the fact that Jesus does not ever specifically claim to be Messiah. The closest point comes in Mark 14:61–62 when in response to the direct question of the High Priest, "Are you the Messiah, the Son of God?" Jesus answers, "I am ..." Even with this statement, however, there are those who still deny that Jesus ever claimed to be the Messiah. This title, they argue, was a later interpretation of the church read back into the ministry of Jesus. Whether that is correct is open to debate, but it is certain from the text that each gospel writer viewed Jesus as the Messiah and depicted him as understanding himself to be such.

The major question as presented in the gospels was not whether Jesus was the Messiah but rather what kind of Messiah Jesus understood himself to be. The Synoptics are again in agreement on this point. Jesus' ministry was interpreted as a Servant ministry. He was, therefore, a Servant-Messiah. This is clear from the moment of the baptism, the temptation accounts, through his public ministry, his teaching to the disciples, and continued to the time of the crucifixion. His life consistently was a life of service dedicated to God in the proclamation and inauguration of his Kingdom.

Son of God

As important as the idea of Messiahship was, it became very quickly (perhaps because of the teaching of Jesus) relegated to a secondary position. The title that was even more important for the early church was "Son of God." As stated earlier, there were "sons of God" all over the ancient world, but to the early church Jesus was uniquely Son of God in a way and to a degree no one before or after could ever be. Mark's gospel, as has been seen, is a consistent portrait of Jesus as Son of God. Even the demons who have supernatural insight recognized that this was no ordinary mortal, but "the Holy One of God" (cf. Mark 1:24, et al.).

There are other episodes which point to this close relationship of Jesus with God: Jesus' claim to be able to forgive sins (Mark 2:5 and parallels), his claim to be "lord of the Sabbath (Mark 2:28 and parallels), the episode of the cleansing of the Temple (Mark 11:15ff. and parallels), the parable of the vineyard (Mark 12:1ff. and parallels), and the reply to the High Priest (Mark 14:61–62 and parallels). All these assume a unique relationship between Jesus and God.

Son of Man

The last title is in some ways the most interesting and most controversial. It is the title "Son of Man." The first question to be answered is that of the meaning of the term. In the Semitic background the phrase "Son of Man" could designate simply "man" (either individually or collectively). Usually when found with this designation, the idea was that of a human being in a state of creaturehood or a state of weakness. The usage of Ezekiel (cf. Ezekiel 2:1, 3, 8 et al) falls under this category.

A second meaning that is sometimes pointed out by linguists is that the phrase can be a substitute for the first person pronoun, I. A speaker could say, "son of man," when "I" would be the intended meaning, much as is sometimes done today with "the present writer," "your speaker," etc. It is true, however, that not all scholars agree that this was a usage for the term, but it does appear likely that in some instances it was.

A third usage of the term is found in titles. The phrase is found in Daniel 7 where one "like a son of man" appears. In that context the term is found to represent a "corporate" figure, "the saints of the most high." There is another document in which the term appears, this time designating an individual figure. This is the intertestamental book known as I Enoch. In this writing the "son of man" appears to be a type of "heavenly" being who exercises at least some of the functions of a Messianic figure (cf. I Enoch 46, 62, 69). The background, therefore, of the term is varied.

Upon turning to the usage of the phrase in the Synoptic gospels one finds that the term seems to be used as a title most frequently, and further that the term carries an individualistic connotation (even though there are some few New Testament scholars who interpret it as a corporate entity), and that it is almost always found on the lips of Jesus. In addition one finds also that the sayings about the Son of Man in the Synoptics can be grouped together under common headings, of which there are three. First, there is a group of sayings in which the Son of Man is viewed as a human being, a person of this world. Secondly, there is a group of sayings that connect the Son of Man and suffering. And there is a third group which depicts the Son of Man as a figure who would appear sometime in the future.

New Testament scholars are divided as to exactly how these categories should be interpreted. Some scholars reject all three categories as being from Jesus, arguing that this was a title given to him by the early church and subsequently read back into the traditions about Jesus and his teachings. It seems odd, however, if this is true, that the term is not used anywhere else in the New Testament as a title for Jesus—except in Acts 7:56 and Revelation 1:13. A title that had been created for Jesus by the church would surely have left some trace in the writings of the church for the church! It is much more likely that the term was one used by Jesus which was preserved in the traditions about Jesus, but which the church did not use, preferring instead to use what they considered to be the more exalted titles.

Other suggestions have been made, one being that Jesus used the term but not of himself. His reference was to a coming figure who would bring in the new age and the judgment of God. Some of these scholars argue, therefore, that the only category which is authentic as far as Jesus' teachings are concerned is the third category. Some others accept only the second category as going back to Jesus directly. One can readily see that unanimity of opinion on this topic is difficult to determine.

The most practical method of interpreting the sayings would seem to be an open-minded approach to each saying, examining it in its context against the three possible interpretations and the three possible categories. It may be that in the translation of the term from Aramaic to Greek there were some nuances which were missed. For example, if one examines carefully the saying in Mark 2:27–28, there are several possibilities for interpreting the meaning. *As it stands,* Mark understands the saying to be a claim by Jesus to be Lord of the Sabbath as the Son of Man. In other words whatever Jesus thought appropriate for his disciples to do on the Sabbath was acceptable since he exercised authority over it as Son of Man, Son of God. Originally, however, the saying may have had a different meaning. In the context of the story the basic point seems to be that human need takes precedent over the pedantic rules of religious authorities. Citing an example from the Scriptures about no less a person than King David, Jesus made the point that, "The sabbath was made for man, not man for the sabbath ..." (2:27). The subsequent saying is the crucial one. "So the Son of man is lord even of the sabbath." It is just possible that originally the saying may have meant, "so man is lord even of the sabbath." This would make the saying then consistent and can easily be explained as a misunderstanding of the common Semitic term "son of man." Since, however, the term was usually used by Jesus as a title, it was so understood here as well.

This simple illustration points to the complexity of the situation. That Jesus used the term and used it of himself seems clearly established. Whether one can establish a standard methodology to determine the authenticity of each saying or the accuracy of its being understood by those who passed along the tradition is uncertain. What is before the interpreter are the texts of the gospels. Each gospel writer used the term as a self-designation of Jesus and understood it to be Jesus' own special phrase to illustrate His interpretation of His ministry. It was a ministry characterized by service and suffering but one which Jesus strongly affirmed would ultimately climax in victory. The Son of Man sayings fit these ideas quite closely. Whether they go back to the teachings of Jesus (which is most likely) or whether they are inventions of the early church, these sayings fit the ministry of Jesus as presented in the Synoptic gospels almost perfectly. It is against that background that the sayings must ultimately be judged.

**Notes
Chapter II**

[1]Cf. C. H. Dodd, *The Apostolic Teaching and Its Development* (New York: Harper & Row, 1951), for the classic discussion of the *kerygma.*

**Suggestions for
Further Study**

Synoptic Gospels

For an introduction to the discipline of form-criticism, the following sources are very good.

R. C. Briggs. *Interpreting the New Testament Today.* Abingdon Press, 1973. Pb. Pp. 87–109.

E. V. McKnight. *What Is Form Criticism?* Philadelphia: Fortress Press, 1969.

E. B. Redlich. *Form-Criticism.* London: Gerald Duckworth & Co. Ltd., 1939.

Bruce Vawter. *The Four Gospels: An Introduction.* New York: Doubleday & Co., 1967.

For the older and classic statements about the discipline and its application to the text, see the following.

M. Dibelius. *From Tradition to Gospel.* Translated by B. L. Woolf. New York: Charles Scribner's Sons, 1935.

Rudolf Bultmann. *The History of the Synoptic Tradition.* Translated by John Marsh. New York: Harper and Row, 1963.

The whole area of source criticism may be seen in its classic form in B. H. Streeter, *The Four Gospels: A Study of Origins.* Rev. ed. London: Macmillan & Co., Ltd., 1930.

Also see R. C. Briggs. *Interpreting the New Testament Today.* Pp. 59–86.

The view that Matthew is the earlier gospel is still argued by a few. The most appropriate source for studying this thesis is W. R. Farmer, *The Synoptic Problem: A Critical Analysis.* New York: Macmillan, 1964.

The study of redaction criticism may be pursued in the following sources.

R. C. Briggs. *Interpreting the New Testament Today.* Pp. 59–86, 110–137.

Norman Perrin. *What Is Redaction Criticism?* Philadelphia: Fortress Press, 1969.

J. Rohde. *Rediscovering the Teaching of the Evangelists.* Translated by Dorothea M. Barton. Philadelphia: The Westminster Press, 1968.

C. H. Talbert. *What Is a Gospel? The Genre of the Canonical Gospels.* Philadelphia: Fortress Press, 1977.

The way Jesus has been interpreted through the centuries is a fascinating and rewarding study. The usual designation of this pursuit is "the quest for the historical Jesus." The following books are quite good for such an investigation.

A. Schweitzer. *The Quest of the Historical Jesus: A Critical Study of Its Progress from Reimarus to Wrede.* Translated by W. Montgomery. 3rd edition. London: Adam & Charles Black, 1954 (original German edition 1906). This is the classic account of the problem up to the time of Schweitzer.

Two more popular and less weighty books should be of great value to the beginning student.

Hugh Anderson. *Jesus.* Great Lives Observed Series. Englewood Cliffs, New Jersey: Prentice-Hall, Inc., 1967.

J. H. Hayes. *Son of God to Superstar: Twentieth-Century Understanding of Jesus.* Nashville: Abingdon Press, 1976.

Other books about Jesus that are of value to the student. These listings include different approaches and viewpoints.

Günter Bornkamm. *Jesus of Nazareth.* Translated by Irene and Fraser McLuskey. New York: Harper & Row, 1960.

Hans Conzelmann. *Jesus.* Translated by J. Raymond Lord. Philadelphia: Fortress Press, 1973.

C. H. Dodd. *The Founder of Christianity.* New York: Macmillan Co., 1970.

H. C. Kee. *Jesus in History: An Approach to the Study of the Gospels.* 2nd edition. New York: Harcourt, Brace, Jovanovitch, 1977.

C. F. D. Moule. *The Origin of Christology.* New York: Cambridge University Press, 1977.

E. W. Saunders. *Jesus in the Gospels.* Englewood Cliffs, New Jersey: Prentice-Hall, Inc., 1967.

Eduard Schweizer. *Jesus.* Translated by David Green. London: SCM Press, 1971.

E. Trocmé. *Jesus and His Contemporaries.* Translated by R. A. Wilson. London: SCM Press, 1973.

G. Vermes. *Jesus the Jew: A Historian's Reading of the Gospels.* London: Collins, 1973.

John Reumann. *Jesus in the Church's Gospels: Modern Scholarship and the Earliest Sources.* Philadelphia: Fortress Press, 1968.

The following commentaries and discussions are recommended for a study of the individual gospels.

Mark

P. J. Achtemeier. *Mark.* Proclamation Commentary Series. Philadelphia: Fortress Press, 1975.

H. C. Kee. *Community of the New Age: Studies in Mark's Gospel.* Philadelphia: Westminster Press, 1977.

Eduard Schweizer. *The Good News According to Mark.* Translated by D. H. Madvig. Richmond: John Knox Press, 1970.

Hugh Anderson. *The Gospel of Mark.* Greenwood, South Carolina: The Attic Press, 1976.

C. E. B. Cranfield. *The Gospel According to St. Mark.* New York: Cambridge University Press, 1959.

W. Marxsen. *Mark the Evangelist.* Translated by R. A. Harrisville. Nashville: Abingdon Press, 1968.

D. E. Nineham. *The Gospel of St. Mark.* Pelican Gospel Commentaries. Baltimore: Penguin Books, 1963.

W. Wrede, *The Messianic Secret in the Gospels.* Trans. by J. C. G. Grieg. Cambridge: J. Clark, 1971.

Matthew
W. D. Davies. *The Setting of the Sermon on the Mount.* New York: Cambridge University Press, 1964. Not for beginners!

————. *The Sermon on the Mount.* New York: Cambridge University Press, 1966.

J. C. Fenton. *Saint Matthew.* Pelican Gospel Commentaries. Baltimore: Penguin Books, 1963.

H. B. Green. *The Gospel According to Matthew.* New Clarendon Bible. Oxford: Oxford University Press, 1975.

David Hill. *The Gospel of Matthew.* Greenwood, South Carolina: The Attic Press, 1972.

Eduard Schweizer. *The Good News According to Matthew.* Translated by D. E. Green. Atlanta: John Knox Press, 1975.

Luke
C. K. Barrett. *Luke the Historian in Recent Study.* London: Epworth Press, 1961.

G. B. Caird. *Saint Luke.* Pelican Gospel Commentaries. Baltimore: Penguin Books, 1963.

Hans Conzelmann. *The Theology of St. Luke.* Translated by Geoffrey Buswell. London: Faber and Faber, 1960.

E. E. Ellis. *The Gospel of Luke.* Rev. ed. Greenwood, South Carolina: The Attic Press, 1974.

A. R. C. Leaney. *The Gospel According to St. Luke.* 2nd ed. New York: Harper & Row, 1966.

Hans Conzelmann. *The Theology of St. Luke.* Translated by G. Buswell. New York: Harper & Row, 1960. A classic redaction-critical approach.

Further Readings on the "Son of Man" Problem
F. H. Borsch. *The Son of Man in Myth and History.* Philadelphia: Westminster Press, 1967.

R. Bultmann. *The Theology of the New Testament.* Translated by K. Groebel. New York: Charles Scribner's Sons, 1951. Vol. I, pp. 26–32.

A. J. B. Higgins. *Jesus and the Son of Man.* Philadelphia: Fortress Press, 1965.

H. E. Tödt. *The Son of Man in the Synoptic Tradition.* Translated by D. M. Barton. Philadelphia: Westminster Press, 1965.

Trial and Death of Jesus
One of the more interesting aspects of Jesus' life revolves around his trial and exactly why he was condemned. The following works are recommended for those interested in this problem.

Paul Winter. *On the Trial of Jesus.* Berlin: Walter de Gruyter, 1961.

J. Blinzler. *The Trial of Jesus.* Translated by I. and F. McHugh. Westminster, Md.: Newman, 1959.

Ernest Brammel, editor. *The Trial of Jesus. Cambridges Studies in Honour of C. F. D. Moule.* London: SCM, 1970.

For the idea that Jesus was a political rebel, see S. G. F. Brandon, *Jesus and the Zealots.* Manchester: University Press, 1967.

———. *The Trial of Jesus.* London: Batsford, 1968.

CHAPTER III

Synoptic Themes

Jesus' Ministry

It is an accepted criterion of New Testament studies that the gospels are not "biographies" but are a special kind of confessional writing. Therefore these documents do not yield "historical" data so as to allow the student to write a biography of Jesus which would be acceptable to the "pure" historian of the twentieth century. (It is, however, often overlooked that we cannot *really* write a twentieth century biography of any personage of antiquity!) The gospels, it must be remembered, are documents written in the light of the resurrection of Jesus, and therefore reflect some theological "growth" in the church's understanding of the nature and significance of this person. The complexity of the situation can be reflected as follows: first of all, there was the "bare fact" of Jesus' life and teaching; then came the oral proclamation of this "fact," probably altered somewhat with theological and religious interpretation; then came the oral traditions selected and remembered usually because of the needs of the early community; some of these traditions were later collected and written down; the gospels writers then used these oral and written sources in the compilation and composition of their gospels. At any and every point in this chain there was the possibility that the purposes of the person(s) involved could and would modify the tradition to fit a particular existential situation. Some scholars have even contended that certain stories or teachings were "created" to meet needs inherent in the early church so that the gospel material cannot be used to determine Jesus "as he really was," or as this concept is usually called, the "Jesus of History."

Having this in mind, we can now understand why some scholars are exceedingly dubious about discovering the "Jesus of History." A few have gone so far as to say that we can know practically nothing about him. Rudolf Bultmann's oft-quoted statement is a classic: "I do indeed think that we can now know almost nothing concerning the life and personality of Jesus, since the early Christian sources show no interest in either, are moreover fragmentary and often legendary; and other sources about Jesus do not exist."[1] Thus one can readily see that the discussion about the historical reliability of the gospel records is exceedingly diverse ranging from those who argue for the complete historicity of the gospel accounts to those who feel that there is little, if any, actual history contained within them. In all probability the truth lies somewhere between.

The problem that the modern interpreter faces is that the questions which are raised now are not the same types of questions which were considered important to the ancient writers. These persons were indeed concerned with history, but that was a secondary not a primary consideration. We recall again that these are religious documents speaking from faith to faith. It may well be that modern investigators expect too much from these documents, much more than was ever intended by the original writers.

A very judicious statement by one of the leading New Testament scholars of today may be in order here.

> We may fairly say that so far no branch of criticism has provided us with any sure or universally acceptable formula for sifting out the authentic historical from the theological or evangelical element in the Gospels. The field of Jesus-research has been all through the scene of a rather painful conflict of conservative and radical tendencies, of confidence in the historical trustworthiness of the Gospels and extreme doubt. But perhaps for too long too many have expected too much from these documents. We have imagined that they should place in our grasp the figure of Jesus "as he really was in himself" as an isolated and idealized individual. But to wish for so much is to wish Jesus out of the historical process, for history has a lot to do with the impact and reaction, impression and response, relationship and encounter between person and person. Insofar as the Gospels do not separate Jesus from the concrete world in which he lived, but show him as a real man in contact with real men, they simply will not yield to our facile and unjustifiable

modernization whereby we hope to extract from them the "timeless essence" of his life in capsule form and in one easy lesson, so to speak.[2]

In other words, the gospel accounts of Jesus' ministry are indeed filled with historical data about the life, teaching, and ministry of Jesus. But the purpose of these writers was not primarily to present a historical reconstruction of Jesus; it was, rather, to present Jesus as a religious being with religious connotations and importance. To ask of these documents, then, only or primarily historical questions is to ask the wrong questions! It is not, however, illegitimate to examine these accounts to learn all that may be possible about the historical setting.

According to the Synoptic picture the ministry of Jesus was located primarily in Galilee and concluded with a trip to Jerusalem at Passover time. It is difficult to ascertain the exact length of this public period from the gospel accounts. Probably the extent was no less than about six months and no longer than eighteen months. The Synoptic chronology (basically Mark's), it has been contended, is essentially that of the actual ministry of Jesus. Some still advocate this, but more and more scholars are beginning to give credence to the Johannine chronology where there is the three-year ministry known to most Sunday school children, and where the ministry in Jerusalem is a significant part of Jesus' life. There are several trips to Jerusalem in John, but in the Synoptics there is only one. According to Mark, Jesus is crucified on the Passover after having eaten the Passover meal with his disciples. (The Jewish day is reckoned from 6 P.M. to 6 P.M.; therefore at 6 P.M. on Thursday the Passover began.) Jesus ate the Passover meal, was arrested, tried, convicted, executed, and buried—all on the Jewish Passover.

At this point the disciples were evidently bewildered and confused. They had apparently scattered with Jesus' arrest. The movement seemed to have been squelched. But after the Sabbath, when some women came to the cave where his body had been placed, they found the tomb empty. At the tomb they found a young man (Mark), an angel (Matthew), or two men in "dazzling apparel" (Luke). The proclamation was the same: "He has risen!" Further, both Matthew and Luke have resurrection appearances and most probably so did the original ending of Mark's gospel now lost to us. Thus one can readily see that the one single event which more than any other transformed the frightened disorganized band of disciples into a courageous group proclaiming the totality of this life which could not be snuffed out by the evil of humankind was the resurrection. The New Testament in general and the Synoptics in particular do not give us any *specific* information concerning the resurrection, neither how it was accomplished, what kind of body Jesus had, etc. The unanimous witness, however, was that he did in fact rise and appeared to numerous people. These appearances did not last for a long period of time—only long enough to convince the disciples and others that this stupendous feat had in fact been accomplished.

There are many persons who think that the resurrection, being such a unique and monumental occurrence, *proved* that Jesus was God's Messiah. This event in itself, however, did not *prove* to these people that this Jesus was God's Messiah. Rather it was the culminating event in a long series of events and association with and learning from Jesus over a period of time that finally convinced them of his Messiahship. While the early disciples were awed by the event of the resurrection, it must not be thought that the event *by itself* led them to the theological interpretation they placed upon it. Their interpretation was based upon the totality of the life and ministry of Jesus situated as it was within the flow of human history at that particular time. It was based, rather than on one stupendous event, on a long series of events of which the resurrection was the crowning validation on a life that, at least to these persons, seemed to manifest in itself those qualities which fulfilled not only the concept of the Messiah who would inaugurate the Kingdom of God but more than that—a person who was uniquely *Son of God*—the revelation of God to the world in terms of a human personality. This life made possible, they believed, a new and more direct access of people to God, an assurance that God loved them and would forgive their sins, a new way of life (Kingdom living) which would differentiate between them and the world, and the assurance of a victory over all the forces of evil and darkness including the last great enemy, death. Thus it was not just in the dying and rising that these people saw in Jesus God's promise, but in the living, day-to-day living, that they could recognize his authority over those parts of one's being and world that separate a person from God.

Even though we know relatively little of the actual events of Jesus' life, the impact that he made through his personality and actions was great indeed. Closely related to this was, of course, his teaching. And it is to that aspect of the Synoptic tradition that we now turn.

Common Themes of Synoptic Teaching

While each gospel writer depicts Jesus in his own peculiar way, there are nevertheless common themes which occur in the teachings of Jesus in spite of editorial redaction and emendation by transmission.

The Kingdom of God

The most prominent theme of Jesus' teaching in the Synoptics is the theme of the Kingdom of God. Most of Jesus' parables and teachings are directed toward the exploration of what the Kingdom is like and how one is to enter into it. The most difficult thing for the modern writer to ascertain is exactly what Jesus intended by the term. There are those who argue that Jesus meant a kind of political state whereby the chosen of God would rule the world. Others believe that the Kingdom was to Jesus a completely other-worldly type of existence. Still others think that it was intended to be a type of earthly Utopia usually characterized by the kind of structures which their particular pre-philosophy dictates. Many of this stripe feel that the Kingdom is *completely* this-worldly. There are varying views which range between the extremes and which attempt to do justice to Jesus' teachings at this point.

It must be admitted that there are various elements in Jesus' teaching about the Kingdom. There are overtones both of a this-worldly as well as an other-worldly sphere. There are also overtones (to be discussed more fully later) of both present and future aspects of this Kingdom. There is considerable evidence that Jesus believed that this new Kingdom life was to be different from ordinary life both under the law and apart from the law.

All of these diverse aspects of Jesus' teaching on the Kingdom (and more) lead one to the conclusion that the Kingdom is not a single, self-contained, easily definable, delimited structure but rather a combination of various ideas which are not presented to us in the gospels in a systematic way. This situation may be the result of the manner and mode in which the tradition was utilized and transmitted by the early church, or it may be that it reflects the lack of a systematic approach by Jesus himself. Nevertheless there are certain aspects to the Kingdom that seem to be fairly consistent. The first is that this is *God's* Kingdom. Human beings do not build it or cause it to come into existence—it is fully a gift of God *to* and *for* the human race. It is expected that individuals will accept the gift, as a child would with openness and eagerness, and also would accept the responsibilities which accompanied this great benefit to themselves. The parables of the Kingdom challenge the hearer to respond to this gracious offer, and Jesus teaches that there are grave consequences if one does not respond positively to the invitation.

This Kingdom is the means by which the Kingdom of Satan, that powerful and, to them, very real factor in the human predicament would be defeated and destroyed. The miracles are signs that the Kingdom of God is already making itself manifest in the lives of men and women. It was a *transforming power* made available to people in a way not previously known. Jesus' teaching about the Kingdom indicates that this Kingdom is neither totally individualistic nor totally corporate, that this Kingdom is not some earthly Utopia nor some apocalyptic catastrophe which would put an end to all human history. It was God's active intervention in the world of human affairs in a way and to a degree not hitherto acknowledged or recognized by the religious leaders. The Kingdom was in fact God's taking decisive action in the sphere of human history to restore humankind to its rightful place in God's created order.

There is evidence that Jesus conceived of this Kingdom as a growing dynamic entity, never static or stagnant, which would some day include persons of all types. The only limitation appears at times to be the commitment of people to work and labor in this

Kingdom and the commitment to dedicate themselves to it totally. It is dynamic because God is dynamic. God's Kingdom then is God's activity to save humanity and to do for people what they are unable to do for themselves. Through this activity his sovereignty is established beyond all doubt and his reign recognized as eternal.

The Eschatology of the Kingdom

A question closely related to that concerning the nature of the Kingdom centers on the "time" of the Kingdom. When was it to come? This is in all probability not the proper question for us to ask, but bitter theological debates have raged over this question. Therefore, a look at this issue is appropriate at this point. There are two basic views representing each of the "extremes."

First of all there is the futuristic eschatological view which places the coming of the Kingdom in the future. The most commonly mentioned name connected with this particular stance is that of Albert Schweitzer and is called "consistent" eschatology. Schweitzer takes as the base for understanding Jesus' views the statement in Matthew 10:23 (paraphrase), "... you will not have gone through all the towns of Israel, before the Son of Man arrives." It is his contention (following in a sense his contemporary, Johannes Weiss) that Jesus was thoroughly indoctrinated with the apocalyptic thinking of his contemporaries who looked for the Kingdom's coming in the immediate future in some dramatic form. Jesus was convinced, according to Schweitzer, at his baptism that he was the "Messiah designate." When, however, his prediction in Matthew 10:23 did not materialize, he was forced to revise the forecast. Jesus then thought that he must suffer and die. His death would constitute the "apocalyptic woes" (i.e., the intense evil which would immediately precede the intervention of God to establish the Kingdom), and this would "force the last things" to take place. Here is Schweitzer's famous statement concerning this point.

> Soon after that [the appearance of the Baptist] comes Jesus, and in the knowledge that He is the coming Son of Man lays hold of the wheel of the world to set it moving on that last revolution which is to bring all history to a close. It refuses to

turn, and He throws Himself upon it. Then it does turn; and crushes Him. Instead of bringing in the eschatological conditions, He has destroyed them. The wheel rolls onward, and the mangled body of the one immeasurable great Man, who was strong enough to think of himself as the spiritual ruler of mankind and to bend history to His purpose, is hanging upon it still. That is His victory and His reign.[3]

A second view is closely linked with the name of C. H. Dodd. The interpretation of those in this school is basically that Jesus thought of the Kingdom as already present in his ministry. While Jesus did utilize futuristic terminology, he nevertheless re-interpreted the apocalyptic content. The references to the future signify events of a wholly "supernatural order." The disciples because they were so much a part of their own world unfortunately misunderstood and continued to interpret the apocalyptic terminology rather literally. Or perhaps, as Dodd argues, the early church had a tendency to give apocalyptic form and meaning to sayings of Jesus which were never originally intended apocalyptically.

> But these future tenses are only an accommodation of language. . . . The Kingdom of God in its full reality is not something which will happen after other things have happened. . . . "The Day of the Son of Man" stands for the timeless fact. So far as history can contain it, it is embodied in the historic crisis which the coming of Jesus brought about. But the spirit of man, though dwelling in history, belongs to the eternal order, and the full meaning of the Day of the Son of Man, or of the Kingdom of God, he can experience only in that eternal order. That which cannot be experienced in history is symbolized by the picture of a coming event, and its timeless quality is expressed as pure simultaneity in time . . ."as the lightning flashes."[4]

One could readily anticipate the criticisms which were directed toward Professor Dodd's thesis. It was argued that his interpretation of Jesus' teachings was more applicable to Plato than to a Semitic mind living in the context of first century Palestine.

These two illustrations serve to show how diversely the eschatology of the Kingdom has been and can be interpreted. Neither of these two extreme positions take account, however, of the numerous passages recorded in the gospels which seem to refer to the Kingdom as either present or future. Both elements are there, and it seems illegitimate to ignore either at the expense of the other. Most scholars today fall between the extremes, recognizing that there are elements in Jesus' teaching which indicate both present and future aspects of the Kingdom. In a real sense the Kingdom was *at least* "breaking in" with Jesus' ministry, and there are sufficient illustrations in his teaching to demonstrate the idea that Kingdom living and Kingdom benefits are not postponed for some later time but begin in the present. It is also clear, however, that the Kingdom is not completed nor is it to be considered final in the present. The parables of growth and the teachings about the future consummation lead one to the firm conviction that there is a very definite futuristic emphasis in Jesus' teaching at this point. Whether the futuristic element should be interpreted as literal apocalyptic is debatable, but it is a fact that some future expectation was central in Jesus' thought about the Kingdom.

Thus there is a tension in the teaching of Jesus as depicted by the Synoptic writers between the present and future aspects of the Kingdom. How one makes a synthesis of them will depend to a great extent on a variety of considerations—for example, how much weight is allowed to form-critical, or source-critical, or redaction-critical methodology, to name only a few components. Much will remain in the mind of the interpreter, but justice must be done to the *evidence* if the search for real understanding of Jesus' teachings is to bring us close to what he really meant.

The Ethics of the Kingdom

Closely related to the questions of the meaning of the Kingdom of God and the time of its coming is that of the ethical obligations which the acceptance of the Kingdom placed upon the individual. Some have viewed Jesus's teaching in the Sermon on the Mount (Matthew 5–7) as "normative" for Kingdom living. But because a literal interpretation of Jesus' statements seems to be impossible, various theories have been suggested to relieve the problem. One of the most famous is that proposed by Albert Schweitzer called "interim-ethic." This view holds that Jesus never meant for his teachings to be followed (or that it was even possible for them to be followed) for a long period of time, but rather they were intended to be followed for that very short period between the present and the soon to be consummated Kingdom of God. One readily understands that this kind of interpretation is closely linked with an eschatology of the Kingdom which is futuristic and imminent.

It can be said that many interpreters make the mistake of viewing Jesus' ethical teaching too narrowly by connecting it only with the Sermon on the Mount. And further many make the mistake of taking Jesus' teaching here literally, not understanding the Semitic inclination toward hyperhbole and also toward practical proverbs and parables. Basically, it can be argued that the ethical demands of the Kingdom are *attitudinal* rather than propositional. In other words, people are not to substitute one set of legal maxims for another! If one has accepted the basic demand of the Kingdom, to accept the One whose Kingdom it is, and has committed oneself to the Kingdom openly and eagerly as a child, that person already has the foundational ethic for the Kingdom life.

One of the best examples is Jesus' oft misunderstood teaching concerning the "Sin against the Holy Spirit," sometimes called the "unforgiveable sin" (cf. Mark 3:21–30). In the context of the passage this refers to the "attitude" of the religious leaders toward Jesus. Because of their intense dislike for him, they were willing to accuse him of being able to cast out demons because he was in league with the demon world. Jesus was not unique in being able to exorcise demons, thus his question to them: "And if I cast out demons by Beelzebul, by whom do your sons cast them out?" (Luke 11:19). Their attitude resulted in calling good, evil, simply because of their own bias and prejudice. Persons with this kind of thought pattern are the self-righteous who cannot be forgiven because they are not and cannot be aware that they need forgiveness!

Closely related to this is Jesus' statement to John, his disciple, concerning the man casting out demons who was rebuked because he was not following the disciples. Jesus said, "Do not forbid him; for he that is not against you is for you" (Luke 9:5; cf. also Mark 9:38–40). Anyone who is doing good for the right reasons, i.e., alleviation of human suffering, cannot be viewed as an enemy. The basic theme of Jesus' ethical teaching is that one is to love God *totally* and to love one's neighbor as oneself. The guidelines for these commandments are to be found in Jesus' teaching. There are no long lists of *dos* or *don'ts* because Jesus was not a legalist. He knew that life is very complex and complicated and that no list could possibly fit into the many situations with which life confronts persons. Thus the important thing is to be prepared in terms of attitude and principle and dedication. These things being properly situated, the individual can then, by using the illustrative guidelines, determine the "Christian" action or reaction to the circumstances. This is not to say that the resultant action or reaction is therefore a positive good as some recent interpreters have intimated, but it is to say that the decision will be the "lesser of the two evils" given the nature of the world one lives in. But, according to Jesus' teaching, each decision made with the proper motivation in the light of the guidelines laid down by the authoritative principles could be viewed as the "Christian ethic." Those actions must be viewed, however, not simply in terms of what they mean for the present but also what they could mean for the future. In short, because the Kingdom is itself both present and future, the ethic of the Kingdom must be viewed in terms of actions which will benefit the Kingdom both now and later. And Jesus makes it very clear that the *means* one uses to attain one's goal are just as important as the goal itself (cf. Matthew 7:21–23).

How the early church attempted to use and apply the teachings of Jesus in the face of new situations and new people who were not of the same thought-world is the story of the remainder of the New Testament writings. To the spread of this new movement and its literature we now turn.

Notes   [1]Rudolf Bultmann, *Jesus and the Word,* trans.
Chapter III   Louise P. Smith and Erminie Huntress (N. Y.: Charles Scribner's Sons, 1934), p. 8.

[2]Hugh Anderson, *Jesus* (Englewood Cliffs, N. J.: Prentice-Hall, 1967), pp. 22–23.

[3]Albert Schweitzer, *The Quest of the Historical Jesus,* trans. W. Montgomery; 3rd ed. (London: Adam and Charles Black, 1954), pp. 368–369. First German edition 1906.

[4]C. H. Dodd, *The Parables of the Kingdom* (London: Nesbet and Co., Ltd., rev. ed. 1936), p. 108.

Suggestions for Further Study

For different viewpoints about the life and ministry of Jesus, see the bibliography at the conclusion of Chapter II.

If one is interested in understanding the *teachings* of the gospels, the following books are highly recommended.

F. W. Beare. *The Earliest Records of Jesus.* New York: Abingdon Press, 1962.

Norman Perrin. *Rediscovering the Teaching of Jesus.* New York: Harper & Row, 1967.

T. W. Manson. *The Sayings of Jesus.* London: SCM Press, 1949. (First appeared in 1937 as part of a larger work.)

J. Jeremias. *The Parables of Jesus.* Translated by S. H. Hooke. Rev. Edition. New York: Charles Scribner's Sons, 1963.

——— *New Testament Theology: The Proclamation of Jesus.* Translated by John Bowden. New York: Charles Scribner's Sons, 1971.

Further Readings on the "Kingdom of God"
Göstra Lundström. *The Kingdom of God in the Teaching of Jesus.* Translated by Joan Bulman. Richmond: John Knox Press, 1963.

Norman Perrin. *The Kingdom of God in the Teaching of Jesus.* Philadelphia: Westminster Press, 1963.

G. E. Ladd. *Jesus and the Kingdom.* New York: Harper & Row, 1964.

Books on the Resurrection of Jesus

Willi Marxsen. *The Resurrection of Jesus of Nazareth.* Translated by Margaret Kohl. Philadelphia: Fortress Press, 1970.

R. H. Fuller. *The Formation of the Resurrection Narratives.* New York: Macmillan, 1971.

I. T. Ramsey. *The Miracles and the Resurrection: Some Recent Studies.* London: SPCK, 1964.

Norman Perrin. *The Resurrection According to Matthew, Mark, and Luke.* Philadelphia: Fortress Press, 1977.

C. F. Evans. *Resurrection and the New Testament.* London: SCM Press, 1970.

G. E. Ladd, *I Believe in the Resurrection of Jesus.* Grand Rapids, Michigan: Wm. B. Eerdmans Publishing Co., 1975.

Wolfhart Pannenburg. *Jesus—God and Man.* Philadelphia: Westminster Press, 1968. Pp. 53–114.

Miracles

R.H. Fuller, *Interpreting the Miracles.* Philadelphia: Westminster Press, 1963.

C. F. D. Moule (Ed.). *Miracles: Cambridge Studies in Their Philosophy and History.* London: Mowbray, 1965.

T. A. Burkill. *Mysterious Revelation.* Ithaca, New York: Cornell University Press, 1963. Pp. 41–61.

R. M. Grant. *Miracle and Natural Law in Graeco-Roman and Early Christian Thought.* Amsterdam: N. Holland Publishing Co., 1952.

CHAPTER IV

The Hellenistic Background and the Book of Acts

There has been a popular misconception prevalent for some time to the effect that the Graeco-Roman world of the first century contained a "religious vacuum." It was argued that the belief in the old gods of Greece and Rome had disappeared, thereby leaving a void waiting to be filled by the proclamation of Christianity. Nothing could be further from the truth, however. Instead of a religious void, the serious student of this era finds religions and religious philosophies of every size, shape, and description.

Even though the old gods of Greece and Rome were not so important as in the centuries past, it is nevertheless true that many people still believed in them. Worship continued to go on at numerous shrines and altars dedicated to Zeus or Apollo or some other deity of the old pantheon.

In addition to this there were many people who were attracted to astral cults, believing that the stars and the planets held certain power over the lives of people. Still others worshipped the goddess *Tyche* (Chance or Fate), and temples were erected in her honor.

Another characteristic religious phenomenon of the period was the popularity of the "mystery" cults. These were very popular among the "ordinary" people and probably evolved from ancient fertility beliefs and cults. The essential idea here was that salvation could be obtained through having the "secret mystery" revealed to a person which would enable the devotee at death to become one with the deity. The most popular of these were the Eleusinian, the Dionysiac, and the Orphic, even though there were many others. Most of them had a myth which supposedly explained the origin of the religious cult.

Another very popular type of "religion" consisted of the "religio-philosophical" groups which appealed more basically to the educated. These were the groups known as the Stoics, the Epicureans, the Cynics, and similar types. Of these the Stoics seem to have been most influential. They believed in a cyclical view of history which would come to an end in a great conflagration when all the elements of the world would be burned. It was their belief that the world was guided by Law or Nature and that a person should be "in tune" with that Law. The ideal life for a Stoic was to achieve a state of *apatheia,* freedom from feeling. This was not seen as a separation from the world or its woes, but the true stoic was not to become "emotionally" involved. One was to work to change things for the better, but one was not to become emotionally entangled so that if the desired goal was attained, well and good. But if the desired goal was not reached, there would be no real regrets if one could be guided by *apatheia.* Therefore, the Stoic attempted to live in accordance with Nature or Law in a state of *apatheia* which led to a life of virtue and worth.

The Epicureans believed that persons could be happy. Too often, however, their views have been distorted into a picture of total, unbridled hedonism. While it is true that the pursuit of pleasure was a key to their lifestyle, it is also true that they seemed to be more concerned with the absence of pain than with the active seeking of pleasure. The true Epicurean would weigh the consequences of an action; if the pleasure to be gained was overshadowed by the pain involved, then the action was to be avoided. These people did not believe that the gods (if they existed) had anything to do with this created order.

There were other philosophies as well, one of the better known being the Cynics whose "diatribe" style of debate is probably reflected in some of Paul's writings. During the period ca. 300 B.C. to 300 A.D. these ideas and "schools of philosophy" continued to exert influence on the society of that time. And naturally there was a generous amount of overlapping and borrowing of ideas one from another.

Another of the characteristics of that time involved a "thought-pattern" analogous in the Graeco-Roman world to apocalyptic in the Jewish world. This was the "system" of ideas known as "gnostic." The term comes from the Greek, *gnosis,* meaning knowledge. As far as we can determine there were no fully developed gnostic systems until the second century A.D., but gnostic ideas were quite widespread and influenced many of the other philosophical and/or religious idealogies of the time. The gnostics were basically dualistic in their thinking, viewing the created world as evil, changeable, and finite. God was the opposite of these qualities and, therefore, could have no relationship with the created order. To account for the world and its creation, many gnostics postulated that there had occurred certain emanations from God which in turn had emanations from themselves. Each of these emanations had a name and/or function, and the structure of the relationship among these entities constituted the "over-world," which was a maze of intricate paths leading from one emanation to another. Sometimes these emanations were called "archons" or "rulers."

The created order was basically weak, evil, but somehow (exactly how depended on the myth that was told to explain the phenomenon) a spark of the divine had permeated the created world. Therefore each person has flesh and soul and spirit; the flesh and soul came from the archons. The spirit, however, is asleep or imprisoned in the person and must somehow be awakened so that it can be released from this realm of evil and darkness. This can only be accomplished through the acquisition of knowledge which has been brought to the world through some kind of transcendent savior. The knowledge is that of how the "over-world" of the archons and emanations has been constructed. If this knowledge is avilable to the spirit at death, then the path to being reunited with the deity can be traveled until the spark of the divine is safely absorbed again and is at peace.

To the true gnostic then this world and its values are no longer appropriate. This type of thinking led to two extremes: (1) the *ascetic* idea that since the world was so evil, corrupt, etc., the true *pneumatic* (i.e., the "spiritual" person) had to shun as much as possible any contact with the present world; (2) the *libertine* who argued that this world and its rules and values were no longer binding on the truly liberated *pneumatic,* therefore one could do anything one pleased. In fact, reacting against the mores of this world order was incumbent upon the one who was "in the know." (These two reactions will also be detected in the history of the early church!)

Even though there were no full-blown gnostic systems until later (ca. the 2nd century A.D.), these ideas were a significant part of the thought milieu of the Graeco-Roman world. There were overtones of gnostic thinking in several of the religions and religious philosophies of the time.

One can readily see that there was no religious vacuum in this period of human history. In fact, "religion" appears to have been a significant part of that culture. It was into such a culture that the early Christians began proclaiming their gospel.

The Book of Acts

For many centuries it was practically assumed that the Book of Acts reflected very carefully the history of the early Christian church. Luke was viewed as a historian—and that was that! In the nineteenth century, however, at the University of Tübingen in Germany, a scholar by the name of F. C. Baur was to leave his mark on New Testament studies in general and on the Book of Acts in particular. Baur postulated that the history of early Christianity was characterized by a conflict between two groups in the early church: one group which revolved around the person of Peter, and a second group which revolved around the figure of Paul. These two groups were divided basically along the lines of attitude toward the Jewish law and consequently the idea of salvation that was attendant to each position.

The history of the early church, and therefore, the New Testament writings were to be understood against the backdrop of this conflict. In such a scheme the Book of Acts seemed to reflect a "conciliatory" approach to the situation, and thus was interpreted as having been composed by a member of the "Paulinist" group who wrote during the second century A.D. to reflect a conciliatory approach toward the situation. The writing places both Peter and Paul in a very congenial framework, each holding essentially the same views! Such an approach naturally points away from the role of the writer as a "historian."

The Tübingen position in many ways is now discarded, but nowhere does it influence still hold sway in New Testament studies as it does in dealing with the Book of Acts. To this day scholars still argue over date, authorship, purpose of the book, centering their debate around the Tübingen ideas.

The beginning student can find good scholars on either side of the issues. It seems, however, likely that Luke thought he was to some degree writing history; but it is also clear that history to the biblical writers was not as narrowly defined as it is today. Luke is really a religiously centered historian. This means that one finds *both* history and religious interpretations in this writing. (For Luke's religious emphases, cf. Chapter II, pp. 58–59.) That Luke does not intend a complete and detailed historical chronicle is obvious from reading the text of the book, but it is also clear the Luke is presenting what he thinks, at least, is a general outline of the spread of the Christian movement from Palestine to the center of the Roman Empire.

Acts: Outline

I. Introduction 1:1–11
II. Early Church in Jerusalem 1:12–8:3
III. Early Church in Judea and Samaria 8:4–12:25
IV. Early Church in the Graeco-Roman World 13:1–28:31

The Book of Acts is loosely structured along the plan given in 1:8: "But you will receive power when the Holy Spirit has come upon you; and you shall be my witnesses in Jerusalem and in all Judea and Samaria and to the end of the earth." In each section the church grows and succeeds only then to encounter persecution. The persecution, however, becomes the means whereby the next period of growth is inaugurated. The first section concludes with the stoning of Stephen (chapter 7); the second with the attacks led by Herod Agrippa I (chapter 12). The stage was then set for the career of Paul.

The First Stage: Acts 1:1–8:3

At the conclusion of his gospel Luke depicts Jesus giving instructions to his disciples to remain in Jerusalem until "power from on high" is received. He then "parted from them" (cf. Luke 24:49–53). The Acts account then begins with the disciples waiting in Jerusalem, but Jesus has *not* "parted from them"! The early verses (1–11) seem to emphasize the return of Jesus but cautions that no one knows the mind of God about such matters (v. 7).

Also clear from the initial chapter is the seeming importance of the Twelve in the minds of the early Christians, so much so that the person who fills the slot vacated by Judas is carefully chosen. But once having given the account of that election, Luke never mentions Matthias again!

At this point the reader finds the initiating experience for the growth and development of the church. According to Luke this occurs with the sending of the Spirit during the Pentecost festival. In this account one encounters for the first time the phenomenon of "glossolalia," i.e., speaking in tongues. There are two basic understandings of this "gift" in the New Testament. One, and the most common, is that of a sudden seizure of the person by the Spirit which sends that person into a state of ectasy. During that ecstasy a message from God was supposed to be delivered, usually in a "tongue" unknown to the world which had to be interpreted by the person upon returning to "normal" or by another person who could interpret tongues.

The second interpretation is found at this juncture in Acts whereby the gift of tongues is the gift to proclaim enthusiastically the gospel message to all kinds of people (in Jerusalem for the feast) in the language of each nationality. The question as to how that could be sets the stage for the first of the many speeches in Acts, here the speech of Peter. This proclamation follows almost precisely the outline of the *kerygma* (cf. Chapter II, pp. 27–29) with the exception that the reference to Jesus' Parousia is omitted. People respond positively to the proclamation and the early church has taken its first step on the road to "all the world."

In this portion of the church's development the basic problem stems from the animosity of the Jews. In every case the Jewish law and leadership are at odds with the Christian leaders. There are two central episodes dealing with these matters. First there is the discussion among the Jewish leaders in which Gamaliel, one of the most respected rabbis, participated. His advice was to leave these people alone since, if they were not acting in accordance with God's will, they would fail (good Pharisaic theology!). If they were acting in accordance with God's will, then those who opposed would be guilty of opposing God (Acts 5:33–39). The Christian leaders were beaten and allowed to go free, but they were also warned not to speak further in the name of Jesus.

The second episode revolved around the person of Stephen, one of the younger leaders of the Jerusalem church. He was accused of blasphemy and when called to defend himself launched into a long history of God's dealing with his unappreciative and unresponsive people (Acts 7). The conclusion of the matter was that Stephen so infuriated the Jewish people present that a mob scene ensured resulting in the stoning of Stephen. This triggered the persecution against the church, and it is at this point that the figure of Saul is introduced into the narrative. At this stage he was a zealous persecutor of the church.

As for the organization of the early church, there seems to have been little, if any, formal structure initially. The Twelve obviously were of great importance, and they seem to have been the focal point of organization. As the church grew, new needs naturally arose. The Twelve could not be responsible for doing everything (cf. 6:2f.); therefore additional persons of ability were selected to fill needs as they arose. The structure appears to have been basically functional rather than political.

The early church also seemed to have a deep concern for the needy among its own membership. To fill that obligation some of the members experimented with a type of communal living wherein many sold their possessions and contributed the money to a com-

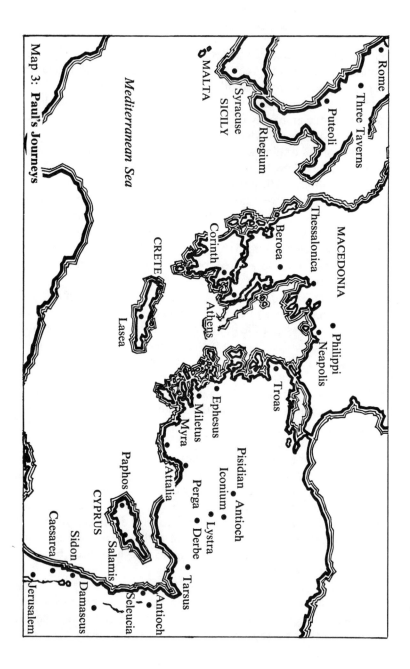

Map 3: Paul's Journeys

Rome
• Three Taverns
• Puteoli
MALTA
Syracuse
SICILY
Rhegium

Mediterranean Sea

MACEDONIA
Thessalonica
Beroea •
Corinth
CRETE
Athens
Lasea

Philippi
Neapolis

Troas

Ephesus •
Miletus •
Myra •
Attalia

Pisidian Antioch •
Iconium •
Lystra •
Perga • Derbe •

Paphos
CYPRUS
Salamis

Tarsus •
Antioch
Seleucia

Sidon
Damascus •
Caesarea •
Jerusalem •

mon fund for use by the church. Several things need to be observed at this point. First of all, there is no indication from Luke's account that this was mandatory. Neither the sale of property nor the contribution of *all* the proceeds seems to have been obligatory. The second item to keep in mind is that this sale of property must have stemmed from the idea that the Parousia was imminent, so near in fact that no provision for the future needed to be made. This miscalculation obviously put the church in Jerusalem in a bad situation since the prople were in dire circumstances on at least two different occasions, one when the people in Antioch sent relief to them (cf. Acts 11), and later when Paul collected money from the Gentile churches to assist the distitute in Jerusalem (cf. 2 Corinthians 8, 9; 1 Corinthians 16; Romans 15:25f.).

The Second Stage: Acts 8:4–12:15

The second segment of Luke's "history" is to a great degree a transitional section. To be sure, the reader encounters a description of the growth of the church into the area of larger Palestine with the center of activity moving on to Antioch in Syria. The apostles help to spread the gospel to others—to Samaria, to an Ethiopian eunuch, to a Roman centurion.

The emphasis is, however, upon building a foundation for Paul's spread of the gospel into the Graeco-Roman world. The account of the call of Saul on the road to Damascus is recorded in Acts 9, and the vision of Peter (10:9–16) which taught him that "God shows no partiality" are the two key events recorded in this second section of the account.

It was also in this time that the term "Christian" was first applied to these followers of Jesus. In all probability the term was initially a term of ridicule or derision (the "Messiah people"!), but like many such terms it became a badge of distinction. Up to the coining of this term the Christians were known as followers of the Way, or Nazarenes, or Galileans.

More persecution was heaped upon the leaders of the movement, this one led by Herod Agrippa I. Nevertheless, according to Luke, the movement continued to grow, and the stage was now ready for the third phase in the spread of the gospel.

The Third Stage: Acts 13-28

This third section of the Book of Acts, and the largest, deals primarily with the figure of Paul and his work. The account depicts three basic "missionary" forays of Paul and the events which ultimately brought him to Rome.

Operating from Antioch in Syria Barnabas and Saul set out on the first journey. At Cyprus, the first stop, the first recorded convert is none other than the Roman governor of the island, Sergius Paulus. Luke's emphasis upon the political innocence of the Christian movement is highlighted at the very beginning, for the Roman governor was not simply a Roman citizen but a proconsul, i.e., a Roman senator! It was at this point that the name of Saul is changed to Paul in the Acts account. There is, in all probability, no esoteric significance to this change; Paul simply seems to be the Greek equivalent of the Hebrew-Aramaic Saul.

From Cyprus the group sailed to Asia Minor, specifically Perga, where John Mark left and returned to Jerusalem. They went further into the hill country to Antioch of Pisidia. Here the basic method of the preaching tours is outlined. First the group would go to a synagogue, where they would proclaim their message. Usually some would believe, but most would not. Then the group would move out on its own, the group consisting of the Jews who had accepted the truth of the message along with some Gentiles who had heard and were attracted to the new teaching. These were, at first, drawn from a group of persons commonly known as "God-fearers." These were Gentile people who were attracted to the religion of Judaism because of its strict monotheism and high ethical standards. These people were unwilling to become Jewish proselytes because they did not want to conform to the legalistic obligations of the law, especially at the points of circumcision and food requirements. Paul's basic message which did not emphasize these requirements naturally appealed to these people. And the third group then consisted of other Gentile people who were receptive to the message.

According to the Acts account the proclamation was basically kerygmatic in nature. And some significant success (but not countless multitudes!) was achieved. In each place Paul encountered severe opposition to himself and his message usually from the Jewish community. This pattern was to continue throughtout his career.

An interesting episode occurred at Lystra where Barnabas and Paul were mistaken for gods, recalling the famous mythological story of Baucis and Philemon. Barnabas was hailed as Zeus, since he was the leader on this first journey, and Paul was taken to be Hermes, the spokesman for the gods. According to the Acts account, Jews from Antioch and Iconium later followed the group to Lystra and stirred up the crowd against them, so much so that Paul was stoned, and they dragged him out of the city thinking that he was dead. Recovering, however, Paul and the group went on to Derbe, after which they retraced their steps to Antioch in Syria with the exception of Cyprus.

At this point in the narrative, Luke includes the account of a Council which took place in Jerusalem to determine what kind of attitude should be taken toward the Gentiles who were now beginning to compose a large part of the church's constituency. Debates over when this occurrence actually took place are numerous among New Testament scholars, some even arguing that the episode is nothing more than a creation of Luke to suit his theological purposes. It seems best to understand the story as an account of an actual event, the contents of which would by necessity have been a matter of concern early in the period when the movement had begun to spread to the Gentile world.

Luke's emphasis can be clearly detected in the narrative, however, with his concern that the gospel be offered to the entire world. It is interesting to note that the Council does not seem to issue a binding edict, but rather a general concensus loosely agreed upon seems to be the ultimate outcome. There are two basic matters of concern. The first and most important has to do with idolatry (i.e., "... the pollutions of idols and unchastity...." (15:20a). The risk of syncretism is always a threat when bringing a new religious ideology to a new area, and the church had to be on the alert not to "blend" religions.

The second matter seems to be more directly related to the Jewish food laws, ". . . from what is strangled and from blood" (15:20b). Rather than being a requirement that the Gentiles were subject to, this injunction seems to be more practical than theoretical. Do not offend the sensitivities of those who had formerly been Jews at the point of dietary customs.[1]

Whatever the exact meaning, it is clear that a degree of friendship and community existed between the two groups at the conclusion of the Council. This prepared the way for a second excursion, but Paul and Barnabas could not agree on whether to take John Mark with them on this journey. Barnabas argued that they should; Paul did not want to take a chance with someone who had deserted the mission earlier. Therefore Barnabas took Mark and sailed to Cyprus—we hear no more of them. Paul takes Silas and departs via the land route to revisit the churches in Asia Minor established on the first journey.

At Lystra Paul came in contact with a young man, Timothy, the son of a Greek father and a Jewish mother. Timothy obviously had the talents Paul knew were necessary for the work of the spread of the gospel and was selected to assist Paul on the journeys. Paul circumcised Timothy, not as a matter of adhering to the ritual precepts of the law but in all probability as a practical consideration. After all, they would be working much of the time among Jews, preaching in Jewish synagogues, and an uncircumcised person in that setting would have been an offense to the very people they were attempting to reach. This seems to be the meaning of Luke's explanation (16:3).

After going through the region of Phrygia and Galatia (exactly where those are is still argued among New Testament scholars), Paul came to Troas. Here he encounters a call from the people in Macedonia, and the gospel is now taken to the mainland of Europe. In keeping with Luke's emphases, the first recorded convert on European soil is a woman, Lydia. And further, Paul and Silas are imprisoned at Philippi but released and given an apology when it is learned that they are Roman citizens. After leaving Philippi, they encountered the opposition of the Jews again in Thessalonia and then Beroea. Even though Timothy and Silas remained in Beroea, they sent Paul on to Athens.

It was in Athens that Paul delivered his famous Mars Hill or Areopagus speech. This speech differs from the other speeches in Acts in that it does not basically follow the kerygmatic outline. Paul here argues more in concert with the Greek culture and background and only toward the end introduces any mention of Jesus or other kerygmatic ideas. Some scholars find nothing in this presentation by Luke to be unusual, while others make much of the fact that very few responded to Paul's message and that there is no evidence of a growing church in Athens in this early period. These latter scholars, argue therefore, that Luke is trying to get across the point that when the basic kerygma is abandoned, success of the Christian movement is severely limited. Whether this is what Luke intended is difficult to determine and scholars still debate the issue. No matter what position one takes interpretatively at this point, there is no question that there is very little success in Athens, and we hear of it no more.

Paul then moves on to Corinth, a very unlikely place for success in proclaiming the new religion. Corinth was infamous for its immorality, so much so that the word "corinthianize" in the Greek of that era meant "to participate in gross degeneracy." Nevertheless, Paul stops in Corinth for eighteen months! And a strong and active church emerges out of his work, even if it is not always a "proper" church (cf. 1 Corinthians).

It is during Paul's sojourn in Corinth that the only datable event in his life occurs. Toward the conclusion of his stay there Paul was brought before the Roman proconsul, Gallio, at the instigation of the Jews in Corinth (18:12ff.). (Naturally, no wrong was found in Paul by the governor.) We know from an ancient inscription that Gallio took office in July, 51 A.D. According to Acts, the episode before Gallio took place at the end of Paul's stay in Corinth and not too long after Gallio had taken office, i.e., late summer, early fall of 51 A.D. All other dates for Paul's life are figured forwards and backwards from this episode.

Shortly thereafter Paul left Corinth, visited Ephesus briefly, and sailed back to Palestine. It is unclear from the Acts account whether he visited Jerusalem at this time. In all probability he did not, but either way he did not tarry long. He left Antioch in Syria, traveling

again by the land route through Asia Minor almost directly to
Ephesus.

During this "third" journey Paul's activity centered in Ephesus
where he remained for two to three years. It was during this time
that there was a riot directed against Paul because he argued against
idols. This preaching seemed to upset those who made their living
fashioning and selling images of the goddess Artemis (Diana).
Again the matter is shown to be personal, not connected in any way
with Roman law (19:35–41).

Even though Acts tells us nothing about them, we can learn from
Paul's letters that other matters were also pressing while he stayed
at Ephesus. One major concern revolved around the "Judaizers,"
those who were arguing that all Christians should be forced to keep
all the ceremonial aspects of the Jewish law in order to participate
in the new community of the faithful. In arguing for their position,
they also attacked Paul as an apostle and the gospel which he was
preaching.

A second problem which emerged during this same period involved Paul's relationship with the Corinthian church. Someone(s)
in the church at Corinth questioned Paul's authority; and when
Paul visited Corinth, he was rebuked rather rudely. This caused him
to leave and to write to them a "tearful" or "painful" letter which
helped to clear the air and to restore the broken relationship. All
these events are known to us from Paul's letters but are not mentioned in the Acts account.

We do know from the Acts narrative, however, that Paul left
Ephesus, went to Macedonia, and stayed in Greece (probably Corinth) for three months. He returned through Macedonia to Troas
(where he put a young man to sleep with his preaching so that the
young man fell out of a window!); after which he traveled to Miletus where he summoned the Ephesian elders. Here he delivered to
them a farewell discourse. From this point he set his goal as Jerusalem and went there in spite of warnings not to go.

When he did arrive at the Temple in Jerusalem, there was a riot
which resulted in his arrest by the Roman soldiers as a rescue. The
soldiers arrested Paul, or took him into protective custody, but they
allowed him to speak to the people. The people listened until he be-

gan to speak about preaching to the Gentiles. At that point there was another commotion, whereupon the Roman soldiers decided to scourge Paul to find out what all the trouble was about. Paul reminded them that he was a Roman citizen. This caused the tribune to arrange a meeting between Paul and the Jewish Sanhedrin.

In that setting Paul emphasized his Pharisaic beliefs which caused confusion in the council. Since some were Pharisees and some Sadducees, the two factions began fighting among themselves. Again Paul was taken from the midst of the confusion by the Roman authority. Shortly thereafter a plot against Paul's life was discovered, so that he was removed to Caesarea, the Roman provincial capital. This placed Paul under the direct jurisdiction of the Roman governor, Felix. According to Acts, Paul remained in custody for two years since Felix did not really know exactly what to do with him.

When Felix left the governorship, a new ruler was appointed, a certain Festus. This man wanted to do the Jews some favor to ingratiate himself to them and asked Paul to go to Jerusalem to be tried there. Paul, knowing the dangers involved, refused to go and appealed to take his case to Caesar. At this point, again in accord with Luke's emphasis, Herod Agrippa II (a puppet ruler over part of Palestine) heard Paul's defense. Both he and Festus agreed that Paul had done nothing to deserve either death or imprisonment (26:30–32). But Paul had already appealed to Caesar, and now the time for the journey to Rome had come.

On the way to Rome there was trouble with the weather, and they were shipwrecked on Malta. After three months the journey was resumed in another vessel, and ultimately Paul finally arrived in Rome. The Book of Acts concludes with the statement that Paul lived in Rome for two years at his own expense and that he preached about Jesus "openly and unhindered." At that point the Book of Acts ends.

What happened to Paul? The reader is not told. Why did Luke conclude his account so abruptly and leave so many questions unanswered? Various suggestions have been made. Some have argued that Luke planned to write a third volume but for whatever reason was not able to do it. Some have argued that the Book of Acts ends here because this is the time at which it was written or perhaps Luke died before he was able to finish the book. Some have even argued that the two-volume work was written (especially Acts) as a defense for Paul at the time of his trial. The most plausible explanation is that Luke knew the final events of Paul's life, i.e., that according to tradition Paul, along with Peter, was martyred in the Neronian persecution in Rome somewhere ca. 64–66 A.D. But if he had recorded that conclusion, it would have nullified a significant point that had been running through his narrative, i.e., the political innocence of the Christian movement and its leaders. Therefore Luke concluded his work with Paul in Rome preaching the gospel "openly and unhindered" because that is the image he wished to leave with his readers.

**Notes
Chapter IV**

[1]Even though the components of this "decree" are open to various interpretations, and exact interpretation is difficult indeed (especially since the wording of the two statements is different, cf. 15:20 and 15:29), it seems that this explanation makes the most logical sense.

**Suggestions for
Further Study**

For some insight into the Graeco-Roman world the following books are helpful.

Robert M. Grant. *Gnosticism and Early Christianity.* New York: Columbia University Press, 1959.

Hans Jonas. *The Gnostic Religion.* Boston: Beacon Press, 1958.

A. N. Sherwin-White. *Roman Society and Roman Law in the New Testament.* London: Oxford University Press, 1962.

Harold R. Willoughby. *Pagan Regeneration: A Study of Mystery Initiations in the Graeco-Roman World.* Chicago: University of Chicago Press, 1929.

R. McL. Wilson. *Gnostics and the New Testament.* Oxford: Blackwell, 1968.

Books on Acts

F. F. Bruce. *Commentary on the Books of Acts.* Grand Rapids, Michigan: Wm. B. Eerdmans Publishing Co., 1954. The New International Commentary on the New Testament.

H. J. Cadbury. *The Book of Acts in History.* New York: Harper & Row, 1955.

W. W. Gasque. *A History of the Criticism of the Acts of the Apostles.* Grand Rapids, Michigan: Wm. B. Eerdmans Publishing Co., 1975.

Ernst Haenchen. *The Acts of the Apostles: A Commentary.* Translated by B. Noble and G. Shinn under supervision of Hugh Anderson. Philadelphia: Westminster Press, 1971.

R. P. C. Hanson. *Acts: Introduction and Commentary.* Oxford: Clarendon Press, 1967. The New Clarendon Bible.

L. E. Keck and J. L. Martyn, editors. *Studies in Luke–Acts.* Nashville: Abingdon Press, 1966.

G. H. C. MacGregor. *Acts: Introduction and Exegesis,* in G. A. Buttrick et al., editors. The Interpreters Bible. Nashville: Abingdon Press, 1954. Vol. IX.

William Neil. *The Acts of the Apostles.* London: Oliphants, 1973. The New Century Bible.

J. C. O'Neill. *The Theology of Acts in its Historical Setting.* 2nd edition. London: SPCK, 1970.

J. W. Packer. *Acts of the Apostles.* Cambridge: Cambridge University Press, 1966. The Cambridge Commentary on the New English Bible.

C. S. C. Williams. *A Commentary on the Acts of the Apostles.* 2nd edition. London: Adam and Charles Black, 1964.

Books on Paul and His Writings

F. W. Beare. *St. Paul and His Letters.* Nashville: Abingdon Press, 1962.

Günther Bornkamm. *Paul.* Translated by D. M. G. Stalker. New York: Harper & Row, 1971.

W. D. Davies. *Paul and Rabbinic Judaism.* Revised edition. London: SPCK, 1955.

C. H. Dodd. *The Meaning of Paul for Today.* New York: Meridian Books, 1957.

John Knox. *Chapters in a Life of Paul.* Nashville: Abingdon Press, 1950.

Johannes Munck. *Paul and the Salvation of Mankind.* Translated by F. Clarke. Richmond: John Knox Press, 1959.

H. J. Schoeps. *Paul: The Theology of the Apostle in the Light of Jewish Religious History.* Translated by Harold Knight. Philadelphia: Westminster Press, 1961.

CHAPTER V

The Letters and Teaching of Paul

When one turns to examine the letters of Paul, there are several points that need to be kept under consideration. First of all, and most importantly, there is the matter that Paul's letters are "occasional" writings. This means that each was written for a specific "occasion," usually to answer questions that were matters of concern for the churches addressed. This realization must make one aware that nowhere does one find a systematic statement of Paul's theology. What one does find are answers to questions and problems faced in the daily existence of the churches and Paul's relationship to these problems and these churches!

Two closely related points in dealing with the letters of Paul which have been raised by the advent of the historical-critical methodology are the questions concerning "authenticity" and unity. Are the letters genuine in terms of Pauline authorship? This question was acutely formed by the Tübingen school and remains one of the chief issues even yet. And further, are the letters as we have them a "unity," or does the individual letter appear to be a composite made from several letters or fragments of letters? These are two crucial points in dealing with Paul's teaching as found in his letters.

Another factor that should be remembered is that, in all probability, Paul dictated his letters. This would account for "hanging statements," incomplete arguments, and perhaps sudden changes of mood. It may also answer the question which sometimes arises about slight differences in style and/or vocabulary. Whether one wishes to make a great deal of this is a matter of individual judgment, but it is part of the broader picture.

When examining the individual letters by Paul, one finds that they usually follow the basic pattern for the writing of letters in that period. First there is a short salutation giving the author's name and the persons to whom (and whence) the letter is directed. Following this there is a short thanksgiving for the persons addressed. At that point there follows the major section of the letter dealing with the matters at hand. In Paul's letters, the body of the letter seems to fall into two categories, a section dealing with the problems *per se* and a section dealing with ethical exhortation (called *paraenesis*). The correspondence then concludes with a personal statement about the author and includes personal greetings and comments to persons in the church addressed. Most of Paul's letters generally follow this pattern.

The Thessalonian Correspondence

Upon turning to Paul's letters, we shall attempt to deal with them, as best as can be determined, in chronological order. The first of his extant correspondence was directed toward the Thessalonian church.

As to the issue of authenticity there is some debate over these two letters. The old Tübingen school denied that either was genuinely Pauline, but the basis for their arguments has been by and large discounted in current scholarship. Nevertheless, there is still some argument since these letters appear to be so similar in tone and language. Some argue that Paul would not have written two letters so similar within such a short time to the same church! To answer that problem some have argued that Paul wrote 1 Thessalonians but that 2 Thessalonians was not written by Paul. Another theory is that Paul wrote both the letters but one (1 Thessalonians) was written to the Gentile element in the Thessalonian church while the second (2 Thessalonians) was written to the Jewish element in the church. Theories still abound, but the basic consensus now is that both these letters are genuinely Pauline. And this seems to be a quite legitimate and sound assumption.

As to the issue of unity, even though there are those who question the unity of both these letters, again the consensus seems to be that each one is understood best as a unity and that there is no real evidence to argue for a composite letter formed from two or more fragments in either of these two short epistles.

As to the historical problems there is very little debate that the letters were composed by Paul at Corinth on his second journey ca. 50 A.D. The only real question seems to revolve around the issue of which letter was written first. When the Pauline corpus (i.e., body of letters) was assembled, the letters were arranged in order of length. Therefore when two letters were addressed to the same church the longer was placed in the order according to its length but the shorter one was not separated from it. Therefore simply because 1 Thessalonians was placed first, there is no reason to assume automatically that it was written first. Some scholars do indeed argue for the priority of 2 Thessalonians, but these are in the minority.

What "occasion" fostered the writing of these two letters. This must be determined from the internal evidence of each letter. Since both of the letters mention persecution and discuss various aspects of the Parousia, it is safe to assume that reports about the church and questions by the church lay at the base of Paul's concern for them. Perhaps the best approach is to concentrate on the content of each letter.

1 Thessalonians: Outline

   I.   Salutation 1:1
  II.   Thanksgiving 1:2–10
 III.   Body 2:1–5:24
       A.   Paul's work among them 2:1–16
       B.   Paul's concern for them 2:17–3:13
       C.   Christian conduct towards each other 4:1–12
       D.   Problems relating to the Parousia 4:13–5:11
       E.   General exhortation 5:12–24
 IV.   Conclusion 5:25–28

This letter to the Thessalonians follows the usual epistolary pattern with the primary emphasis being in the body of the letter. Paul first of all emphasized his own example of working among them, obviously attempting to counter some people who had probably become idle waiting for the return of Jesus. (He will speak to this issue more pointedly in 2 Thessalonians 2.) Paul then expressed to the people in the church his deep concern for them because he had heard about the persecution which was being directed at them. Upon Timothy's return he was informed that they had kept the faith and that the trials (at least momentarily) were over.

A warning then was given about immorality and an exhortation to right and proper conduct. But the major discussion evolved from a question which the people had put to Paul. "What happens to our loved ones who die before the Parousia? Do they miss out on the glory of that event?" These people obviously had taken the idea about the imminence of the Parousia very seriously (cf. 2:1ff.). It was, therefore, a serious matter to them when some of their loved ones began to die and the Parousia had not yet taken place. Thus the question to Paul.

His answer, which covers a relatively large proportion of this short writing, was directed at alleviating their fears about this matter. He writes to them as a pastor in this context, and his basic words of comfort are simply that the persons who have died are better off than the living since they have already gone to be "with God." In the process he also described what most interpreters take to be certain events which will characterize the Parousia. And the description is basically that of an apocalyptic scheme literally interpreted. The exact time cannot be known, Paul argued, but the analogy he gives of a woman about to bear a child indicates that he believed that the time was near.

The final section of the letter contains general exhortations to honor those who work diligently, to help those who need assistance, and an admonition not to seek revenge (perhaps in retaliation for persecution?). The people are urged to do what is right and abstain from evil. The letter then concludes with brief greetings and a short benediction.

2 Thessalonians: Outline

After the salutation Paul, in the thanksgiving, congratulated the people in the church for bearing up and keeping the faith in spite of the persecutions that were at that moment in process (1:4). He assured them that God would set all things aright, that those who were persecuting them would receive their just reward.

The major portion of this letter, however, is taken up with a discussion of the Parousia, probably because of the persecution and the fact that some were arguing that the event had already occurred (2:1–3a). Paul gives here a typical apocalyptic picture of evil increasing until it becomes so intense that God intervenes and destroys it. But there are in Paul some twists that seem to be unique with him. The basic one involves the idea of a "restraining force" and a "restraining figure" (2:6–7) which are to delay the final events. Exactly what Paul meant by these terms is not clear, and several theories have been suggested. One is that God or the Holy Spirit is the restraining force and person, holding back the end to enable people to have opportunity to hear the gospel proclaimed. Another is that the restraining force is the Roman empire and the peace it has established, and thus the restraining one would be the emperor. A third theory is that Paul thought the act of proclaiming the gospel was the restraining force and that he, as the chief proclaimer of that gospel to the Gentiles, was the restraining one. Each of these three theories assumes that the delay is for the purpose of allowing the gospel to be preached to the entire world before the Parousia could occur. It is entirely possible that this is the correct interpretation, but it is not so evident, however, exactly what the "restraining" elements are.

Whatever the exact interpretation of that matter, the outline of the events leading to the Parousia in chapter 2 is typical apocalyptic. Evil increases, and in this description is led by a "man of lawlessness." Whether a specific person was in Paul's mind is not known to us; but when he appears, the typical apocalyptic motifs of increasing evil and its power, horrible persecution of God's people, the intervention of God, and the removal of the persecution are enumerated clearly. (For a similar outline cf. Mark 13.) Paul exhorts them to remain faithful through the times of horror, because God has a special reward for those who persevere.

Now there is a request from the apostle for the people of the church to pray for him and his work. He is satisified that they are firm in their commitments to God and to Christ.

He turns at this point to discuss a matter which he has already mentioned in 1 Thessalonians, namely the problem of people who fail to shoulder their responsibilities and are not working. This state of affairs was probably born out of the expectation of many that the Parousia was coming soon, so soon that normal duties and responsibilities could be ignored. Paul spoke rather sharply to this issue here, using his own example as a guide. Even if the Parousia does come tomorrow, normal duties should be continued so that one does not become a burden to others and also because responsible behavior is expected of a Christian any time in any circumstances.

The letter concludes with a short written statement by Paul which, he says, will authenticate his letters. Obviously there were some who were writing in his name in order to popularize some of their own understandings about certain matters, especially the Parousia (cf. 2:2).

The Corinthian Correspondence

The most productive part of Paul's ministry in terms of literary output took place during and around his three-year stay at Ephesus ca. 54–57 A.D. It was in this period that at least six letters were written, perhaps even more. Of these at least four letters were written to the church at Corinth.

As best we can determine, Paul wrote to the Corinthians a letter warning the church there not to associate with "immoral people" (cf. 1 Corinthians 5:9). This letter is sometimes designated letter A. The next correspondence which Paul has with the people at Corinth resulted from a twofold occurrence. First the people of Corinth wrote Paul a letter (or letters) asking his advice and counsel on certain matters. And Paul learned from "Chloe's people" that there were some other problems also current which were not included in their letter to him. Therefore the letter known as 1 Corinthians contains Paul's ideas and advice on many problems, some of them very serious. This letter is known as letter B.

Shortly thereafter someone(s) in the church at Corinth questioned Paul's authority and right to be called an apostle. At the same time whoever this was stirred up some sort of trouble among the church's membership. Upon hearing of these events Paul made a visit to Corinth where he was treated rather rudely. He left, wrote to them a "painful" letter, a letter of "tears" (cf. 2 Corinthians 2:1ff. and 7:8), in which he obviously castigated the people in the Corinthian church for their treatment of him and rejection of the gospel he preached. This letter is designated letter C and was taken to Corinth by Titus.

Paul waited for the return of Titus in Macedonia (perhaps at Philippi). When he returned, he informed Paul that the Corinthians had responded positively to his letter and wished to be reconciled with him. Upon hearing this news Paul wrote another letter, a "thankful" letter , known as letter D.

Thus far, the correspondence looks something like this.

Letter	Place of Origin	Time
A	Ephesus	54/55
B	Ephesus	55
C	Ephesus or Macedonia	55/56
D	Macedonia	56

The full situation, however, is not yet clear, for the problem of unity is still to be examined. There is virtually no question among New Testament scholars as to the unity of 1 Corinthians. 2 Corinthians is a very different matter, however. 2 Corinthians 1–9 seems to reflect generally the conciliatory theme of letter D, but chapters 10–13 are of a different tone altogether. These chapters are harsh and chiding, and for that reason many scholars feel that these chapters are part (if not most) of the "severe" letter C. But there is no real evidence, textually speaking, that chapters 10–13 ever existed apart from 1–9. Because of these two factors several scholars have recently argued that after Paul had written 1–9 in the light of Titus' good news, that something had caused the situation to deteriorate again. Upon hearing that Paul added chapters 10–13. The change in the situation then caused the change in tone. (In this scheme chapters 10–13 are sometimes referred to as letter E.)

There are other problems as well in dealing with the issue of unity in 2 Corinthians. For example, 6:14–7:1 seems to interrupt the flow of the passage. If one reads 6:13 and 7:2 without the intervening verses, there is one smooth and continuous line of thought. Since the verses 6:14–7:1 speak to the issue of immorality and idolatry, some have suggested that 6:14–7:1 is a fragment of the first letter, letter A.

Others have argued that since chapters 8 and 9 both speak to the same matter (the collection of money to assist the church in Jerusalem) but in a somewhat different way that these chapters may have originally been separate from the main letter. Also there are those who think that 2:14–7:4 (sometimes less 6:14–7:1) was also part of yet another letter! And the possible combinations of these fragments into original letters become quite complicated. It may be well to note that some scholars recently have begun to argue again for the unity of 2 Corinthians!

It appears, however, when one reads the letter that some explanation must be found for the drastic change in tone of 10–13. Otherwise the argument for unity in chapters 1–9 *can* be made, and in the absence of any unanimity among the scholars on this topic perhaps should be held.

Therefore the correspondence can be outlined as follows: Exactly how one finally arranges the data is a matter of personal preference after studying the evidence, however.

Letter	Place of Origin	Time	Existing Letter
A	Ephesus	54/55	2, 6:14–7:1(?)
B	Ephesus	55	1 Corinthians
C	Ephesus or Macedonia	55/56	2, 10–13(?)
D	Macedonia	56	2, 1–9 (1–13?)
E(?)	Macedonia	56	2, 10–13(?)

1 Corinthians: Outline

I. Salutation 1:1–3
II. Thanksgiving 1:4–9
III. Body 1:10–15:58
    A. Problem of factionalism 1:10–4:21
    B. Problem of gross immorality in the church 5:1–13
    C. Problem of Christians suing each other 6:1–11
    D. Problem of men and prostitutes 6:12–20
    E. Problems dealing with marriage and sex 7:1–40
    F. Problem of food offered to idols 8:1–13
       (1) Excursus on Christian liberty and responsibility 9:1–11:1
    G. Problem of proper decorum for women in worship 11:2–16
    H. Problem of proper decorum in celebration of Lord's supper 11:17–34
    I. Problem of spiritual Gifts 12:1–14:40
    J. Problems dealing with the resurrection 15:1–58
IV. Concluding Remarks 16:1–23

After the usual salutation and a short thanksgiving Paul began to deal with this multitude of problems that were causing concern and trouble in the Corinthian church. The first ones with which he wrestled were those Chloe's people had related to him.

The first issue is that of factions in the church. Some of the people there were beginning to become cliqueish by advocating allegiance to one or another of the religious leaders. And some were claiming their own superiority by attempting to show that they belonged to Christ. Paul argued that Christian leaders were gifts from God in one sense, but as far as superiority is concerned they were all human beings together. God is the one to whom honor is due, God alone! This is made plain in 3:3b–8:

> For while there is jealousy and strife among you, are you not of the flesh [i.e., still in a state of being opposed to God and apart from God], and behaving like ordinary men? For when one says, "I belong to Paul," and another, "I belong to Apollos," are you not merely men? What then is Apollos? What is Paul? Servants through whom you believed, as the Lord assigned to each. I planted, Apollos watered, but God gave the growth. So neither he who plants nor he who waters is anything, but only God who gives the growth. . . .

The next problem addressed was a case of gross immorality, a man living with his step-mother! Paul reminded them that even the pagans had laws forbidding this sort of activity. He commanded them to remove this man from the fellowship of the church. His reason for this very harsh command was two-fold. First of all the church, even though it must by necessity be composed of people who are still far short of perfection, is compelled by its nature to draw the line on such examples of gross immorality. The reason for this is to keep the witness of the church open to the world and as "pure" as human beings can make it. The second reason is equally important; this act of judgment is to be executed for the ultimate purpose of redemption for the wayward brother.

Paul argued that the church has to rid itself of any extraordinary evil, but he reminded the people of the church that they still live in the world and must take seriously their responsibilities toward the people of the world. That means they are to seek diligently to spread the good news of their faith to all who have not heard or have not responded positively. The Christian is not to shun the people of the world, but there is to be a difference in attitude and approach towards those outside the church since they are in a different category as far as the Christian community is concerned. Christians are to exercise discipline over their own numbers; those outside fall into another grouping.

The next problem concerns that of Christians who cannot agree among themselves as to what is right and fair in their dealings with one another. Because they could not agree, they were suing each other in the Roman law courts. Paul argued that Christians, above all, should be able to judge fairly even when they themselves were involved. To have to resort to litigation demonstrated a failure of Christian growth and commitment.

Another problem was concerned with a certain type of activity being practiced, the rationale for such actions being supported by an argument which reflected a gnostic thought pattern. One recalls that the true gnostic held that only that which belongs to the "Spirit" is real; therefore, it makes no difference what one does with the material body. Since the flesh by nature craves certain things, such as food, for example, it does not really matter what food is eaten or where (cf. 6:13a). From this kind of *a priori* rationale, these people were obviously arguing that there should be no restraints on anything relating to the flesh. Therefore these people were frequenting the "houses of ill repute!" To counter their arguments Paul emphasized the Old Testament view of the makeup of the human personality as a "psycho-physical" totality. That idea was understood to mean that the physical dimension of life cannot be separated from the spiritual dimension. In Old Testament thought the two elements, i.e., the physical and the spiritual, were combined into *one* person, or personality. When a person then has sexual relations, it is not simply the physical element that is involved but the entire person. Therefore the one who "joins himself to a prostitute" becomes "one body with her," i.e., their personal beings become one. Thus the person sins wholly; and even if the spiritual dimension could be separated ultimately from the physical, at the moment of such action it too was involved and tainted by that activity. Paul further argued that such activity affected not only the individual but also the church and even Christ himself! Therefore, "Shun immorality" (6:18a).

Beginning with chapter seven Paul turned to the matters about which they had written. And it is interesting to note the arrangement of his discussion. He had just completed a section dealing with sexual license, and in chapter seven he turned immediately to discuss what was perhaps the other side of the coin, namely people arguing over whether a person should marry. Some had even argued for abstinence from sexual contact in the marriage covenant!

First of all Paul realized that the sexual drive in human beings was the strongest of all natural drives (beyond that of survival), and he obviously had seen firsthand some of the more extreme manifestations of sexual "freedom." He argued, therefore, for the marriage context for sexual activity, emphasizing that in this relationship the husband does not rule over his body but the wife does and vice-versa (cf. v. 4). Each belonged to the other in every aspect of life.

As to whether people should marry at all, Paul thought it best to remain single but not for the reason that sex *per se* was sinful. He was concerned about the Parousia. In view of the "impending distress" he felt that it was better not to marry and to abstain from sexual relations not because these are wrong but because of the practical considerations. It was thought that when the Parousia came there would be a time of intense suffering and distress at which time the people of God would encounter the intensity of evil (a typical apocalyptic motif). Married persons have responsibilities and burdens that others do not have, and children are a natural consequence of sexual activity. Paul wished to spare them (and the children) these added anxieties. But, he argued, if a couple cannot behave properly, they should marry—and there is no sin (v. 36).

There is another problem alluded to in this discussion, the possibility of divorce. According to Paul there seem to be circumstances in which divorce is acceptable, but under exactly what circumstances is not clearly specified. It is clearly related to the idea of "peace," i.e., total well-being. He seems to indicate that in a situation where there is no "peace," divorce is permissible. Would it be permissible to remarry? Paul does not say precisely, but he leans in the direction of a negative response. Is that negative an absolute one —or is it conditioned also (as in his other views on marriage given here) by his idea that the Parousia is coming very soon? Probably that is the case.

The next problem concerned whether Christians should eat meat which had been offered to idols. It was thought that once an animal had been sacrificed to a god, the god somehow in a quasi-physical way entered the meat. When the devotee ate the meat, the god became a part of that person's very being. Since the one who brought the sacrifice could not eat all the meat, especially of a larger animal, the remainder belonged to the priests who sold the meat in the marketplace. This was the means whereby the priests and the temples were supported.

The question which had obviously arisen among the Christians in Corinth revolved around two points of view: (1) it is wrong to eat the meat saturated with a god, for in so doing we are commiting an act of blasphemy and denying our Lord; (2) the other gods are nothing, and we can eat all of that meat we wish.

Paul agreed initially with the latter group. He argued that there were no other gods; therefore to eat the meat was not an act of idolatry. But the issue is far more complex than that. While it is true that there are no other gods and there is no idolatry involved in eating the meat, the Christian has a responsibility beyond resolving the question of right and wrong *for oneself.* There is, more importantly, the question about responsibility for one's neighbor. What is "morally right" for an individual standing alone may not be acceptable in certain contexts. For example, there were those in the Christian community who were weak and continued to think about other gods. Because of these weaker persons a true Christian should refrain from doing that which will "destroy" the weaker person. The responsibility for one's neighbor is clearly laid upon the Christian. And the rights and feelings of others are to come before personal rights and feelings.

The enunciation of this principle led Paul into a longer discussion of Christian liberty and discipline in chapters 9–10, for there is a difference between what it takes to destroy one's neighbor and what simply annoys that person!

After that excursus Paul began a discussion which dealt with certain matters of decorum related to worship practices in the church. This discussion continues through chapter 14. The first problem discussed under this category concerned a matter related to the idea of proper apparel for women, namely the wearing of a veil over the head while participating in the worship service. Exactly why not wearing this garment was a problem is simply unknown to us. That this was the problem is clear (vv. 4–5). There is no suggestion here that the women keep silent; it is frankly assumed that women were to pray and prophesy in church! What was at stake was a sense of propriety and decorum to make certain that the sanctity of the church be guarded from attacks from non-Christians. It was especially important that such attacks not be fueled by church members abusing Christian freedom and flaunting cultural standards (even when these were not concerned directly with moral issues).

The second problem focused on the manner in which the Eucharist was celebrated. In all probability the early church (since it was composed of small groups) celebrated the Last Supper by eating a communal meal together. This was probably called the *agape*, or love-feast, and it appears that this was the procedure in the church at Corinth. But there were those who came early, ate all the food, and even got drunk! In response to this situation Paul outlined his own understanding of the tradition concerning the events at the last meal Jesus ate with his disciples. This is the oldest *written* account of that event recorded in the New Testament (11:23ff.). Paul viewed the service as a "remembering memorial" of Jesus' death. Again the problem was basically one of proper decorum in the church's order of worship.

The third matter of concern in this area was twofold, one part general and one more specific: there was a general argument among the members of the church in Corinth as to who had the "highest" or "best" spiritual gift; the second part was more specific in that one of the spiritual gifts was not being utilized properly and thus had become a disturbing factor in the worship service.

In chapter 12 Paul discussed the general problem. He argued that all gifts come from the same Spirit, and each gift was to be used for the common good. It was in connection with this point that Paul used his famous figure comparing the church and its members to a human body. Each individual part has a function to perform, but the health of the larger organism is of first concern. Each part is to perform as best it can without jealousy or envy of other individual parts.

It was into this context that Paul wrote those words which comprise one of the best known sections of Paul's writing–the thirteenth chapter of 1 Corinthians. But that chapter is set within a specific and particular context, that of Christians quarreling with each other over who has the "best" talent for use in the church. Paul argued here that neither talent alone nor bare accomplishments are enough for a Christian. Any achievements, in order to be classified as Christian, must be the result of the proper motivation, namely faith, hope, and especially love. Paul called these elements a "more excellent way" and argued that love determines whether an action is "something or nothing!"

The discussion moves on to the more specific problem in this area, namely the problem of speaking in tongues, *glossolalia.* This highly animated and emotionally charged experience had obviously become a source of disruption in the church services. Paul argued, therefore, that this type of experience had to be handled properly so that the church's worship would be meaningful and edifying to all present—both believers and non-believers. The guideline, therefore, was that the practice be kept orderly, and a limit placed on the number of such occurrences. And further, if there was no one present who could interpret the tongues, no tongue was to be spoken.

The last group of problems revolved around the idea of the resurrection. Was Jesus *really* raised from the dead? Are Christians really raised from the dead? If so, what kind of bodies do they have in the resurrection? These seem to have been the basic questions put to Paul to answer.

First of all Paul simply stated that the resurrection of Jesus really happened. He appealed to eyewitnesses who had seen Jesus after his death and challenged anyone who did not believe to ask one of them about the truth of the matter. He then used a circular type argument to support his belief that others are raised too. Since Jesus was raised, those who are identified with Jesus will be raised.

The last response grappled with the question as to *how* people are raised. To the Semitic mind there could be no thought of any type of life apart from a body of some kind. To attempt to explain this unknown and unexplainable phenomenon Paul resorted, as he often did, to the use of an analogy. He compared the body one has presently with a seed which when planted produces another "body" quite unlike (in form) the seed itself. But the new plant is a direct continuation of the essence of the seed planted. Something like this happens with the Christian in the resurrection. The old body which is "physical" is a form suited for existence in this life; in the resurrection there will be a "spiritual" body, i.e., a body suited for existence in the spiritual realm. But the implication is clear from the analogy—what one is in the spiritual realm is directly related to and is an outgrowth of what one is in the present life. According to Paul the Christian no longer fears death, since death no longer has dominion over the Christian. It appears that Paul was still expecting the Parousia shorthy (15:51). But apart from that expectation he believed that one's personality continued in a relationship with God unbroken by physical death.

He concluded this rather long letter dealing with all sorts of problems with some directions to the Corinthians for the collection he was making for the Christians in Jerusalem. In the near future he planned to make a trip to see them via Macedonia.

There are some personal greetings and messages also included.

2 Corinthians: Outline

   I. Salutation 1:1–2
  II. Thanksgiving(?) 1:3–7
 III. Body
     A. Joy at being reconciled 1:8–7:16
     B. The collection 8–9
     C. Paul's defense of himself 10:1–13:10
 IV. Conclusion 13:11–14

It is difficult to follow a logical sequence in this letter since Paul obviously is writing out of the intense emotion of the situation. This fact could account for the seeming breaks in the "flow" of the letter which some argue are caused by letters or fragments of letters which have been put together to form the document as it now exists.

The deeply felt emotion of the problems Paul had just experienced with the Corinthian church is clearly seen in the early part of the writing. He refers (2:1–4) to the "painful" visit and to the "tearful" letter. There is some defense of himself in these early chapters (1:8ff.; 3:1ff.), but it is guarded and muted. It also appears that he is at least beginning to think about the possibility of his own death (4:7–5:10), something he has not alluded to before in his writings.

The most important element, however, in this letter appears to come in 5:16–21. Out of this experience with the Corinthian church Paul has learned something about God and his relationship with the world. Sin has caused the human race to become estranged from God. The relationship was broken and needed to be repaired. Something had to be done, but the human race was incapable of such action. And, further, they did not really want to be reconciled to God. By the sending of Jesus and the events which surrounded him God made it possible for people to be reconciled to God. The act of God in Christ was for the benefit of humanity. And as the reconciliation between two human beings or factions is a beautiful event, how much more marvelous is the reconciliation between God and the world. As usual, however, Paul emphasized that this act of God and new relationship carried with it very serious obligations—Christians must become the agents for God's reconciling work in this world, "... entrusting to us the message of reconciliation. So we are ambassadors for Christ, God making his appeal through us" (5:19c–20a).

The latter part of these chapters (1–7) is filled with more expressions of joy that they have settled their differences. Chapters 8 and 9 contain Paul's appeal to the church in Corinth to contribute to the collection he was making to assist the people in the church at Jerusalem.

No matter how one interprets chapters 10–13, as part of Paul's "severe" letter or as a later letter (written after 1–9) or as a part of letter D but after a "mood" change by Paul, it is indisputable that the tone of these chapters is quite different from that of 1–9. He defended his right to preach the gospel and presented evidence that he had, humanly speaking, earned the right to have respect shown to him and even to boast (cf. especially 11:21b–28). He concluded with an appeal for all to live in peace.

As one can readily ascertain, the study of Paul's relationship with the Corinthian church is, as fascinating as it is, at points, complicated.

The Problem With the Judaizers: Galatians

While Paul was stationed in Ephesus on his third journey, a problem arose in the churches in Galatia over whether Gentile Christians should be required to keep all the precepts of the old Jewish law. This discussion centered particularly in the rite of circumcision. There was a group which argued very emphatically that all Christians should indeed keep all of the old laws. Since Christianity was supposedly the outgrowth of the old Israel and in fact claimed to be the true Israel of God, it was necessary to keep the old laws which governed and regulated the people of God from ancient times.

Exactly who these people were poses a problem for the modern scholar. Some argue that the "Judaizers," as they were called, were Christians in the Galatian churches who had been converted from Judaism to Christianity. They were now insisting that the Gentile converts submit to the old regulations. Others argue (and there is some evidence for this in Paul's comment in Galatians 2:11–12) that the Judaizers were people from the Jerusalem church who claimed to have the support of James, the leader of the church there. A third theory is that these dissidents were actually Gentile Christians from the churches in Galatia who felt so strongly about the historical roots of their new-found religion that their zeal caused them to argue for complete adherence to all the past requirements of the "mother" religion. There is no real agreement concerning the identity of these people but in all probability they came initially from Jerusalem (whether they actually had James' blessing is not known), but their ideas found receptive minds among some of the church members of that area. To make their case they were forced to attack Paul personally and to deny that he had any right to be called an "apostle." And further, they questioned the validity of the gospel he preached.

Upon hearing the news of this attack upon him and his gospel and fearing the damage that this sort of situation may have on the newly converted people, Paul "fired off" the letter to the Galatians in the heat of anger. The letter literally bristles with harsh words and bitter comments for those who are unsettling the young converts in these churches. The authenticity and unity of this letter are not usually questioned.

A further critical question has to do with where these churches were located! The older idea was that these churches were located in central Asia Minor among the people who were by race known as *Keltai* (Galatians). If so, these are churches about which we know nothing insofar as their origin is concerned. Acts does not mention *specifically* any missionary work of Paul among these people, indicating only that Paul went through the region. But traditionally, it was assumed that these were the people to whom the letter was written. This view of the destination of the letter is called the "North Galatian" theory.

After historical-critical research emerged, some questions began to be raised about the destination of this letter. Since Acts does not mention any specific churches in the northern part of Asia Minor, and since Paul usually used the Roman designation for provinces, and since Barnabas was not with Paul on the journey when these churches were formed, many scholars developed a new theory as to the recipients of this letter. They argued that the Galatian churches were those formed during the first journey (Pisidian Antioch, Iconium, Lystra, and Derbe) in the Roman province of Galatia. This view is sometimes called the "South Galatian" theory.

Which of these two views one accepts as to the destination of this writing does not really affect the interpretation of the letter. The major point, however, at which any problem arises is with the date. Most interpreters are agreed that the letter, whether addressed to North or South Galatia, was written from Ephesus ca. 55 A.D. But since Paul did not mention the Jerusalem Council (which according to Acts took place between the first and second journeys), some think that the Council had not yet taken place. If one followed that argument, the destination of the letter would have to have been directed to the "South," since the "North" Galatian churches would not have been founded as yet. And the date of the letter would have to be ca. late 48 or early 49 A.D. The place of writing would then probably have been Antioch in Syria. Very few hold to that position now, however, most preferring the 55 A.D. date and Ephesus as the place of origination.

Galatians: Outline

There are really few "niceties" in this letter. Even in the salutation Paul is already defending his status as an apostle (1:1), and he immediately proceeded to defend the content of the gospel he preached. In the process Paul gave a description of where he was and what he was doing after his conversion experience. (These data are difficult at points to fit into or coincide with the Acts account.) During that period he came briefly to Jerusalem, and later he returned with Barnabas to "lay before" the people there the gospel he preached among the Gentiles. It was then agreed that Paul should continue his work among the Gentiles, and even the issues of circumcision and, later, food laws were deemed to be approved as Paul saw them.

The real issue under discussion in this letter is whether the law has anything to do with the new life that can be given by God to the human race. According to Paul's opponents it does. Certain aspects of the law were considered to be essential for the proper relationship of a person with God. Paul argued that it is only the Spirit that can give new life and used Abraham, the Father of Israel, as the chief example. It was not the law that placed Abraham in the proper relationship with God, but rather Abraham's faith, i.e., trust in God and commitment to him. To prove the point Paul reminded his readers that the law came 430 years *after* Abraham (3:17)!

Further, Paul argued that if one attempts to make the law the key in the salvation process, that person has no hope, for if one seeks to keep the law, it must be kept in all of its precepts—and no one can do that. The real purpose in the giving of the law was to give guidance to people in their relationship with God and each other and to serve as a pointer to the full revelation of God given in Jesus. He called the law a "pedagogue" (3:24). In those days a pedagogue was a slave or servant who had responsibility for oversight of the children especially at the point of education. The pedagogue was not the children's teacher *per se* but rather took the children to the teacher, saw to it that the children did their studies, and assisted them in the learning process. The law, Paul says, is analogous to that. It helped, it assisted, it pointed the way to the real teacher, who, to Paul, is Jesus the Messiah. In fact now that the true teacher has come, there is no real need of the pedagogue. Through God's Messiah all human value systems are nullified: "There is neither Jew nor Greek, there is neither slave nor free, there is neither male nor female; for you all are one in Christ Jesus" (3:28). Jesus has brought back again the original intent of the call of Abraham, i.e., that the human situation is made right by the promise and action of God not through external human acts! The new life comes only to human beings through trusting God and commiting their lives to him.

In this historical setting Paul argued mightily for Christian freedom, to be relieved from the burdens of attempting to keep the law in all of its manifold aspects. He emphasized that if anyone argues that one element of the law is essential for salvation, the whole law must be kept. But he believed that Christ has set people free from such external requirements. Knowing, however, that this teaching could be easily misunderstood and distorted, Paul quickly added that this new freedom was not to be used as an occasion for doing whatever one wishes. There are weighty responsibilities involved in this new relationship with God; the Spirit enters one's life to transform it, not simply to set it free from legal requirements.

There are characteristics of this new life which Paul described as walking "by the Spirit." This life is diametrically opposed to the life "in the flesh," i.e., the life of a human being apart from God. There is here no dichotomy between flesh and spirit as understood so often in Greek thought. When one walks by the Spirit, one lives a life in accordance with God's will and way. When one walks by the flesh, one lives a life against God's will and way. That there is no line between material and spiritual here can be seen clearly in Paul's delineation of the characteristics of the "works of the flesh"

(5:19–21) and the "fruit of the Spirit" (5:22–24). In each list there are things "material" and "spiritual"; that is not, therefore, the contrast Paul wished to make.

Paul argued that the Christian life is a lifestyle that is different from the world, and it is a lifestyle that will in fact fulfill the deeper meaning of the law. "But the fruit of the Spirit is love, joy, peace, patience, kindness, goodness, faithfulness, gentleness, self-control; against such there is no law." But all these are gifts from God to be appropriated only by faith.

Even in his concluding remarks (6:11–18) Paul still argued for his position. Externals such as circumcision count for nothing; all is involved in the new life. And, further, he appealed to the fact that he had suffered for the sake of this gospel (6:17).

This letter is filled with intense emotion. Some are perplexed that such a person as Paul could tell his enemies to "go to hell," not once but twice (cf. 1:8–9), and to suggest to them that if circumcision is of such import, why not go the whole way and castrate themselves (5:12)! At first reading this strikes the reader as pompous and arrogant. But on further reflection and a more careful reading, the intensity of Paul's outburst is not so much directed at defending himself, even though that is a part of the picture, but rather he was more concerned about the well-being of these new Christians who were being confused by all of those charges and countercharges. He did not want to have them confused or disturbed in these very crucial moments in their Christian growth. It is for them that Paul is more concerned; he was committed to them and felt responsible for them. That seems to be why this letter is so intense. Paul himself was not really hurt by the charges of these people; he was well-grounded in his faith, but the Galatian people were not yet so mature.

The Summary of the Third Journey: Romans

Even though the Letter to the Romans has often been interpreted as a "theological treatise," this writing is basically, as are Paul's other letters, an "occasional" document. It is true that this letter is the least occasional of Paul's writings because he did not found the church at Rome and probably knew very little about it. The purpose for the writing of the letter was Paul's desire to go to Spain to preach the gospel there. He wanted to use Rome as his base for this operation as he had used Antioch in Syria as the base for his other endeavors.

Therefore in the winter of 56–57 Paul wrote to the Romans from Corinth. But what exactly did he write? If Romans is a theological treatise, as some argue, it is peculiar that so many themes and issues are either ignored or relegated to insignificant status. It is more likely that Paul wrote to the Romans simply what was "in his mind" at the moment. This was the end of his last missionary journey in this part of the world. That time had seen problems with the Corinthian church and problems with the Judaizers. And if one reads Romans carefully, one will find that *every* matter discussed is related to these experiences. Because Paul did not know the people or the church at Rome intimately, he wrote to them a reflective letter which revolved about the issues which he had most recently encountered.

There is almost no question about the authenticity of this letter. What critical questions there are revolve around the destination of the letter and its unity. And these two issues are interrelated to a degree. There is the problem of chapter 16 which many scholars do not think could have been addressed to the church of Rome. So many persons are named and spoken to personally; some of them are known to have been at Ephesus quite recently, during Paul's stay there; and the situation presupposed in chapter 16 seems to reflect an "Asian" background. Because of these factors it is argued by some that chapter 16 is a separate short letter of commendation for Phoebe (a deaconess at the church at Cenchreae, a port near Corinth) written to the church at Ephesus. If this is correct, a question is raised about the integrity of the letter; and further, how this short note came to be attached to the Roman letter.

It may be that Paul knew these people in Rome and that some of those who had recently been with him in Ephesus had traveled to Rome. After all, Priscilla and Aquila had originally been from

Rome. And the extreme emphasis on personal connections in this short note may have been a way of establishing a closer contact between himself and the Roman Christians. In fact, some of the people in Ephesus may have been going ahead to Rome to assist Paul with his work there.

Whatever the answer to this perplexing question, it is nevertheless true that there is no explicit textual evidence which separates this chapter from the remainder of the book. There are some peculiarities in certain texts which do support the idea that the text of Romans may have circulated in a shorter form, but exactly how or why is not known explicitly. If chapter 16 is separated from the body of the letter, there are really no concluding remarks which usually are a part of Paul's style. The short blessing at 15:33 could be interpreted as a conclusion, but it was quite unusual for Paul to conclude so abruptly.

There is another problem connected with the issue of unity. Many commentators cannot fit chapters 9–11 into the "flow" of the letter, arguing that one can omit these chapters and not lose any of the basic thought that Paul seems to be discussing in this letter. There is no textual evidence for this, however, and the tendency to find these chapters an intrusion into the text is prominent among those who interpret Romans from a particular viewpoint and perspective.

In the light of the Protestant Reformation which owed much to Luther's understanding of Romans and Galatians, most Protestant scholars have interpreted Romans as the classic statement regarding justification by faith alone. And there is no question that this theme is quite prominent in Romans. But there are other issues and themes as well, which has led some more recent scholars to argue that there may be a different theme to Romans other than that of justification by faith. The most popular of these newer "themes" is the concept of the "righteousness of God." If indeed God acts in accordance with his own righteousness and expects righteous lives from his people, then chapters 9–11 become a crucial, if not focal, discussion in this writing. There are some others, fewer surely, who argue that the theme of Romans is the "universality of the gospel." Under this theme also chapters 9–11 would be a central point in the overall structure of the book.

It is probably superfluous to argue which, if any, of the proposed themes is *the* theme of Romans. All three of them appear frequently and usually together (cf. 1:16–17; 3:21f.). It is doubtful that Paul sat down and consciously wrote or dictated a letter with one central theme. As has been argued here, these themes are connected with his recent experiences, and others appear in the writing also.

Romans: Outline

- I.   Salutation 1:1–7
- II. Thanksgiving 1:8–15
- III. Theme(s) of the Letter 1:16–17
- IV. Body
    - A. The universal sinfulness of the human race 1:18–3:20
    - B. God's new way of dealing with the human situation 3:31–4:25
    - C. Ultimate goal of reconciliation 5:1–11
    - D. Results of God's action
        - (1) Freedom from sin 5:12–6:23
        - (2) Freedom from law as a means of salvation 7:1–25
        - (3) Assurance of God's victory and love 8:1–39
    - E. Problem of the rejection of the Jews 9–11
        - (1) Problem of election 9
        - (2) Salvation 10
        - (3) God's purpose 11
    - F. Application of the Christian life
        - (1) To other Christians 12:1–13
        - (2) To enemies 12:14–21
        - (3) To the state 13:1–14
        - (4) Relationship of strong and weak 14:1–15:13
    - G. Reasons for his coming to Rome 15:14–33
    - H. Personal Greetings 16

It would be impossible in a short space to do justice to the contents of Paul's letter to the Romans. A brief summary is given here but the letter deserves to be studied in some depth and with some intensity. The results will be worth the effort!

After his lengthy salutation and a warm thanksgiving, Paul presents a portrait of the human race enmeshed in sin. The Gentiles and the Jews are both guilty of the same sin, idolatry, and idolatry to Paul is basically the worship of the human self caused by human pride. Idols are in reality only extensions of the self. Therefore when one is an idolater, that person is simply worshipping oneself. The manifestations of this basic principle of sin vary from the Gentile world to the Jewish world. Among the Gentiles the results of such an attitude of life are perversions and debauchery and gross evil. Among the Jews, who have been entrusted with the covenant and God's law, the result of such an attitude of life is hypocrisy. Therefore, Paul argues that there is no one in the world who can stand before God in anything other than a state of sinfulness.

But God has taken action on behalf of the human race to restore the broken relationship and to make available a new force to release persons from the power and bondage of sin and to endow them with the righteousness of God. This new relationship with God is a transforming force in the life of the believer which will give that person a new life. This new life is characterized by a reconciliation with God which gives hope for the future.

Even though Christians are now a part of the new age, they still live in the old age under the dominion of sin and evil. This evil is both personal and individual and also impersonal and collective. These old ties and temptations continue to pull at the Christian. Can a Christian caught in this kind of situation be separated from sin? The answer which Paul gives is that while the Christian may at points commit *acts* of sin, that person has been freed from the *dominion* of sin. A Christian life is one that is given over to righteousness as its master and is, therefore, characterized by righteousness not sin.

The law was given to God's people as a guideline for the relationships between God's people and God, and God's people with other people. But human sin being what it is caused people to interpret the law as an external code to be kept, the keeping of which would ensure salvation. No human being can keep the law perfectly, however, so in that sense the law only served to intensify human sinfulness not remove it. The true Christian feels the tension between what a person is and what that person ought to be in a way that those who are apart from God do not realize. In fact Paul himself feels this so acutely that he cries out, "Wretched man that I am! Who will deliver me from this body of death?" (7:24). He is sure, however, that there is hope for a person who has faith in Jesus, so sure that the entire eighth chapter is a proclamation of assurance to the Christians. The Spirit of God transforms their lives and sets them apart. Whatever is necessary for the well-being of those who entrust their lives to God has already been done by God himself! There is nothing in all the created order that can separate a Christian from the love of God (8:35–39).

At this point in his discussion Paul wrestled with the problem which arose out of the fact that the Jewish people no longer were considered to be the elect people of God. The Christian church, predominantly Gentile, was now considered to be the new Israel of God, called to carry out God's elective purpose. Paul argued that true descendants of Abraham were people of faith, not people born of a physical descent. God's election should not be considered an automatic phenomenon which magically passes along from generation to generation with no commitment or response on the part of the people involved.

But what about God's promise and righteousness and what about the idea that the new gospel was for everyone, if now the Jewish nation was no longer the elect people of God? Has God's word been shown to be false? Not so, says Paul, for the human response is very important to the idea of election (and salvation). The Jews have been set aside because of their incorrect response to God's election. This is clear from chapter 9 which deals with the problem of election.

Chapter 10, however, turns to the issue of salvation, a different issue here! But again the human response is central. One must accept the gifts of God offered to the human race, and anyone who will can receive salvation (10:12–13). In chapter 11 Paul attempts to show that God's ultimate plan is for all people to be the people of God! But again the human response is crucial (11:19–22). In concluding this discussion Paul acknowledged that these are matters above human understanding. God's ways are "inscrutable" and his judgments "unsearchable" (11:33). Paul knew that he was dealing with matters here that really transcend human understanding and intelligence.

Beginning with chapter 12 the discussion moves on to ethical exhortation. The Christian is urged to present the very "self" in the service of God and to use whatever talents one has for the benefit of the church. And even when treated harshly by others, vengeance is not to be a part of the Christian's lifestyle. Rather, good is to be rendered to one's enemy in the hope that these acts of kindness may cause repentance (12:20).

The Christian also has a responsibility to the state. According to Paul it was incumbent on the Christians to obey the civil laws, not because the state was perfect but because there was more positive good in this system than evil. For several centuries the Graeco-Roman world had been in turmoil with wars both civil and international. The *Pax Romana* (peace of Rome) had just recently settled on this part of the world, and some very positive elements were emerging as a result of this peace. One aspect, for example, was the good system of roads which facilitated travel and trade. These two items, peace and easy travel, had allowed Paul to pursue his work of preaching the gospel to the world. Therefore, to Paul, even though he was very much aware that there were abuses of power and evils, the Roman government was a positive good. Order was better than chaos and anarchy. Progress can only be made where there is order.

There is then a discussion about the relationship between the "strong" and the "weak" which is reminiscent of the problems in 1 Corinthians. Here Paul encouraged both groups to exercise some restraint in their judgment on each other.

Finally there are the concluding remarks where Paul told the people in Rome that he wished to come to them and to go on to Spain to preach the gospel there. His travel plans included going to Jerusalem with the collection and then to journey to Rome. The final chapter (16) includes numerous personal greetings whether addressed originally to Rome or not (cf. above).

The Prison Correspondence

Traditionally Paul is supposed to have written four letters from prison. The understanding was that these letters were written by Paul from prison in Rome ca. 60–62 A.D. The letters specifically are Philippians, Colossians, Philemon, and Ephesians. That, at least, is the tradition.

There are, however, a number of problems concerning this correspondence both collectively and with the individual letters. First of all there is the general question concerning where Paul was actually imprisoned when he wrote these letters. The tradition says Rome, but there are numerous comments contained in the writings which cause some problems when attempting to understand them as having originated in Rome ca. 60–62, e.g., "I am coming to visit when I am released." Therefore, two other possibilities have been suggested: Caesarea and Ephesus. We know from Acts that Paul was held at Caesarea for two years before he was sent to Rome; therefore this is a viable option. There is no evidence, however, that Paul was ever imprisoned in Ephesus. It is known that he remained there for almost three years and that during that period some intense feelings erupted into a riot. It is also true that Paul refers to "fighting with the wild beasts at Ephesus" (1 Corinthians 15:32), in all probability a comment to be taken metaphorically not literally. A later tradition (probably emerging from this comment) did understand Paul to have been imprisoned at Ephesus, but this tradition cannot be relied on by itself.

In spite of the problems involved there are a number of scholars who still hold that Paul was imprisoned in Ephesus and wrote the prison letters there. If the letters did originate other than at Rome, the Ephesus origin explains more logically more of the problems encountered than a Caesarean source. But the lack of any specific, concrete evidence of an Ephesian imprisonment is still a major stumbling block to such a theory. Therefore, there is a real burden of proof incumbent upon those who would argue for a place of origin for these letters other than Rome.

In addition to the overall problem of origin there are specific questions related to each of the letters individually. These shall be discussed with each letter.

Philippians: Outline

I. Salutation 1:1–2
II. Thanksgiving 1:3–11
III. Body
    A. Paul's personal situation 1:12–26
    B. Paul's plea for unity of people in church 1:27–2:18
       (1) Hymn to Christ 2:5–11
    C. Personal plans 2:19–3:1
    D. Comments against Judaizers 3:2–16
    E. Exhortation to Christian living 3:17–4:13
IV. Concluding Remarks 4:14–23

It is difficult to outline precisely the Philippian letter because of all Paul's letters this one is the most personal. Therefore, personal comments and feelings are interwoven throughout the various portions of the letter. Paul was basically writing to thank the people in the church at Philippi for a gift they had sent to him to assist him during the time of his imprisonment. The one who brought the gift, Epaphroditus, became ill while he was there. Part of the letter reports on this illness and recovery. Some of the ambiguity of the letter results from the fact that Paul had difficulty in accepting gifts gracefully. He always stubbornly worked and earned his own way wherever he went, "to set an example" so he said. Now he obviously needed the assistance, and it was difficult for him to express his thanks.

There is very little question today concerning the authenticity of this letter, but there is question about its unity. There seems to be an abrupt change in subject matter and mood at 3:1, so much so that some have argued that 3:2–4:3 (or perhaps 4:9) is part of another letter. Some even argue that 4:10–20 may also be a brief note that was written separately. It is, therefore, possible that this letter, as we have it, is a composite of several fragments. But the letter seems to hold together rather well; and read for what it was intended to be, very personal greetings and admonitions, it seems best to regard this letter as a unity.

The date of the letter will vary accordingly as one determines the origin of the writing. If it did originate in Rome the date would have been 60–62 A.D. If Caesarea, 58–60 A.D.If Ephesus, perhaps 55 A.D. There is an internal problem of content which has some bearing on the date. This is connected with the passage beginning at 3:2. Here Paul is harshly attacking the Judaizers with the same zeal as he had shown in Galatians. Some, therefore, think that the letter (or at least this passage) reflects the earlier period when the Judaizing controversy was at its height, i.e., 55–56 A.D. By the time Paul went to Rome that episode had cooled off considerably. This is the primary (but not the only) reason for questioning the Roman origin of the letter or at least that portion of the letter.

There seems to be good reason, therefore, in assigning to Philippians a date of ca. 55 A.D. Since we know Paul was in Ephesus during that period, Ephesus would then be the originating place for the letter. From the writing itself it is quite apparent that Paul is in prison as he wrote. It is true that there is no specific external evidence to prove that Paul was imprisoned at Ephesus, but there is enough indirect evidence to make the conjecture "plausible," to say the least.

The traditional view of the Roman origin still holds major sway but other possibilities can be argued with some cogency.

There are several points which call for close investigation in the examination of the contents of this letter. First of all, there is the eschatological dimension which arouses some interest because Paul seems to have altered somewhat his perspective at this point. In Paul's earlier letters his basic eschatological viewpoint seems to have been an apocalyptic viewpoint, perhaps literally interpreted (cf. 1 Thessalonians 4:13ff.; 2 Thessalonians 2:1ff.). It was considered unusual for anyone to die before the Parousia in the earlier writings; even in 1 Corinthians Paul said that "not all will die" (15:51). But in this letter Paul seems to face death for himself and prefers that alternative! "For to me to live is Christ, and to die is gain. . . . My desire is to depart and be with Christ, for that is far better." (1:21–23)

This statement seems to shift the emphasis away from the futuristically oriented apocalypticism of the Thessalonian correspondence with its emphasis on an external Parousia to a more private and individual type of eschatology. There are those who believe that Paul ultimately gave up the idea of the Parousia and cite Philippians as an example to substantiate their theory. It is true that Paul does seem to have shifted his emphasis here, but it is probably going too far to say that Paul has given up the idea of the Parousia. In 4:4 he says, "The Lord is at hand." Even though this comment can be interpreted to mean that God is near to all who call upon him, the usual nuance of such a statement in Paul's letters designates the Parousia. It appears that Paul's situation here is very serious, and he faced the fact that he could die. Because of this his emphasis naturally shifted to a more personal and private understanding of physical death and the Christian's relationship with it. There seems to be no real evidence that Paul has given up the idea of the Parousia, however.

Another major point in the study of this epistle relates to the famous Christ-hymn of 2:5–11. It is generally agreed that this is a pre-Pauline hymn which was probably used in the worship liturgy of the early church. As Paul was exhorting the Philippians to live in harmony and be of one mind, he inserted this hymn to illustrate humility and unselfishness. As Christ was willing to sacrifice, so should the people of Christ be willing to learn humility.

This hymn, however, gives to Christ a dimension not really found before in Paul's letters. And there are weighty matters of interpretation which lie hidden in the Greek of the poem, some of which have not yet been fully resolved. Further, there is no general agreement as to the overall structure of the hymn; different scholars divide the poetry in different ways. It is usually agreed, however, that the phrase, "even death on a cross" (2:8c), is a Pauline addition to the hymn.

The exact meaning of the hymn, while debated, is used by Paul to illustrate a point he is trying to make to the Philippian Christians. Be unified in spirit; be humble; be dedicated to the cause of God; be dedicated to the well-being of each other. In the development of the Christology (the doctrine about the nature of Jesus) in the early church, however, this hymn played an important part.

As already indicated, at 3:2 there is a change in tone where Paul warned against the Judaizers and defended his own place in the Christian church. But the defense here was so very personal that he exposed more of his inner feelings than perhaps in any of his other writings. The passage contained in 3:7–14 is a poignant revelation of his deepest feelings about himself, his own value, the value system of the world, and the real values that come only from God. He says, very bluntly, that all of his worldly claims to success and prestige (of which according to his culture there were many) could be placed in a heap, and they would be to him as a "heap of dung!" The things that really count can be given only by God through Christ; and even these must be used in a life and death struggle against the world. The Christian life is not an easy life. It is a constant struggle and challenge to become what one cannot be by oneself, but can be through the grace of God. ". . . Forgetting what lies behind and straining forward to what lies ahead, I press on toward the goal for the prize of the upward call of God in Christ Jesus." (3:13b–14)

In his own way Paul has tried to thank the Philippians for their gift and assistance. A letter as intimate and revealing as this from such a one as Paul is in itself a gift returned to the Christians of that place.

Colossians: Outline

I. Salutation 1:1–2
II. Thanksgiving 1:3–12
III. Body
    A. Description of God's Christ 1:13–20
    B. Personal exhortations 1:21–2:7
    C. Challenge not to fall prey to false teachings and false living 2:8–3:17
    D. *Haustafeln* (social concerns and relationships) 3:18–4:6
IV. Concluding Remarks 4:7–18

Paul's letter to the church at Colossae originated from Rome ca. 60–61 A.D. according to tradition. There are here no real stumbling blocks in the way of accepting this part of the tradition. The basic problem with this epistle is that of authenticity, i.e., is it genuinely Pauline. Because of the somewhat different vocabulary and the gnostic-type heresy involved at the church (a heresy that includes elements from a much later time, some argue), and the advanced teaching about Jesus there are some scholars who deny this letter to Paul.

If one examines the letter carefully, one finds that the difference in style is rather slight, and the vocabularly deviation consists mainly in the sections dealing with the heresy, one that has not been encountered before. And further the cosmic teaching about Jesus is also directly related to the heretical problem Paul is attempting to solve. Therefore there seems to be no real basis for denying the authenticity of this letter—nor its unity.

Exactly who the heretics were in the church at Colossae is not known. Interpreters of this writing have detected two possibilities: a Greek-oriented heresy closely related to gnostic thought, and a Jewish-oriented heresy closely related to an ascetic lifestyle centering in food laws and feast days. Since this was not a church which Paul knew personally and since the only evidence for the problem must be surmised from the letter, it is difficult to be certain about the people or even the problems. It seems clear, however, that the false teachings were generally gnostic in nature.

Gnosticism, with its sharp dichotomy between matter and flesh, usually tended toward two extremes. One was a depreciation of "material" things and activities to the point of withdrawal from normal society, while the other considered "material" things so unimportant that one could do *anything,* physically speaking, without harming in any way one's "pure spirit." There are portions of Paul's teaching in this letter which seem to be directed toward both these extremes, both explicitly and implicitly. And, further, there is the teaching which is found in most gnostic systems involving the network of "entities" or "elemental spirits" that comprise the "overworld" between God and the created world. The argument used by the people at Colossae obviously went something like this: If Christ was a connecting element between God and the world and was to be worshipped, should not the other elements be worshipped as well?

In the light of the issues that are discussed in this letter and since they appear to be related basically to gnostic thought, it seems best to consider the heresy in Colossae as basically Greek, gnostic in origin. The references to the Jewish food laws and feast days probably emerged from a combination of the ascetic gnostic tendency and the knowledge of the Old Testament (their Bible!) with which they had become familiar.

After his usual salutation and thanksgiving (which really flows into the discussion of the problem), Paul first discusses the idea that the other "beings" in the *pleroma* structure (i.e., the structure of the "overworld") were to be worshipped along with Jesus. His answer to this is similar to his basic answer concerning the existence of idols and gods in 1 Corinthians 8. Obviously those who had been puzzled over this matter considered Christ the last link in the superstructure between God and the created order, i.e., the lowest of all the beings there. Paul immediately argues that Jesus is the first-born of all creation (1:15) and was an agent in the creation of all things visible and invisible. Rather than being the last and lowest link he is the first and highest! He then goes on to say that ". . . in him all the fulness of God was pleased to dwell . . ." (1:19). The word "fulness" in this verse is the Greek word, *pleroma.* In other words, Paul with this seemingly simple statement has destroyed the idea of the *pleroma.* If it ever existed, it exists no longer, for all the connective elements between God and the created order are contained within the person of Jesus. He repeats that again, emphatically, in 2:9.

Here again is an instance where Paul in arguing against certain problems in the church has introduced an additional dimension into the ideas connected with the person of Jesus (cf. also Philippians 2:5–11). In the Philippians passage it was fairly clear that Paul was using an existing hymn in honor of Christ. There are some scholars who argue similarly here, but there is not anything like universal recognition that a hymn was used in this Colossians passage. Some find a hymn here; others do not. This particular passage is so specifically oriented toward the problems of the church in Colossae that it seems a bit strained to see in these verses (1:9–20) a hymn. Paul seems to be speaking simply to the problems of the moment.

As for the second element in the heresy, the emphasis upon ascetic tendencies (cf. 2:20–23), Paul argued that simply abstaining from certain "worldly" things does not really get at the matter of a new life freed from bondage to the "flesh." In order that the other extreme (i.e., the libertine gnostics) not latch on to this teaching and distort it into a license to do anything, Paul immediately began to talk about the characteristics of the truly Christian life (cf. 3:1–17).

There is then a short but significant section dealing with *Haustafeln,* i.e., social concerns and relationships. He discusses the relationships between husband and wife, parents and children, masters and slaves. In this context Paul appears as a person of his own time, accepting the usual order of relationships that were commonly held then. But he makes it plain that the Christian life is supposed to make a large difference in these relationships. It is interesting to note that the master-slave relationship occupies most of the discussion (3:22–4:1)! Perhaps this can be explained by remembering that the letter to Philemon concerning a runaway slave was written and delivered at the same time as Colossians!

The letter concludes with personal greetings and comments. An interesting point here is that Paul refers to another letter, a letter from Laodicea (4:16), which has not (so far as we know) been preserved.

Philemon: Outline

I.   Salutation vv. 1–3
II. Thanksgiving vv. 4–7
III. Body
    A.   Appeal for Onesimus' life and well-being vv. 8–22
IV. Concluding Remarks vv. 23–25

Whatever the date and origin of the Letter to the Colossians may be, the Letter to Philemon is undoubtedly to be considered the same in these two areas. The letters were dispatched at the same time by the same hand (cf. Colossians 4:10–17 with Philemon vv. 23–24).

In all probability the letter was written from Rome since that would have been a good place for a runaway slave to have gone to gain a large degree of anonymity. Traditionally this letter was written by Paul on behalf of a slave, Onesimus, who belonged to Philemon, a Christian in the church at Colossae. Onesimus had obviously run away and in the process had stolen some money or property. In Rome somehow Onesimus came into contact with Paul and became a Christian. This set of circumstances put Paul in a very difficult position. Under the Roman law Paul was obligated to send Onesimus back to Philemon, but by so doing he would place the slave in a dangerous situation.

According to the law Philemon would have been within his rights to do with Onesimus as he wished. And under such circumstances it was often the case that a runaway slave having been returned would be made an example. Paul was, in a sense, placing Onesimus' life on the line. In this short letter, then, Paul is literally trying to save the life of this man! He sent Onesimus back, but the letter he dispatched on his behalf placed enormous pressure on Philemon to accept Onesimus' return without harm coming to him.

To accomplish this Paul addressed the letter not simply to Philemon but to his wife, the leader of the church there, and even to the entire church! In fact, there is a reference in Colossians 4:16 to a letter "from Laodicea." No such letter has been preserved, and it has been presumably lost. There are some scholars, however, who argue that the letter which is known as "to Philemon" may be the letter from Laodicea since it is addressed to a church rather than an individual.

Further, Paul appealed to Philemon's sense of pride in complimenting him on his faith in Christ and the love which he had shown for all the saints (i.e., Christians). He then asked Philemon to do "what is required" by accepting Onesimus back as a Christian brother. He even hinted that Philemon might send him back to serve during the time of Paul's imprisonment. Paul agreed to repay anything that Onesimus owed; he writes the I.O.U. in his own hand (v. 19a). And he cleverly added, "I would not mention the fact that you owe me your very life!" (v. 19b, paraphrase). In addition Paul mentioned that he would like Philemon to prepare the guest room for him, the implication being that he was coming to see what Philemon had done with Onesimus!

The letter is short and to the point. Each word seems carefully chosen to convey exactly the proper nuance. After all, a man's life was on the line here; and what Paul said could make a difference in what Philemon did with Onesimus.

Interestingly enough we do not know what happened to Onesimus. Paul certainly brought enough pressure to bear on Philemon both externally and internally! But the real settlement of the matter is not known.

Basic Ideas in Paul's Writings

After one has studied and examined the epistles of Paul, there is usually a feeling that one has not really been able to understand the man fully. There seem to be some inconsistencies and contradictions in the writings. How does one make sense of all that one finds in these letters?

One of the problems that is involved in the attempt to understand Paul stems from the fact that throughout Christian history the theologians have turned to Paul when they wanted to structure a theological system for the church from the New Testament. This is a curious phenomenon for of all the writings contained in the New Testament, Paul's letters are the least theological in origin; these letters are the *most* occasional of the New Testament canon! This means that they are directed toward very specific situations and problems in an attempt to solve problems and effect reconciliations. Whether it is legitimate to derive from such writings a theological system is open to question. But it is frustrating to attempt to fit all the pieces of Paul's "theological" thinking together into one coherent whole. The author of 2 Peter, writing later, said, "So also our beloved brother Paul wrote to you according to the wisdom given him, speaking of this as he does in all his letters. There are some things in them hard to understand, which the ignorant and unstable twist to their own destruction, as they do the other scriptures"

(3:15–16). There are very few who have ever tried to understand Paul who would argue with that assessment!

But if one approaches Paul's letters as presentations of religious beliefs instead of strict theology, one is more likely to find a key to assist in understanding the writings of this complex and intense man. It is perhaps best to acknowledge that one cannot from the writings as they now stand compose a systematic theology of the apostle Paul. Is there, however, a thread of continuity which one can detect that holds all the diverse ends of Paul's teaching together?

There does seem to be such a thread. In spite of all the ambiguity and incongruity which one encounters in examining many of Paul's favorite topics the essential element in the teaching of Paul seems to be "new life." This is the one consistent point that he continually reiterates in his writings. This element springs from a new relationship with God made possible through God's action in Jesus. And this new life is effected through the Spirit of God given to those who have accepted God's offer of grace. This new life, new style or manner of living, transforms a person into something different from the style and manner of this world. It gives a new value system which is different, sometimes directly opposite, from the value system of the world. It is a new life that is characterized by a new motivation in one's activity and thinking, the motivation now being love–love of God and one's neighbor–instead of pride and selfishness. To the Christian it is not enough simply to do the right thing. One must do the right things for the right reasons! (cf. 1 Corinthians 12–13).

Paul seems to keep a delicate balance between the importance of individuals as individuals and the understanding that basically Christians are a group, the people of God. In such a setting it is impossible for each person to do exactly what that person wishes without regard for the group. The individual Christian has responsibilities both for the other Christians and to the world at large, to witness to the world that God has made possible a reconciliation between humanity and himself. The Christian, therefore, is always charged with responsibility for others (cf. 1 Corinthians 8). This new life and its attendant responsibilities cause a person to live in a different manner. Each person will not be the same, not at all, but each person will be motivated by the same force, genuine care, concern, and love for others; and each person will be committed to the same God and be subject to his demands.

All of Paul's ideas and concepts are basically related to this understanding. And this is also the probable explanation for the seeming inconsistencies and contradictions that one finds in Paul's writings. It is, for example, very difficult to understand Paul's teaching in the area of eschatology. At certain points he seems to espouse a rather literalistic apocalyptic view (cf. 1 Thessalonians, 2 Thessalonians, 1 Corinthians) while in other places that emphasis seems to be totally different (cf. 2 Corinthians 4–5; Philippians 1:21ff.). In speaking, therefore, to the various churches with different problems and circumstances, he applied the basic principle of the new life in Christ as best he could to the manifold problems and questions of those early churches. The world as it is, is ambiguous and difficult; therefore the answers to the problems of life and death cannot always be clearly delineated. As for the seemingly confusing ideas related to the Parousia, Paul obviously felt that as long as one had accepted the new life offered by God and as long as one was committed to that new life, it would not really matter whether the Parousia came tomorrow or never. The most important part of the Christian life was the new transforming relationship with God which formed the basis of real religious experience.

Paul and Women

Because so much has been made in recent times about Paul's teaching concerning women, it is perhaps in order to examine briefly his teaching on this specific point. To understand better his ideas one needs to be reminded about the context of the times. For good or ill the world of Paul's day afforded very little status to women. Generally speaking, women were little educated or, more likely, totally uneducated, were trained basically to perform domestic duties, and were overall considered to be weaker vessels. As a group they were considered to be of little value, and in some places were considered no more than property. There were some exceptions to this general attitude, naturally, but all in all the status of women in that time (both in Jewish and Hellenistic cultures) was exceedingly low. This must be understood when considering the New Testament position.

In the early church it seems that women played a fairly important part in the ministry of Jesus (cf. Mark 15:40–41; Matthew 27:55). This is especially emphasized in Luke's writings where women are quite often featured. It seems also that women played an important role in the early church. Women were permitted to speak and prophesy and pray in the church meetings, and in several writings there is reference to "deaconesses" which seems to have been some sort of office or function in the early church.

It is not surprising then to learn that women played a significant role in the churches which Paul founded. Priscilla and Aquila were leaders both in Corinth and at Ephesus. And in Romans 16 there are no fewer than eight women greeted—and these are obviously significant persons in the work of the church.

In Paul's teaching he states clearly that: "There is neither Jew nor Greek, there is neither slave nor free, there is neither male nor female; for you all are one in Christ" (Galatians 3:28). In relationships between husbands and wives he seems to indicate that there is an equality here. "Each man should have his own wife and each woman her own husband. The husband should give to his wife her conjugal rights, and likewise the wife to her husband. For the wife does not rule over her own body, but the husband does; likewise the husband does not rule over his own body, but the wife does." (1 Corinthians 7:2b–4). It would be difficult to find a more "equal" statement than this.

There are, however, several passages which have been cited by some persons to demonstrate that Paul was totally and absolutely anti-female. From the letters that are most probably Pauline there are three passages frequently discussed: 1 Corinthians 11:2–16; 1 Corinthians 14:34–35; and Colossians 3:18–19.

The two passages from 1 Corinthians are found in a section of that letter which deals with proper decorum in the worship services. The first has to do with a rule that women should have their heads veiled when they pray or prophesy. The exact problem which called forth this explanation from Paul is simply not known to us; it would certainly assist in understanding the passage if the background were evident. Nevertheless there are certain points which can be made. Paul never says that a woman cannot pray or prophesy—only that he considers it proper decorum for a woman to have her head covered when so doing. And further he explicitly states that "... in the Lord woman is not independent of man nor man of woman; for as woman was made from man, so man is now born of woman. And all things are from God" (11:11–12). There seems to be no anti-feminine teaching here.

The second passage is found in the context of a problem, again connected with proper order and decorum in worship. This arises out of the phenomenon fairly common in the early church of glosso-lalia, speaking in tongues. This was a highly excitable and emotional experience in which persons sometimes lost control of their senses. Paul's basic instruction to them at this point was to regulate such activity carefully, especially in the worship services.

Toward the conclusion of his discussion of this matter he makes the statement, "... the women should keep silence in the churches. For they are not permitted to speak. . . . If there is anything they desire to know, let them ask their husbands at home" (14:34–35). There are at least four ways to interpret this passage. One could let it stand at face value, but that would directly contradict Paul's statement in chapter 11. It would be strange to say that women could pray and prophesy and immediately thereafter compel them to keep silent! So there must be some other explanation.

One could, secondly, interpret the passage to mean that Paul does not wish for women to speak "in tongues" in the church service. Perhaps this could cause embarrassment to them or could possible give the wrong impression about Christian women to people outside the church. This is a possible meaning but the comment about "asking their husbands at home" seems to indicate a broader interpretation here.

A third explanation revolves about a textual problem. In some early Greek manuscripts these verses are either omitted or placed after verse 40. This indicates that these verses may not have been a part of the original text of the passage. These verses then would be an early scribal comment which was copied into the text here (in some manuscripts after verse 40). If one omits these verses, the text reads just as well without them. This explanation may be a correct understanding of what has happened, but the vast majority of early texts does contain these verses, and it is difficult to omit them on the evidence we possess now.

A last alternative is to remember that Paul is speaking to specific problems in the Corinthian church. And in this context the problems are related to improper practices and occurrences within the worship life of the community. There may have been something which had been occuring in this context, done by certain specific women in the church, which was disturbing the worship of the community. If this is true, it had to do with improper talking or questioning. In such a setting Paul's advice is for order in the service, and questioning later at home. This advice would no more be anti-female than would Paul's refusal to allow the men to frequent the houses of ill-repute (6:12–20) be anti-male! There are certain obligations one has as a Christian to oneself and to others. And the Christian life is supposed to be different.

The last passage is that found in Colossians 3:18–19. Again exactly what problem lies behind Paul's admonition here is not known to us. And even in this context Paul emphasized the obligation not simply of the wife to the husband but also of the husband to the wife. It is also interesting that in this list of social relationships, husband-wife, parent-child, slave-master, the slave-master discussion dominates over half of the discussion. It is quite possible that this is because of the problem with Onesimus since this letter was sent at the same time as the letter to Philemon—and may well have been sent to the same church! The basic purpose, therefore, of the entire passage may have been to establish a setting for Paul's thoughts about that situation. If that is so, the reference to the relationship between husbands and wives, parents and children, may be used simply to establish a more intimate context for the master-slave relationship.

And it is also quite possible that Paul was simply arguing for some kind of order in human relationships, and he naturally used the accepted order of authority in his time. That is, of course, a principle that is applicable in any age. There has to be some kind of order and authority so that progress can be made in human life. And respect for such order is very important. The accepted order of authority may change in the development of human relationships, but the principle still stands.

We have examined the primary texts where Paul mentions women explicitly. The worst that can be said from an examination of these texts is that he was a product of his time and culture, accepting the place of the male as the primary element in the political and social structures of that period of history. But it is also clear that he emphasized equality within marriage, the equal dependence of male and female on each other, the right of women to participate in religious worship in the church, and seemed to encourage all people to join together in the church as equals. For his time these were significant advances. And some of the principles which he set forth have led, and could only lead, to a more acute awareness of the inherent equality of all people *in the Lord.* Humanly speaking all people are not equal because the world's value system is different. But in Christ all are truly equal, not because each has the same talent or is exactly alike, but because each one belongs to the Lord and to each other.

Suggestions for Further Study

For a study of the overall theological teachings of Paul these books are especially helpful.

The Theology and Religious Teachings of Paul

Rudolf Bultmann. *Theology of the New Testament.* Translated by K. Grobel. New York: Charles Scribner's Sons, 1951. Vol. I. Pp. 185–352.

James M. Efird. *These Things Are Written: An Introduction to the Religious Ideas of the Bible.* Atlanta: John Knox Press, 1978. Pp. 121–138.

J. Fitzmyer. *Pauline Theology: A Brief Sketch.* Englewood Cliffs, New Jersey: Prentice-Hall, Inc., 1967. For beginners.

V. P. Furnish. *Theology and Ethics in Paul.* New York: Abingdon Press, 1968.

G. E. Ladd. *A Theology of the New Testament.* Grand Rapids, Michigan: Wm. B. Eerdmans Publishing Co., 1974. Pp. 359–568.

Calvin J. Roetzel. *The Letters of Paul: Conversations in Context.* Atlanta: John Knox Press, 1975.

D. E. H. Whiteley. *The Theology of St. Paul.* Philadelphia: Fortress Press, 1964. A non-technical presentation of Paul's theology.

For the student who wishes to study individual letters of Paul, the following list of commentaries will provide a sound beginning. *Many* other good works are available, however.

The Thessalonian Letters
Ernest Best. *A Commentary on the First and Second Epistles to the Thessalonians.* New York: Harper & Row, 1972.

A. L. Moore. *1 & 2 Thessalonians.* London: Nelson, 1969.

Ronald A. Ward. *Commentary on 1 & 2 Thessalonians.* Waco, Texas: Word Books, 1973.

D. E. H. Whiteley. *Thessalonians in the Revised Standard Version: Introduction and Commentary.* London: Oxford University Press, 1969.

The Corinthian Correspondence
C. K. Barrett. *A Commentary on the First Epistle to the Corinthians.* New York: Harper & Row, 1968.

C. K. Barrett. *A Commentary on the Second Epistle to the Corinthians.* New York: Harper & Row, 1973.

F. F. Bruce. *1 and 2 Corinthians.* London: Oliphants, 1971.

Galatians
Donald Guthrie. *Galatians.* London: Nelson, 1969.

William Neil. *The Letter of Paul to the Galatians.* Cambridge: Cambridge University Press, 1967. Cambridge Bible Commentary on the New English Bible.

Romans
C. K. Barrett. *A Commentary on the Epistle to the Romans.* New York: Harper & Row, 1957.

Matthew Black. *Romans.* London: Oliphants, 1973.

F. F. Bruce. *The Epistle of Paul to the Romans.* Grand Rapids, Michigan: Wm. B. Eerdmans Publishing Co., 1963.

John Murray. *The Epistle to the Romans.* Grand Rapids, Michigan: Wm. B. Eerdmans Publishing Co., 1959–65. 2 vols.

Philippians
F. W. Beare. *A Commentary on the Epistle to the Philippians.* 2nd edition. London: A. & C. Black, 1969.

R. P. Martin. *The Epistle of Paul to the Philippians: An Introduction and Commentary.* Grand Rapids, Michigan: Wm. B. Eerdmans Publishing Co., 1959.

Colossians and Philemon
G. B. Caird. *Paul's Letters From Prison: Ephesians, Philippians, Colossians, Philemon in the Revised Standard Version: Introduction and Commentary.* Oxford: Oxford University Press, 1976.

Kenneth Grayston. *The Letters of Paul to the Philippians and to the Thessalonians.* London: Cambridge University Press, 1967. Cambridge Bible Commentary on the New English Bible.

Eduard Lohse. *Colossians and Philemon: A Commentary on the Epistles to the Colossians and to Philemon.* Translated by W. R. Poehlmann and R. J. Karris. Edited by Helmut Koester. Philadelphia: Fortress Press, 1971.

R. P. Martin. *Colossians: The Church's Lord and the Christian's Liberty.* Grand Rapids, Michigan: Zondervan Publishing House, 1972.

G. H. P. Thompson. *The Letters of Paul to the Ephesians, to the Colossians and to Philemon.* London: Cambridge University Press, 1976. Cambridge Bible Commentary on the New English Bible.

J. L. Houlden. *Paul's Letters from Prison: Philippians, Colossians, Philemon, and Ephesians.* Philadelphia: Westminster Press, 1977.

CHAPTER VI

The Post-Apostolic Age

After the deaths of Paul and Peter in Rome, the fall of Jerusalem in 70 A.D. to the Roman armies, and the realization that the first generation of Christian believers were almost all deceased, the church entered a period in which certain changes were becoming inevitable. This period, called the post-apostolic age, in many ways was similar to the post-exilic era of Jewish history. There was much discussion about how to cope with the new times with new challenges and new dangers. To some degree the issue was simply *survival.*

The early church had believed so sincerely that the Parousia was near that little thought had been given to the structural organization of the church for the long-range future. Very little systematic thinking had been done about "exact and orthodox" views concerning Jesus. There had been little thought about what Christian ethics should be over a "long haul." To be sure these matters had been discussed but usually in an occasional manner when a specific problem necessitated such thinking. But as time moved on it became more and more evident that some further thought was necessary in order for the church to survive and cope with the world in which it existed.

There were three basic areas of concentration with which the church wrestled during this period, dated approximately 75–150 A.D. These were the areas of Christology, i.e., thinking about the nature and person of Jesus; ecclesiology, i.e., thinking about the nature and structure of the church; and eschatology, i.e., thinking about the "end" or ultimate matters which centered in the problems basically caused by the failure of the Parousia to materialize as had been expected.

The setting for this development was a Graeco-Roman society that basically looked upon the Christians as at best unusual and at worst traitorous or immoral. During this period Christians were just beginning to be viewed as separate and distinct from Judaism. The association of the Christian movement so closely with the Jews during the early period of development had worked to the advantage of the Christians; now, however, the stigma attached to the Jewish religion following the war with Rome (66–70 A.D.) caused some in the ancient world to think of Christians as troublemakers and treasonous also. (This was in all probability part of the background, at least, for Luke's writing early in this time span.)

This, coupled with natural skepticism about any new movement and the misunderstandings some had of the Christians (they were cannibals, they held secret orgies, etc.), led the church into a period marked by periodic persecution. As yet this persecution was not an official, empire-wide state of affairs, but sporadic and isolated instances of persecution obviously did appear. In some forms it probably was simply directed at the Christians by their neighbors. There may have been a drought in an area, for example, and the people in that place felt that the old gods were angry at this new belief. At other points the persecution may have been conducted by the state in certain areas where imperial worship was being demanded. This situation occurred in Asia Minor during the latter part of the reign of Domitian (90–96 A.D.). And there were instances where for unknown reasons Christians were persecuted simply for being Christians, such as during the reign of Trajan (112–117 A.D.) again in Asia Minor.

The issue for the church was basically survival in the midst of a hostile world. This, coupled with the normal "growing pains" of a developing organization in terms of administration and ideology, provides the setting for the literature of this period.

The Deutero-Pauline Writings

There is a group of writings from this period which claim to have been written by Paul or were at some time attributed to Paul. This literature can best be described as Deutero-Pauline. There are five writings included in this group: Ephesians, 1 and 2 Timothy, Titus, and Hebrews.

Ephesians

As was indicated in the preceding chapter, the Letter to the Ephesians is traditionally attributed to Paul during the time of his imprisonment at Rome ca. 60–62 A.D. The tradition has, however, been questioned for some time since there are numerous problems which must be addressed in attributing this writing to Paul prior to 65 A.D.

In the first place the letter was not originally intended for Ephesus but was in all probability a circular letter written to a member of churches in a certain area. This is evidenced by the fact that in the earliest Greek manuscripts of the New Testament the words "in Ephesus" are omitted. There are, in addition, no personal greetings such as are usually found in Paul's letters. These factors have led most scholars to the conclusion that this letter, even if by Paul, was intended originally as a circular document. The destination in all probability was to the churches in the area of Asia Minor around Ephesus. The letter itself was then preserved in this church center and was later viewed as having been written to that church. It is interesting to note that in the early second century, Marcion (an early heretic) compiled his canon of authoritative writings which chiefly centered in Paul's letters (and Luke's writing). In Marcion's canon Ephesians was designated as the letter to the Laodiceans.

The style and language of the letter shows numerous divergencies from Paul's other letters. The vocabulary is different; for example, over 90 words are found that are not used in the other Pauline epistles, and the particles (the *nows, therefores, whereases,* etc.) are also different. In addition, whereas in Paul's letters the style is somewhat definite and pointed, in the Letter to the Ephesians the style is flowing, phrases rushing out tumbling one over the other in a manner that is never found in the other Pauline letters.

Coupled with this is the curious phenomenon that we find in the midst of these vocabulary and stylistic differences numerous phrases and clauses lifted almost directly out of Paul's letters, especially Colossians. This raises the question as to why Paul would quote lines directly from himself since he usually never does that sort of thing. Some scholars, therefore, have conjectured that the Letter to the Ephesians was written by a person who admired Paul greatly, had access to a collection of his letters, and who was attempting to give a summary of Paul's teaching directed, of course, toward the church situation now at hand.

The letter also seems to reflect a church situation that is later than the period when Paul wrote. There is no mention of the Parousia, and it appears that the author is attempting to prepare the church for a long period of conflict with the world. In addition, there are some terms which are used differently in this letter from the Pauline letters. For example, in Paul's writings God is always viewed as the Reconciler of human beings to God through Christ, whereas in Ephesians Christ is the Reconciler. In Paul's letters there is a strong emphasis on the cross as the central aspect of Jesus' life, but in Ephesians the central aspect seems to be the exaltation of Jesus. And, further, the word "church" is always used in Paul's letters to denote a local congregation, but in Ephesians it denotes the entire church in the world.

Because of these problems scholars are divided as to whether Paul wrote Ephesians. Those who follow the traditional view argue that the letter claims to have been written by Paul and that the burden of proof is on those who wish to deny that claim. Those who deny Pauline authorship refer to arguments such as have been cited above and also argue that pseudonymity, i.e., writing works in the name of someone else, appears to have been a common practice in that time. These persons argue that to write something in the name of someone else at that time was not an attempt to defraud but rather an expression of appreciation and esteem for the person in whose name the work was written. It is true that the practice of pseudonymity was widely practiced then and that there was not the stigma attached to such activity as there is today. Whether this proves then that Ephesians is pseudonymous is, nevertheless, an open question.

There is a distinct problem which arises as to the origin of this letter if indeed Paul did not write the letter from Rome. The question then becomes: what kind of setting called for the composition of such a work? There is one fairly detailed theory that has been postulated, and almost everyone who deals with Ephesians takes this hypothesis into account if only to reject it. It is the theory set down by E. J. Goodspeed which goes something like this.[1] After the death of Paul, the early church basically forgot him and his work. With the writing of Luke–Acts, however (which Goodspeed dated ca. 85–90), there was a revival of interest in Paul and his work. Someone who was probably very familiar with Paul's letter to the Colossians, because of the Acts account decided to collect the letters of Paul into a corpus (body). Using Acts as a guide, this person collected as many letters and fragments from Paul's churches as could be found and put them together. As an ardent admirer of Paul, this person decided to write a letter which would summarize Paul's teaching as he understood it. Since Colossians was so familiar to him, that became the basic source used in this composition. Therefore, the Letter to the Ephesians is a kind of introductory letter for the entire Pauline corpus.

Goodspeed speculated further about exactly who could have done this writing and made the collection. Since the letter seems to reflect a setting in Asia Minor and since the letter later was associated specifically with Ephesus, it seemed logical to assume that this work originated at Ephesus. Who then was this admirer of Paul? We know that an early church leader from Antioch in Syria, Ignatius, was being taken to Rome ca. 110–115 A.D. to be martyred. On the way he wrote several letters to churches in the area, one of which was directly sent to Ephesus. In this letter Ignatius tells the people there to honor the bishop, whose name happened to be Onesimus. Goodspeed argued that this must be the same Onesimus for whom Paul had written many years earlier. Since Onesimus was from this area, he would have had access to the letter to the Colossians dispatched at the same time as the letter on Onesimus' behalf. Who else would have owed Paul so much? Therefore, Onesimus was the author of the Letter to the Ephesians, and he wrote in Paul's name as a tribute to his former friend and benefactor.

Even though many cannot follow Goodspeed's theory *in toto,* there is here a possible setting given for the writing of Ephesians. Since Ephesians seems upon close examination to have quotations from each of the Pauline letters, it is plausible that the author of this work had before him the text of each of Paul's writings included in the New Testament canon. If something like Goodspeed's theory is accepted, the Letter to the Ephesians would then have been written ca. 90–95 A.D. in Ephesus by some admirer of Paul writing to present Paul's thought to the churches of his own time.

No matter the conclusion one reaches in attempting to determine the critical problems of date and authorship and setting of this letter, the letter itself remains a masterpiece of literature which soars to great heights in proclaiming its message.

Ephesians: Outline

I. Salutation 1:1–2
II. Purpose of the Church in God's Plan 1:3–3:21
   A. Unity of all things in Christ 1:10; 2:11ff,; 3:6, 9
   B. God's mystery now made plain 1:9; 3:9–12; 3:14ff.
   C. Church is founded on God's plan 2:19–22; 3:10; 20–21
III. Exhortations to the Church 4:1–6:20
   A. Unity in the Spirit 4:1–16
   B. A righteous life 4:17–5:20
   C. Proper human relationship 5:21–6:9
   D. Plea for constant combat against evil 6:10–21
IV. Conclusion 6:21–24

The Letter to the Ephesians is a marvelous writing. It speaks about the mystery of God's will which is now revealed through Christ and the church for all the world. God's will is that all the discordant portions of the universe should come together in Christ and the church to unity, for God's purpose and to fulfill his plan for all creation. The writer of this letter describes the church as founded on the "apostles and the prophets" (2:20) which should indicate in all probability that both groups were past and gone. It is also interesting that according to this writer the church seems to be almost entirely Gentile, a situation not fully reached in Paul's setting.

The second major portion of this work contains strong exhortations. The first is that arguing for unity in the church. This unity is not described as conformity or uniformity, but rather it is defined as right action on the part of the members to "build up the body of Christ" (4:11–12). There is also a strong emphasis on the proper kind of life which is fitting for persons who have been the recipients of God's grace. The true Christian has in reality put on a "new nature" (4:24). Not only is there to be no immorality but the Christian life in all its aspects is to be regarded as a serious matter (5:3ff.).

Closely paralleled with Colossians at this point (5:21–6:9) are the exhortations concerning close human relationships. The Ephesian admonitions are much fuller, however. In human relationships there has to be, for the sake of order (and this writer is speaking from the context of the order of his time), certain understood authorities, the husband in the family, the parent with the child, the master with the slave. But within the Christian life these persons are to exercise their authority for the good of those with whom they are related. Their well-being is as important, if not more so, as one's own well-being! For example, the relationship between a husband and wife in a real marriage is, ideally at least, to be so mutually sustaining and supportive that such a relationship can be used as a symbol of the relationship between Christ and the church.

The final exhortation to fight against evil depicts the Christian putting on the armor of God, faith, truth, righteousness, etc. In this exhortation there seems to be an underlying presupposition that this fight is for a long time to come. Could it be that this author has given up hope of an imminent Parousia? It seems so. Even in 2:7 there is a reference to the "coming ages."

This author, then, while attempting to write a summary of Paul's thought for his own situation has risen to great heights of eloquence in challenging the church to be the instrument of God's grace in this world. Only through this instrument can the loose ends of the universe be tied together. Unity in the church consists of building together toward the goal of proclaiming to the world what this author so eloquently calls "the unsearchable riches of Christ" (3:8).

The Pastoral Epistles: 1 & 2 Timothy, Titus

The three letters known as the Pastoral Epistles (1 and 2 Timothy and Titus) are so designated because they are directed toward the concerns of a "pastor" with his congregation. These writings purport to be from Paul giving instructions to his two younger lieutenants, Timothy and Titus. There are, however, as was the case with Ephesians, serious questions concerning the Pauline authorship, much more even than with Ephesians.

The vocabulary and style of these letters are very different from Paul's letters. Over 170 words are used here that are not found in other Pauline writings. And the typical particles, i.e., the *nows, buts, therefores,* etc., are different from Paul's.

It is also true that certain ideas seem to be different, especially the content of the term "faith." In Paul's letters one recalls that the term is basically relational, representing a trust commitment of one's life to God which issues then in a new lifestyle. The word as it is used in these three short writings seems to mean "the faith," i.e., an "orthodox" system of teaching (cf. 1 Timothy 4:1, 6; 6:12; 2 Timothy 2:18; Titus 1:13, etc.), almost an institutionalized understanding of the term.

There is, even further, the recognition of a church order and structure that was not yet so developed in Paul's time. Even though Paul refers to bishops (once) and deacons these do not seem to be "political" offices in the church in his time but rather functional duties to be performed along with other gifts such as teaching, prophesying, and the like (cf. 1 Corinthians 12:27ff.). In these letters the terms seem rather to refer to distinct political offices in the church which have certain standards and qualifications which should be met for anyone who would aspire to fill the position. If so, this reflects a time when the church was struggling with long-range goals and planning and had given up the idea of an imminent return of Jesus. Structure and organization were necessary for the orderly development of the church and for its internal stability and purity.

When one couples these considerations with the fact that the earliest evidence which witnesses to the content of the Pauline corpus does not include the Pastoral Epistles among Paul's writings, there is very good reason to question the Pauline authorship of these letters. Again an admirer of Paul is speaking to a situation in the name of Paul, a not uncommon practice in those days. And there was no stigma attached to such a practice then, in spite of the fact that this would be frowned upon in our culture. There are a few scholars who still argue for the position that Paul wrote these letters, but the vast majority of New Testament scholarship would not agree with that position.

One other possibility remains, however, in the area of authorship. There are those who argue that even though Paul did not write these letters in the form in which we now know them, the author did use some genuine fragments of letters Paul sent to Timothy and Titus in the composition of these writings. While such a theory is difficult to demonstrate clearly, there does seem to be some good grounds for such a hypothesis. The other letter which purports to be from Paul (Ephesians) was written with the other Pauline letters before the author. These letters then could very well have been suggested to an admirer of Paul by fragments of some letters directed by Paul to his young proteges. There are several passages which seem to support such a theory (cf. 2 Timothy 1:16–18; 3:10–11; 4:6–8; 4:9–17a; Titus 3:12–15, and possibly some others).

As for the date of these writings, if one accepts the Pauline authorship, the date would have to be ca. 63–64 A.D. not long before his martyrdom in Rome. If someone other than Paul wrote these letters, the date could be anywhere between 75–125 A.D. In all probability, however, the most likely date would seem to be sometime shortly after the collection of Paul's letters was made, ca. 95–100 A.D. This would explain the interest in Paul at this late date and would also give time for the development of the church structure which is reflected in these writings. There is also a reference to persecution (2 Timothy 3:12) which could very easily fit the situation in Asia Minor ca. 95–100 A.D.

In all probability these letters were written by an admirer of Paul ca. 100 A.D. in the region of Asia Minor to speak to the problems of the church at that time.

Exactly what the nature of these problems were is not known, but one can conjecture concerning them rather accurately on the basis of the material in these epistles. There seems to have been several problems which are discussed in the writings. Most prominent is the admonition to beware of false teaching. In the later New Testament writings this seems to have been a frequently recurring problem, but contrary to what many have believed the problem was not so much "orthodox" teaching *per se*. The crux of the matter was whether the false teaching led to activity and manner of lifestyle that was inconsistent with the Christian ethic as it was founded in the Old Testament writings and in the teachings of Jesus and the paraenesis (ethical exhortation) of Paul. In other words false teaching was dangerous and to be combatted at the points where such teaching led Christians into immoral ways of life and/or unconcern for one's neighbors. But at this point "orthodoxy" was not centered in correct teaching as much as it was centered in correct lifestyle!

The false teaching in the churches here addressed appears to have been of the gnostic type which manifested itself in the two extremes usually associated with this type of teaching, asceticism and libertinism. All three of these epistles therefore warn against the dangers of such false teaching which leads to false living.

A second priority for this writer seems to center in proper order and authority in the church. The primary reason for this emphasis is to keep the church pure in its witness to the world and the individual members alert and with proper respect for the church officials. To ensure the best leadership, specific guidelines are given by which the church should choose its leaders.

The third major problem seems to center in specific social concerns which were internal to the church itself. One of the concerns was what to do with widows in the congregation. Obviously there were numerous widows, and the church felt an obligation to assist these people. But there were those who were taking advantage of the situation; therefore, guidelines needed to be set down to determine who was to be given assistance and who was not eligible.

There is some debate among scholars as to the order in which the letters were written. Most agree that Titus was written between the other two. There is no real agreement as to which Timothy was written first, however.

1 Timothy: Outline

    I. Salutation 1:1–2

   II. Warning Against False Teachers 1:3–11

  III. Personal Comments and Warnings 1:12–3:13
      A. Personal word about himself 1:12–17
      B. Advice to Timothy about worship in the church 1:18–2:15
      C. Qualifications of a bishop 3:1–7
      D. Qualifications of a deacon 3:8–13

  IV. Advice to Timothy About Specific Matters 3:14–6:2ab
      A. Introduction 3:14–16
      B. Warning against asceticism 4:1–10
      C. Encouragement to Timothy 4:11–16
      D. General conduct toward others 5:1–2
      E. Advice about widows 5:3–16
      F. About elders 5:17–22
      G. About wine 5:23
      H. About sin and good deeds 5:24–25
      I. Slaves and masters 6:1–2ab

   V. Final Exhortations 6:2c–21
      A. Warning against conceit and selfishness 6:2c–10
      B. Exhortation to fight the fight of faith 6:11–16
      C. Warning against riches 6:17–19
      D. Final exhortation for Timothy 6:20–21

The content of this letter revolves around proper order, procedure, and most importantly, lifestyle in the church. Those who advocate abstinence (4:1–5) and subjugation of the body (4:8) as well as those who are lax in ethical matters (1:8–12; 6:3–10) are to be shunned. Both these extremes are the result of "false" teaching, probably of a gnostic type.

There is throughout, however, a major concern for the good order of the church. Proper conduct on the part of the membership is essential for the life of the church. And when specific internal problems develop, guidelines should be established so that the truly deserving are cared for; in this instance the concern of the church is for real widows. Incidentally, the specific recommendation of the writer is that young widows remarry—quite a difference from Paul's teaching in 1 Corinthians 7!

2 Timothy: Outline

I. Salutation 1:1–2
II. Thanksgiving 1:3–7
III. Exhortations to Timothy 1:8–4:5
    A. To keep the faith in spite of suffering 1:8–2:13
    B. To guard the faith from false teaching 2:14–26
    C. Warnings to avoid evil people 3:1–13
    D. Encouragement to do the work of the gospel 3:14–4:5
IV. Personal Comments and Greetings 4:6–22

In this letter there is much more similarity, at least in form, to the genuine Pauline letters. But the content again seems to reflect a much later period in the church's history. It is interesting that in this writing Timothy is warned against those who use religion for their own selfish gain (cf. 3:1–7). This seems to reflect some of the situation discussed in a writing known as the *Didache* (the Teaching of the Twelve Apostles) which is generally dated late in the first or early in the second century. Again, however, the emphasis on false teaching is primarily concerned with the effect it has on ethical conduct rather than on the truth or falsity of the doctrine itself.

In this letter there does seem to be incorporated some fragments of letters which were probably from Paul himself.

Titus: Outline

This letter is quite similar to the other Pastoral Epistles in that guidelines for the church and its offices are given, and there is a stern warning against false teaching, again especially that which leads to improper conduct. It is interesting that this letter seems to have been directed toward Crete while the other two seem to have been directed toward Ephesus or Asia Minor.

Here again there is the admonition to shun "stupid controversies" (3:9), since these lead to dissension in the church. The rationale for good conduct is two-fold: God requires it (3:8), and it is necessary for the witness of the church to the world (2:8).

In this letter and in the two short notes to "Timothy" it is clear that the church is in for a long relationship with the world. The hope of the Parousia has not been totally given up, but the references to it are few. And further, when reference is made to it, there is no real dwelling on the issue nor is there more than a slight indication that the idea is important enough to mention. The references to it, therefore, make no real difference in the discussion, a sign that the author considers this idea to be far removed from his present situation. (cf. 1 Timothy 6:4; 2 Timothy 1:12 (?); 3:1; 4:1; Titus 2:13.)

Hebrews

The letter designated "To the Hebrews" does not, as the other Deutero-Pauline writings, claim to have been written by Paul. It is a totally anonymous composition. The authorship of this letter has traditionally been attributed to Paul, but this tradition is late and very early numerous church fathers recognized the broad divergency in style and content from Paul's letters. Various theories were put forth to deal with that problem. Clement of Alexandria postulated that Luke had translated into Greek a writing of Paul which he originally had written in Hebrew. Others suggested that Apollos had composed this writing since the description of Apollos in Acts (18:24–28) certainly fits the qualifications of the person who wrote Hebrews. This suggestion has been a popular one throughout the ages of the church history, Martin Luther himself arguing for this position. Another theory holds that Prisca and Aquila wrote the letter since they were from Rome and were formerly Jews. Barnabas has also been suggested as the author of this writing. The truth is probably contained in the famous *dictum* of Origen (a church father of the 3rd century A.D.) when he postulated that in reality only God knows who wrote this composition.

Because there is as little evidence internally for the other critical questions (date, place of origin, destination, audience) as for the authorship, most of these problems can be answered only tentatively. There may be an allusion to the place of origin or destination in the last chapter when the author writes, "Those from Italy salute you" (13:24, paraphrase). Most scholars interpret this saying to mean that those from Italy (who are here with me) send greetings home to you. In other words the destination of the letter is somewhere in Italy, perhaps Rome. Some evidence of this is seen in the fact that the author of I Clement (a writing from Rome ca. 96 A.D.) surely was acquainted with Hebrews. But the fact is that the saying of 13:24 can just as easily be interpreted as "those from Italy (where I am) send greetings to you (wherever you are!)." It would seem, however, that the destination of the letter or the origin of the letter had to be somewhere in Italy, most probably in Rome. Most favor the hypothesis that the destination was Italy.

If that destination is accepted, then where did the letter originate? Various theories have been suggested: Syria (probably Antioch), Asia Minor (probably Ephesus), and Egypt (probably Alexandria). Again there is no concrete evidence as to the answer, but given the style of writing and type of interpretation of the Old Testament contained in this exposition, it is likely that Alexandria in Egypt should be given a slight advantage.

The date likewise is open to speculation. Many take very seriously the fact that the fall of Jerusalem and the destruction of the Temple (70 A.D.) are not mentioned by this author. How can such a momentous event not be alluded to, especially when the writer is showing that Jesus and the new religious faith are better than the old way? Some argue that this is proof that the date should be prior to 70 A.D. Others argue, however, that this writer is not interested in Temple analogies but in the older cultic apparatus of the Hebrew customs. Therefore, reference to the Temple and/or its destruction is not appropriate to the writer's argument. Further, there seem to be pointers to a later period, i.e., the delay in the Parousia, the apathy of the people addressed, the appeal for a faith that is dedicated to a long-term commitment. Therefore, a date of 80–90 A.D. is suggested by many for this book. It had to have been written before 96 A.D. since the author of I Clement obviously knew it. Since there are some overtones of persecution alluded to, it is not unlikely that the book, since it surely has ties either of origin or destination with Rome, was written shortly after 70 A.D. This would not be long after the Neronic persecution and would also explain the disappointment in the delay of the Parousia. Since many in the early church believed that the Parousia would take place after a period of persecution and many also believed that the destruction of the Temple would be *the* incident preceding the return of Jesus (cf. Mark 13), this dating would explain the feeling of despair and growing apathy of the intended hearers and readers of this message.

The last major problem other than content has to do with audience. The superscription, "To the Hebrews," was attached to this writing very early. In all probability this title was a conjecture based on the large number of references to and interpretations of the Jewish Scriptures. But the early Christians also held firmly to their roots in the traditions of Israel. One recalls the importance placed on the fulfillment of the Scriptures in numerous New Testament writings (cf. Matthew, Luke, Paul's letters, for examples). The difference here is not so much in the citing of the Old Testament texts as it is the manner of interpretation, which in all probability has little if anything to do with the intended audience. This phenomenon speaks more to the author and his purpose and perhaps the origin of the letter. It is quite probable that the intended audience was composed basically of Gentile Christians.

The purpose of the writing is a bit clearer. Simply put, it is to bolster the faith of those who had become apathetic to the new faith and were on the brink of giving it up altogether: whether this situation was caused by persecution, or the delay in the Parousia, or simply human apathy, or a combination of all three cannot be specifically known. There are, however, hints that persecution and the delay are the major factors in this situation. The author felt strongly that this new faith brought by Christ is the highest revelation of God to the human race; therefore to fall away from such a gift is the greatest tragedy one can imagine. He used strong language and even ominous warnings, therefore, to encourage steadfastness.

The basic methodology which the author utilized was to interpret the Old Testament in accordance with principles of an Alexandrian type exegesis, which was a kind of combination between Rabbinic exegesis and Alexandrian allegorizing interpretation. By this methodology the writer attempted to show that Christianity, this new religion and life made available by God's activity in Christ, is better than the best that the world had known up to that time or would ever know. Jesus is better than Moses, the angels, the law, the old priesthood, the old sacrifices, the old covenant. It is, therefore, a fearful thing to neglect so great a salvation (2:3)!

Hebrews: Outline

To divide the Book of Hebrews into neat sections is a difficult task, for the writer weaves together his "theology" and his paraenesis (ethical exhortation) in such a way that one section flows into the other. The overall outline is clear, however. The author wants to use every means and argument available to him to keep the people to whom he is writing from falling away from their religious obligations and commitments. He even goes to the extreme of arguing that if one does become apostate, there is no second chance (cf. 6:4–6)! This teaching has been interpreted absolutely by many causing a great deal of consternation since there is no other such teaching in the New Testament. If one recalls, however, that the writing is occasional and directed to a specific situation for the purpose of emphasizing how important the author felt it to be to remain within this superior religious faith, the teaching becomes very understandable. It is simply one method which is utilized to demonstrate to his audience how important it is to remain faithful.

The author's understanding of faith reflects his thinking on this very point. Faith is "the assurance of things hoped for, the conviction of things not seen" (11:1). In other words, faith is faithfulness to the new commitment, steadfastness in the new way of life in spite of any personal disappointments, persecutions, or tragedies. This is what hope is all about, and hope is of the essence of Christian ideology. The entire eleventh chapter magnificently echoes this theme. If a person is not committed to something in such a way as to persevere in the face of hardship, there is no real commitment there. The author of Hebrews was exhorting his people to make and to keep genuine commitments to this new way of life. Failure to do so brings serious consequences.

There is, therefore, within this book with its soaring figures and intriguing interpretations of Scripture a very simple message. Remain faithful to the Christ of God. In the presentation of this simple yet significant point, he suggests dimensions to the person of Christ that later were taken up into the Christological controversies of the church and became a significant part of the church's doctrine about the person of Jesus and the work which he accomplished (i.e., the doctrine of soteriology, salvation).

Primary in the writer's mind, in addition to his exhortations for hope and steadfastness, was his conviction that this new religion requires new kinds of relationships between persons (chapter 13). There is a very practical and highly moral tone to this piece of literature that, unfortunately, very often is missed. Perhaps the most fitting summary of this book is that given by the author himself:

> Now may the God of peace who brought again from the dead our Lord Jesus, the great shepherd of the sheep, by the blood of the eternal covenant, equip you with everything good that you may do his will, working in you that which is pleasing in his sight, through Jesus Christ; to whom be glory for ever and ever. Amen. (13:20-21)

The Persecution Literature
1 Peter

There are two New Testament writings that seem to be directly connected with the problem of persons suffering because they are Christians, 1 Peter and Revelation. Other writings do reflect the fact that Christians did from time to time and place to place endure sufferings, but there are only two which seem to have been primarily centered on this issue. The first of these is 1 Peter.

Traditionally this epistle has been attributed to Peter the Apostle writing from Rome sometime before his death in the Neronic persecution. This would date the letter then before 65 A.D. There are many, however, who feel that the letter dates from a later period and that this writing is another of those pseudonymous works.

Some of the reasons for the skepticism about the Petrine authorship are: the letter seems to be acquainted with Ephesians (cf. Ephesians 5:22-6:9 especially), which may be a late writing, and also possibly with I Clement (ca. 96 A.D.); the type of persecution seems to be of a sort that is later than the Neronic period; the designation, "Babylon," for Rome does not seem to have been in vogue until after 70 A.D.; the Greek of the letter is quite good indicating someone other than a Galilean Aramaic speaking person; and no church Father earlier than Irenaeus (ca. 180 A.D.) names Simon Peter as the author.

Some argue that the reference to persecution naturally limits the

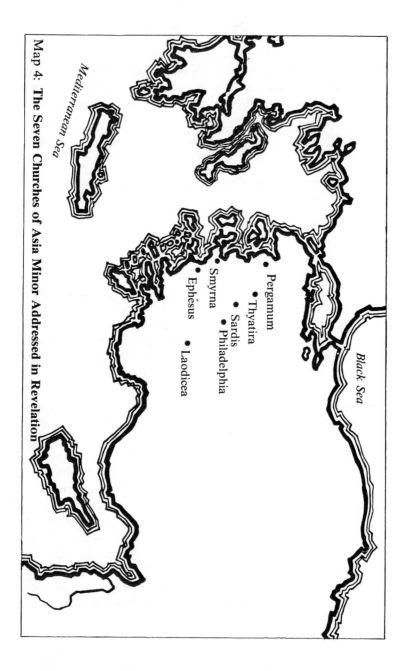

Map 4: **The Seven Churches of Asia Minor Addressed in Revelation**

Mediterranean Sea

Black Sea

• Pergamum

• Thyatira

• Sardis

Smyrna •

• Philadelphia

Ephesus •

• Laodicea

time of the writing to three possibilities, the persecution under Nero (if Simon is the author), or under Domitian (ca. 90–96), or under Trajan (ca. 112). This assumes, however, that the persecution presumed here was an "official" attempt on the part of the government to harass Christians. That such occasions occurred cannot be disputed, but the text of 1 Peter itself does not seem to depict such a setting. There was during the post-apostolic period sporadic and local persecutions directed against Christians by people in the communities. After all, Christians were a new and unusual collection of people with meetings at unusual times and places and talk of "eating flesh and drinking blood." Such activity naturally caused rumors to spread of secret orgies and cannabalism, the slaughter of infants and the like. Such a group would naturally cause resentment, and if anything unusual happened to the community (such as a drought, tragedy, etc.), the most likely cause of such displeasure from the gods would likely be directed at the new Christian group. At least this was probably the thought. Therefore, harassment and even active persecution from the populace would not be improbable or unlikely. 1 Peter seems to reflect this kind of setting, not an official governmental persecution.

The matter of date, then, seems to be quite open if Simon the Apostle is not accepted as the author. Dates from 80–125 A.D. have been suggested. Those who see in this writing an official governmental persecution date the letter ca. 90–95 or 110–115 A.D. The letter itself, however, does not seem to reflect such a late date. There is no reference to developed church organization or offices; there is no evidence of the gnostic tendencies that are associated with most of the later writings (but this may be simply a contextual matter); and there is the pointed belief in the imminent return of Jesus. Together these bits of evidence seem to point to an earlier rather than a later date, probably sometime in the early seventies.

The origin of the letter appears to have been Rome since the writer makes the comment, "She who is at Babylon, who is likewise chosen [the church in Rome], sends you greetings" (5:13). The question of authorship is still a nagging question. If Simon Peter did not write the epistle, how did it become so closely related with him, even written in his name? The answer may lie in what some scholars like to call a "school," i.e., a group of disciples who attached themselves to a person and who preserved and transmitted the teachings of their leader. This was a common practice in the world of that time, Jesus himself being a primary example. There is the tradition that Peter came to Rome and that Mark accompanied him on his journeys to serve as his "interpreter" or translator. (Could someone who needed a translator have written the excellent Greek of this epistle?) And the tradition holds that he was martyred in the Neronic persecution.

It has already been seen that the Gospel of Mark originated in Rome and was traditionally linked with Peter's teaching about Jesus. This indicates that it is likely that some sort of Petrine school remained in Rome and passed along some of the great apostle's teachings. Since Mark is mentioned in 1 Peter (5:13), it is highly probable that this letter originated from this Petrine school shortly after Peter's death. Some such theory as this does explain many unanswered questions about this epistle in terms of origin, date and authorship which fit the facts as they are known.[2]

Another critical problem concerns the exact nature of the content and also the unity of the letter. Many scholars argue that 1:3–4:11 is a baptismal liturgy (or perhaps an Easter baptismal liturgy), or perhaps a baptismal sermon used in the liturgy of the church upon the receipt of new converts into the community of the faithful which most likely was connected with the rite of baptism. If this were true, 4:12–5:14 would be another letter or an addition to the original document. That there is a great stress on baptism in this writing cannot be denied, but the letter as it stands seems to be better understood as a unity even if part of it was taken from a baptismal formula and liturgy. The liturgy itself, even if it is present, probably is comprised of a great deal less than 1:3–4:11.

The destination of the letter seems to be clear. The churches in the northern section of Asia Minor are addressed. The purpose is also clear, to bolster their faith and to give them hope in the midst of persecution which has come upon them. The hope is seen in this writing as connected with the return of Jesus. In typical apocalyptic ideology the present persecution is interpreted as the prelude to the intervention of God for the purpose of removing the persecution and vindicating those who have remained faithful.

1 Peter: Outline

I. Salutation 1:1–2
II. Assurance for Christians 1:3–12
III. Exhortation to Faithfulness and Christian Conduct
    A. Appeal for holiness 1:13–2:3
    B. Appeal to commit oneself to the Christ 2:4–10
    C. Appeal for good conduct in human relationship 2:11–3:12
    D. Challenge to remain faithful in spite of persecution 3:13–4:11
    E. Be prepared for suffering 4:12–19
    F. Challenge to church leaders 5:1–4
    G. Final exhortations 5:5–11
IV. Concluding Remarks 5:12–14

The author of 1 Peter attempts to present his word of encouragement to the churches by emphasizing several points which continually recur in this short writing. Christians are not really citizens of this world but belong to another realm (1:4; 2:11). Because of this the world will neither understand nor appreciate the Christian or the Christian lifestyle (2:9f.; 4:3–5). Therefore, expect persecution as a Christian. If indeed the founder suffered at the hands of the world, so too should his followers expect the same treatment (1:6f.; 2:4; 2:19–24; 3:17; 4:12–14; 5:8–10). The key for this writer is that Christians give the world no cause to direct animosity and persecution against themselves, and he urged the Christians to live in such a way that charges of evil conduct will always be hollow and baseless (2:9; 2:12; 2:16; 4:15–16).

It is clearly the opposition of the world to the lifestyle of a Christian that is at issue here. The admonition to "honor the emperor" (2:17) would hardly be in place if the state were the persecutor in this situation. Christians can expect to encounter the opposition of the world just as did Jesus, and they should not be surprised if it comes. They should expect it, and rather be surprised if it does not come!

Suffering and opposition from the world does not relieve the Christian of the responsibility of adhering to basic Christian principles, however. When the time of accounting does come, the Christian will be judged first (5:17)! The author is certain, however, that the rewards for doing right and adhering to the faith will far outweigh the oppression of the moment (1:3–9; 4:19; 5:10).

Revelation

The Book of Revelation is perhaps the most misunderstood book of the entire Bible. Its use of weird and exaggerated symbolism has caused many throughout church history to view the book with skepticism and doubt. Coupled with this is the fact that the book has been used almost from the beginning by groups who attempt to make of it more than was intended and who claim for it insight into the end of the world. Many church leaders, therefore, have simply shunned the writing with the attitude of Luther who said that his spirit could not tolerate this book! It is true that Revelation (along with Jude and 2 Peter) almost did not become a part of the New Testament canon of inspired writings.

In spite of the wild and unfounded claims made for the book and in spite of the difficulty a twentieth-century person has in interpreting the symbols and deciphering the message, the book had a powerful message for its intended audience.

In the case of 1 Peter, the persecution experienced by Christians was caused by the world and the people of the world who could not understand nor tolerate the new Christian lifestyle. In the case of Revelation, however, the persecution issued directly from the state in an organized and systematic fashion. It is almost universally acknowledged that the Book of Revelation was written during the latter part of the reign of the Roman emperor Domitian (ca. 95 A.D.). Even though most Roman emperors were voted divine status by the Roman senate after their death, there were a few who wanted to be acknowledged as a god during their lifetime. Such a situation arose during the reign of Domitian, who wanted to be known as *Dominus et Deus* (Lord and God) and who pressed imperial worship both of the emperor and the goddess *Roma* in the area of Asia Minor. Failure to participate in this act of devotion brought suspicion upon the person who refused and ultimately persecution up to and including death. Christians refused to participate because this was an act of idolatry to their minds, apostasy of the worst and most unforgiveable kind.

The author of this book is identified only as John. Whether this was John the Apostle (as the later tradition claimed) or someone else named John is not known. It is usually agreed among scholars that the author of this book and the author of the Gospel of John are two entirely different people. Whoever this person was, he was being held in a Roman penal colony (Patmos) for his witness to his faith. From the writing it is clear that this person had some standing among the churches to which he wrote, for he spoke to them with authority and candor (cf. especially chapters 2–3).

The book was intended for the churches in Asia Minor probably to be read in all of them. Its purpose was to inspire hope and confidence in those people who were being asked to hold to their religious convictions in the face of persecution and possible martyrdom.

The instrument chosen by the author to convey his message to the church was the familiar literary genre known as apocalyptic. The characteristics of this literature have already been discussed (cf. pp. 14–15), and the usual ideas and motifs of this type of writing are found in Revelation. The place where this writer differs from most apocalyptic is at the point of naming himself as author. This work, therefore, is not pseudonymous. Its basic message was directed to the Christians to offer them hope and to demonstrate how important it was not to succumb to the pressures of the state and become apostates by participating in the worship of the imperial cultus.

Revelation: Outline

I. Vision of the Son of Man in the Midst of His Church 1
II. Letters to Seven Churches 2–3
III. Vision of God and the Lamb 4–5
IV. Cycle of Judgment: The Seven Seals 6:1–8:1

The message of the Book of Revelation is one of hope, hope in the midst of despair. The first major portion of the book (after the introductory remarks) centers in a vision of the Son of Man standing in the midst of seven golden lampstands (symbolic of the entire church). The emphasis is upon the fact that this is the one who has conquered death; therefore all who are allied with him cannot be harmed by physical death—a challenging and comforting idea for those who were facing death for their witness to this Son of Man.

There are then seven letters written to seven of the churches in Asia Minor, in the order in which one would visit them on a journey. The seven are chosen because of the symbolic number and because the author knew some specifics about them which needed to be discussed. The letters follow a specific pattern: an introduction in which the author refers back to the vision in chapter 1, a word of commendation to the church for what it was doing right, a warning and challenge for places at which they were being negligent in their Christian duties, and a call for endurance with a promise of reward for being faithful. That the letters were intended not only for the individual church addressed but for all the churches of the area can be seen in the continuing refrain, "He who has an ear, let him hear what the Spirit says to the churches."

The vision of God and the Lamb is central to the book. It serves to establish hope by basing all that follows on the sure foundation of the Creator of all and his appointed and deserving agent of judgment, the Lamb. From this scene there issues the unfolding of judgment upon evil and those who are persecuting the people of God. In the chapters that follow there are presented three cycles of judgment based upon the number seven. These three cycles should be interpreted not as a chronological sequence of events but rather as different types of judgment that occur in human history at any given moment or place.

The first cycle of the seals centering in the sequence of the four horsemen teaches that evil is self-destructive. Any person or institution or group which insists on "conquering" begins a cycle which includes strife or war, famine or lack, and finally death. The second cycle of the trumpets teaches that God directly intervenes in and actively judges evil. In each of these cycles, however, the judgment is partial, for the real purpose of judgment is to engender repentance on the part of the people. When it does not, there must ultimately come a judgment that is final. This type of judgment is depicted in the cycle of the seven bowls full of the wrath of God. There does come a time when God's patience and mercy must come to an end, and justice must be served.

As with any apocalyptic work there is a section which can be designated a "historical survey," depicting in symbolic terms how the present situation came to be. This is found in Revelation in chapters 12–13. Here the reader is introduced to a woman clothed with the sun with a crown of twelve stars. She represents Israel, the people of God. The child she is about to bear is the Messiah which the great red dragon (Satan) attempts to devour. But he is unable to do that. Whereupon the dragon makes war upon the woman (now understood to be the church, the continuing Israel of God).

To accomplish the task of punishing the woman, the dragon enlists a great beast from the sea, a horrible creature with seven heads one of which appears to have a mortal wound which has healed. To this beast the dragon gives his power and authority (one of the key understandings of the operation of evil being deception), and the beast makes war on the saints of God. To assist in this procedure another beast is introduced, a lamb that speaks like a dragon! These two creatures represent the Roman Empire with its power centered in the emperors (the heads) and the religious priesthood and cultus which insured the worship of the first beast (Rome).

There is then given the enigmatic number 666 which is, the text says, the number of a man's name. Exactly what the writer had in mind here is not known, but the reader is told that it is a man's name. Perhaps the best conjecture is that which finds the solution in this manner. If one places the name, *Neron Caesar,* into Aramaic letters and adds together the numerical designations assigned to these letters in Aramaic the total of the name is 666. (This procedure was a common practice in those days.) There are some texts, however, which read 616 instead of 666. Can the Nero identification also explain this textual variant? It can, since the final N on Nero is optional in Aramaic; and if that is omitted the number then adds up to 616!

The question is: why Nero? The answer to that seems apparent. Nero was the first real persecutor of the Christians, especially at the state level. The character and personality of this man in his later years was considered despicable even by his friends. He ultimately committed suicide, but there were those who believed that the dead person was not really Nero, that Nero was hiding with the Parthians (successors of the old Persian Empire) and would lead a great army against Rome and all that was good in the world. Several Neronic pretenders arose, but they were proven to be imposters. Finally after ca. 88 A.D. the belief began to grow that Nero would rise from the dead to continue his evil work. This belief in *Nero redivivus* was taken over by this Christian writer to symbolize the intensity of evil and cruelty which the empire had mounted against the people of God. The reference then to the "mortal wound which seemed to have healed" would be reference to the Nero resurrected myth and belief.

In highly symbolic language the writer of Revelation depicts the fall of the great harlot (chapter 17) which he says is the city set upon seven hills which rules over all the earth. That the designation is Rome is really unquestionable. Evil such as this ultimately must be destroyed. When the persecution is over, the people of God can then live in peace and worship as they are required by their God. The figure of the new Jerusalem that comes to earth symbolically teaches that. It is interesting that even in these last few chapters, evil is still present in the world. This has disturbed some interpreters of the book who think that the writing simply lists a chronological history, but in reality the book basically depicts in highly symbolic form and fashion the end of that persecution.

One of the most controversial chapters of the entire book is chap-

ter 20. In this chapter the writer uses a figure known as the mil-
lenium (1,000 years). This passage has been the subject of great
debate for centuries, but the figure as it is given here basically refers
to a special reward for the martyrs (another typical device used in
apocalyptic literature to encourage hope and steadfastness in those
undergoing persecution). The figure 1,000 is in all probability to be
understood symbolically as the other numbers in this book are understood. Wherever people are committed to Christ totally (1,000),
there Satan is bound no matter what happens. Wherever Satan is
not bound, evil is freed to do its dastardly work, wreaking havoc
among the people of God, thwarting the purpose of God.

The clear call of the book is for patience in the midst of this persecution. Evil must be allowed to run its course, partly to give all an
opportunity to repent. But the final outcome is already decided. Evil
has already been defeated, and God will destroy the persecutor.
There are many who interpret Revelation as *the* book which teaches
about the Parousia, but in reality that concept is not explicitly mentioned! It may be that the author understood the destruction of the
persecution and the return of Christ to be coincidental, but it is
equally true that the text does not require such an interpretation.
That God was going to execute his judgment was certain, but the
idea of the end of the world is really not a part of the teaching of
this book. It is simply an apocalyptic writing which encourages faith
and promises a new beginning with the persecution gone.

James

The Epistle of James has had a very difficult time in the history of
the Christian church, first in finding a place in the canon of New
Testament writings and thereafter in being accepted as a significant
and important part of that canon. Well-known is the famous comment by Luther that James is a "right strawy epistle with little of the
gospel about it." He did admit that the book contained a few "good
sayings," however.

Part of the problem perhaps lies in the fact that at first reading
James seems to be at the opposite end of the theological spectrum

from Paul; and since Paul is so powerful, James must be the "lesser light." There is, further, the curious fact that Jesus is mentioned only twice in this writing (1:1 and 2:1), causing some to argue that this work is basically a Jewish document slightly revised to make it appear Christian.

But the book deserves a much more positive hearing than it has received. If one understands that the situation to which Paul wrote and the situation James addressed were quite different, the seeming differences are found to be practically non-existent. And further, if one reads the book carefully, it becomes very clear that this is truly a Christian writing in spite of the paucity of references to Jesus.

The authorship and date of this letter are so closely intertwined that they must be discussed together. The tradition, albeit a late tradition, understood the author to be James, the brother of Jesus. Since the book seems to reflect a Palestinian, even Jewish, background, there are those who argue that James, brother of Jesus, was indeed the writer of this document. If this is true, the date of writing would be sometime before 62 A.D. when James was martyred. The place of writing would be somewhere in Palestine, possibly Jerusalem.

The document itself, however, does not claim for the author kinship with Jesus, and coupled with this is the fact that the book was not cited until the third century and was suspect even into the fourth century. These factors make it improbable that the author was James, the Lord's brother. But exactly who was this James? In truth, we simply do not know. Failure to locate any specific author, therefore, leaves the date wide-open. The author seems to be concerned about a misinterpretation of Paul (cf. 2:14–26), which would then mean that a date after Paul's activity is certain. There are also affinities with 1 Peter (cf. 1:1 with 1 Peter 1:1, and 4:10 with 1 Peter 5:6) which may reflect a similar time and setting for this writing or, more probably, a knowledge of 1 Peter.

There are those who argue that the reference to Pauline thought necessitates a date after the collection of the Pauline corpus, ca. 90 A.D. This does not seem to be a necessary conclusion, however, for the document itself reflects a period of time in which internal problems with the church, here especially at the point of proper conduct, are of primary importance. This fact does point to the post-apostolic age, but there is a reference to the Parousia which is still viewed as imminent (5:7–9). The combination of evidence points to a time shortly after the writing of 1 Peter which has been dated here shortly after 70 A.D. The date then for James' writing should be sometime close to it, probably ca. 75–80 A.D.

The place of writing could be almost anywhere, for the Greek of this letter is very good, and the style of the writing is that of the diatribe. Nevertheless, since the background of the matter points to a Jewish milieu, it is likely that Palestine is the place of origin. Further, there are some very real similarities between the content of this document and the Gospel of Matthew which also originated in Palestine. The book may have been written as a circular letter to a number of churches in that area concerning Christian conduct.

James: Outline

    I.   Introduction 1:1
   II.   Exhortations to Steadfastness
        A.   In the fact of persecution and temptation 1:2–15
  III.   Exhortation to Ethical Living 1:16–27
  IV.   Exhortation to Honor and Care for the Poor 2:1–13
        A.   Argument over faith and works 2:14–26
   V.   Exhortations to Control the Tongue 3:1–4:17
  VI.   Woes on the Rich 5:1–6
 VII.   Exhortations to Patience and Christian Living 5:7–20

The Book of James is difficult to outline or to follow precisely for the writer seems to pick up themes, drop them, pick them up again. Many fail to find any theme or idea which holds the work together. There does appear to be one, however; it is the idea of "double-mindedness" (1:7–8). Upon close reading of the document the concept of the "double-mind" seems to permeate throughout each of the topics discussed. "Double-minded" seems to imply hypocrisy which was viewed as an especially heinous sin in the early church. And this kind of mind-set leads precisely to the kinds of problems the author of James is addressing.

There appears to be an admonition at the beginning (1:2–4) to bolster faith in the face of trials, as active persecution is not really a part of the picture here. The danger in such a situation is to yield to the exigency of the moment and then to argue that God had sent the temptation, the understanding obviously being that if God sent it, one should yield to it! James argued as do others in the New Testament that hardships and bad times do not excuse one from keeping the ethical precepts of the Christian life. Real religion is acted out in the real world, not speculated about or relegated to the realm of theory.

The major portion of the discussion revolves around the conduct of those in the church who discriminate on the basis of wealth, "rolling out the red carpet" for the rich while being less than hospitable to the poor (2:1–3). It is also interesting that the discussion about "faith and works" occurs within the context here of the responsibility of the church toward the poor. Faith in the context here seems to be understood by those against whom James is writing as correct doctrine, intellectual belief in the "right" precepts or theology.

That Paul and James are at odds on this issue seems to be an erroneous conclusion. For Paul, who was facing a situation in which "works of the law" were being espoused as essential and necessary for salvation, faith was a personal relationship and commitment to God who freely offered salvation to the human race. One had to accept this gift humbly and gratefully. Once the new relationship had been established, the believer's life was transformed. There is no letter of Paul's that fails to contain an exhortation to right living and proper conduct. The Christian has responsibilities to others.

James, on the other hand, is speaking to a situation in which faith seems to be understood as correct doctrine. His argument is directed against those who feel no responsibility towards others; therefore, his emphasis is upon the ethical requirements of the new life. James never says that "work saves" anyone; rather he argues that faith apart from works is dead (2:17) and faith is completed (brought to maturity) by works (2:22). Neither Paul nor James would argue that these two elements are separate and distinct, but they both teach that faith and works are rather two aspects of the salvation process freely offered by God to any and all who will respond to his invitation. Such an attitude toward faith as was understood and espoused by James' audience is the direct result of double-mindedness!

And this same attitude is at the root of the misuse of the tongue. James argues that if one can control the tongue, one can control one's life. Again the true believer cannot bless God and curse people; something is amiss in such a person. Double-mindedness is again demonstrating its insidious power to thwart the right kind of life which is required of Christians. Strife between people and within the church is caused by a lack of control over the tongue (chapter 4).

There is a last parting shot at the rich (5:1–6) who obviously are causing difficulty for and within the church (2:1ff. and 5:1ff.). And there is another appeal for patience and steadfastness. The author also believed that the Parousia would occur soon (5:7–8).

In the last few verses of this writing there are three admonitions and instructions which later in the history of the church become significant ideas and even doctrines. First, there was the custom of anointing the sick with oil (5:14–15—in those days oil was believed to have medicinal qualities), which later developed into the practice of unction. Secondly, there was the suggestion to confess sins to one another (5:16). And lastly, there was the idea that by bringing back a sinner from evil, one could accumulate a kind of "merit" which can be used to "cover sins" (5:19–20).

While it is true that this writing is difficult to outline precisely and that no two persons agree totally on the breakdown of the topics discussed, the Book of James deserves better than it has received in the history of the church. This writer has an understanding of God and human nature which is as keen as any in the New Testament. And he is acutely concerned, as were the prophets of old, that this new religion be more than lip service to external rituals or correct beliefs. He understood that no matter how correct one's theology may be, it was worthless if it did not issue in concrete acts in keeping with that belief. "Even the demons believe—and tremble!"

(2:19b, paraphrase) If faith is no more than talk, there is no real faith! And Paul would have said a loud "Amen" to that.

Jude

As to the origin, date, destination, and authorship of this writing, almost nothing is known. The author is simply identified as Jude, brother of James, an obvious attempt to depict him as the brother of Jesus. Since so little is known about this writing it is possible, but not probable, that Jude the brother of Jesus may have been the author. Very few persons argue this case, however, because the work was seriously disputed in the early church, and because the internal evidence seems to point to a date later than the era of Jude, brother of Jesus (v. 17). In all probability the letter is pseudonymous.

As for the place of writing, a Palestinian background is detected by some but there is no real evidence for or against this position. As for the destination of the letter, some have argued for Syria and others for Egypt; some have argued that it was intended for Jewish Christians, others for Gentile Christians. As for the date, various times have been suggested from 80–150 A.D. Around 100–120 would be a close guess. Certainty is very elusive in dealing with this little book.

The letter itself is addressed to "those who are called," perhaps indicating a general writing for an area rather than one specific church. The reason for the writing seems to be very clear, however. There are those who are causing trouble in the church and who are advocating a lifestyle that knows no restraints. Most scholars identify these as persons of a gnostic type who have rejected the "laws" of the world since "spiritual matters" are the only important ones. In addition to this kind of teaching these persons are arrogant and insulting. This letter warns against such people. It is interesting to note once more that correct teaching in the early church's history was not as important as proper ethical conduct.

One peculiarity about this book among the other New Testament writings is that it contains a quotation from one of the intertestamental writings, I Enoch (vv. 14–15). This is one of the reasons why the book was looked upon with suspicion in the canonization process.

Jude: Outline

I. Salutation vv. 1–2
II. Exhortation to Keep the Faith Pure vv. 3–4
III. Warning Against Evil Living vv. 5–16
IV. Exhortation to Persevere vv. 17–23
V. Benediction v. 24

The message of the book is simple and clear: Do not yield to those who claim to be above the law and who are troublesome and immoral. Resist such people. If one does that, God will be there to assist and to keep that person. The final benediction is a beautiful summary:

> Now to him who is able to keep you from falling and to present you without blemish before the presence of his glory with rejoicing, to the only God, our Savior through Jesus Christ our Lord, be glory, majesty, dominion, and authority, before all time and now for ever (v. 24).

2 Peter

The letter known as 2 Peter is almost universally acknowledged to be a pseudonymous writing. The style is quite different from that of 1 Peter; the early fathers recognized only one epistle from Peter; and the internal evidence from the letter itself reflects a late date. For example, the letters of Paul have been collected and are now considered "scripture" (3:15–16); and further, the first generation of Christians and their leaders has already past (3:4). 2 Peter is, therefore, in all probability the latest of the writings contained in the New Testament. The writer also used the Book of Jude in the composition of his work (cf. Jude with 2:1–3:3 of 2 Peter).

As with Jude there is little that is known about the origin and destination of this writing. The situation addressed is quite similar to that of the writer of Jude (gnostic libertines) with an added problem, the concern and disillusionment over the delay in the Parousia (3:4). As for the date, this letter has to have been later than Jude, the suggested dates ranging from 120–150 A.D. A date of ca. 125–135 is quite probable.

2 Peter: Outline

I.   Salutation 1:1–2
II. Exhortation to Keep a Pure Life 1:3–15
III. Beware of False Teachers 1:16–2:22
IV. Discussion of the Coming of the Lord 3:1–10
V.   Exhortation to Keep Oneself in Righteousness 3:11–18

The gnostic teachers have caused problems among the people, arguing that laws are no longer binding upon those who are in the spirit. This author attempts with great intensity to discredit such teaching. His argument is essentially the same as several other writings from this period. False teaching which leads to false living must be abolished.

That there was embarrassment over the failure of the Parousia to materialize is evident from several of the New Testament books, but especially in this letter. It may well be that the gnostic teachers were using this issue to support their claim to be the "true" interpreters of Christian doctrine and morals. Since these people have looked for the Parousia and have been wrong about it, that indicates a change is necessary in basic Christian teaching. The gnostic teachers then claimed that they knew the "truth." The argument used by the author of 2 Peter to explain the delay in the Parousia is interesting and is still in vogue among many Christian groups. What seems "long" to human beings is really "short" with God (3:8–9).

The teaching of this writer is that God will execute his justice and that there will be a final judgment. The old idea about the unexpected nature of the occurrence is coupled here with the belief that the world would be destroyed by fire (a Stoic idea!). Whether the writer meant this literally or whether he was using the figure of fire symbolically as a refining judgment is not known. What he does emphasize, however, is that there will come a time of ultimate reckoning. Therefore, the true Christian must live accordingly or else suffer the same penalties as the godless.

Summary

The literature of this post-apostolic age is, as has been seen, varied and interesting. The problems of surviving in the world that was still going along, "business as usual," were sometimes difficult and disillusioning to the Christians of this time. These people had to overcome many things: being misunderstood by the people with whom they lived; persecution by these people and by the state; dissenters and troublemakers within their own number; lack of organization and structure needed for survival; a growing need for more precise theological understanding to undergird their faith; and just having to cope with the usual problems inherent in life in this world. That they did survive and that they did lay the foundation for the development of the church in the centuries ahead are to their credit.

There is yet one other segment to be studied in the post-apostolic period, the person or persons who left to the church the Johannine literature. The issues and complexities of this grouping deserve to be discussed separately.

Notes   [1]Cf. E. J. Goodspeed, *The Meaning of Ephesians*
Chapter VI   (Chicago: University of Chicago Press, 1933). Cf.
                   also John Knox, *Philemon Among the Letters of
                   Paul,* revised edition. (N.Y.: Abingdon Press,
                   1959).

                   [2]For a full discussion of this position, cf. Ernest
                   Best, *1 Peter* (Greenwood, S. C.: The Attic Press,
                   1971), pp. 49–63.

Suggestions for   The following books are useful in attempting to
Further Study   understand and study the development of the
                      early church.

Walter Bauer. *Orthodoxy and Heresy in Earliest Christianity.* 2nd edition. Translated and edited by R. A. Kraft and G. Krodel et al. Philadelphia: Fortress Press, 1971.

J. C. Beker. *The Church Faces the World.* Philadelphia: Westminster Press, 1960.

F. F. Bruce. *New Testament History.* Revised edition. London: Oliphants, 1971.

Henry Chadwick. *The Early Church.* Grand Rapids, Michigan: Wm. B. Eerdmans Publishing Co., 1968.

Hans Conzelmann. *History of Primitive Christianity.* Translated by J. E. Steely, Nashville: Abingdon Press, 1973.

Oscar Cullmann. *The Early Church: Studies in Early Christian History and Theology.* Edited by A. J. B. Higgins. Abridged edition. Philadelphia: Westminster Press, 1966.

J. G. Davies. *The Early Christian Church.* London: Weidenfield and Nicolson, 1965.

W. H. C. Frend. *The Early Church.* London: Hodder and Stoughton, 1965.

J. N. D. Kelly. *Early Christian Creeds.* 3rd edition. New York: D. McKay Co., 1972.

C. F. D. Moule. *Worship in the New Testament.* Richmond: John Knox Press, 1961.

Eduard Schweizer. *Church Order in the New Testament.* Naperville, Illinois: Alec R. Allenson, 1961.

B. H. Streeter. *The Primitive Church.* London: Macmillan, 1929.

Commentaries on the New Testament books discussed in this chapter which may be helpful are as follows.

Ephesians

F. W. Beare. *Ephesians: Introduction and Exegesis.* G. A. Buttrick et al., editors. The Interpreters Bible. Nashville: Abington Press, 1953. Vol. X.

C. Leslie Mitton. *Ephesians.* London: Oliphants, 1976.

E. F. Scott. *The Epistles of Paul to the Colossians, to Philemon, and to the Ephesians.* London: Hodder and Stoughton, 1930.

F. C. Synge. *St. Paul's Epistle to the Ephesians: A Theological Commentary.* London: SPCK, 1959.

The Pastoral Epistles
C. K. Barrett. *The Pastoral Epistles.* Oxford: Clarendon Press, 1963. The New Clarendon Bible.

Martin Dibelius and Hans Conzelmann. *The Pastoral Epistles.* Translated by Phillip Buttolph and Adela Yarbro. Philadelphia: Fortress Press, 1972. Hermeneia.

P. N. Harrison. *The Problem of the Pastoral Epistles.* Oxford: Humphrey Milford, 1921.

James L. Houlden. *The Pastoral Epistles: I & II Timothy, Titus.* Harmondsworth: Penguin, 1976.

J. N. D. Kelly. *A Commentary on the Pastoral Epistles.* New York: Harper & Row, 1963.

Ronald A. Ward. *Commentary on 1 & 2 Timothy & Titus.* Waco, Texas: Word Books, 1974.

Hebrews
F. F. Bruce. *The Epistle to the Hebrews.* Grand Rapids, Michigan: Wm. B. Eerdmans Publishing Co., 1964.

Hugh Montefiore. *A Commentary on the Epistle to the Hebrews.* New York: Harper & Row, 1964.

The Epistles of Peter and Jude

Ernest Best. *1 Peter.* London: Oliphants, 1971.

J. N. D. Kelly. *A Commentary on the Epistles of Peter and Jude.* London: A. & C. Black, 1969.

A. R. C. Leaney. *The Letters of Peter and Jude.* Cambridge: Cambridge University Press, 1967. The Cambridge Bible Commentary on the New English Bible.

B. I. Reicke. *The Epistles of James, Peter, and Jude.* Garden City, New York: Doubleday & Co., 1964.

James

James B. Adamson. *The Epistle of James.* Grand Rapids, Michigan: Wm. B. Eerdmans Publishing Co., 1976.

M. Dibelius and H. Greeven. *The Epistle of James.* Translated by Michael A. Williams. Edited by Helmut Koester. Philadelphia: Fortress Press, 1976.

B. S. Easton. *The Epistle of James: Introduction and Exegesis.* Edited G. A. Buttrick, et al. The Interpreters Bible. New York: Abingdon Press, 1957. Vol. XII.

C. Leslie Mitton. *The Epistle of James.* Grand Rapids, Michigan: Wm. B. Eerdmans Publishing Co., 1966.

E. M. Sidebottom. *James, Jude and 2 Peter.* London: Thomas Nelson & Sons, Ltd., 1967.

Revelation

G. R. Beasley-Murray. *Revelation.* London: Oliphants, 1974.

G. B. Caird. *The Revelation of St. John the Divine.* New York: Harper & Row, 1966.

James M. Efird. *Daniel and Revelation: A Study of Two Extraordinary Visions.* Valley Forge, Pennsylvania: Judson Press, 1978.

T. F. Glasson. *The Revelation of John.* Cambridge: Cambridge University Press, 1965. Cambridge Bible Commentary on the New English Bible.

CHAPTER VII

The Johannine Writings

There is yet another group of writings from the post-apostolic period to be examined. These are known as the Johannine literature: 1, 2, and 3 John and the Gospel of John. Also usually included in this grouping is Revelation, but most scholars are in agreement today that Revelation belongs in a category by itself. Therefore, since Revelation has already been discussed above, the Johannine grouping will include only the three letters and the Fourth Gospel.

The critical problems associated with this literature are enormous. Theories about the various problems (authorship, date, origin, purpose) are almost without number! Because most scholars agree that these writings came from the same author and approximately the same time and place, the critical problems connected with all four documents can be discussed together.

The tradition which developed in the church is that John, the brother of James, one of the disciples of Jesus, lived to a considerably old age at Ephesus. Toward the end of his life he wrote these works associated with his name. Upon close examination, however, there are some very real difficulties involved in accepting this tradition. First of all, this tradition did not originate early in the history of the church, appearing first in Irenaeus' writing ca. 180 A.D. There were some in the early church who even attributed the Fourth Gospel to the work of a gnostic heretic and refused to allow authoritative status to be attributed to it. Further, some modern scholars think that the author of this gospel used the Synoptic gospels in the composition of his work, thereby casting doubt on the validity of an eyewitness account. Others argue that since the Synoptics and John are so different in some ways, this gospel could not have been written by an apostle. The most telling argument, however, against the tradition that John wrote these works is the fact that three early church leaders who were associated with Ephesus and who wrote to Ephesus in the early second century failed to mention either John's presence there or the existence of the gospel attributed to him. This is certainly strange since other writings and persons (such as Paul) were specifically mentioned. These leaders were Justin Martyr, Polycarp, and Ignatius of Antioch. Their omission of reference to the gospel and John the Apostle cannot be overlooked lightly.

Another factor enters into the discussion also. From church tradition there is known to have been another respected church leader at Ephesus about the end of the first century who was called John the Elder. In some early traditions it is clear that John the Apostle and John the Elder had been confused. Some have found in this the solution to the problem, i.e., the author of these writings under discussion was John the Elder who in the course of the passing along of the tradition became John the apostle. And evidence for this can be drawn from 2 and 3 John where the author calls himself, "the Elder." But even so, there is still the pressing question of why the Fourth Gospel is not mentioned in early traditions connected with Ephesus and why those three leaders mentioned above do not mention either a John the Apostle or a John the Elder as being the author of such a work.

Other identifications have been postulated as to the identity of the author. Since the Fourth Gospel depicts a figure known as the "disciple whom Jesus loved" and points to that figure as the author (or source) of the traditions for this writing, several attempts have been made to identify this enigmatic figure. The most usual connection is, of course, with the Apostle John, an attempt which is ordinarily related to those who wish to prove the late tradition concerning the apostolic authorship. Other identifications which have been suggested are Lazarus, John Mark, Matthias, an unknown man who was host at the last supper, and others! The truth is that specificity at this point is almost impossible. It is also true, however, that behind the traditions of these writings there is an emphatic emphasis on eye witness authority (cf. 1 John 1:1–4; John 21:24). And this is difficult to understand unless there is some truth in the claims.

The origin of these writings is directly related to the problem of authorship. If the tradition is correct, Ephesus was the place of origination. But the same difficulties arise as to Ephesus as the source of origin as to John the Apostle as the author. Some scholars, even though denying apostolic authorship, still hold to Ephesus as the place of writing. Others argue for some place in Palestine, probably Syria, partly because some of the traditions in that area are quite similar to those found in the Gospel of John. There is also a strong anti-Jewish polemic in the writing which suggests as likely an origin somewhere in Palestine where the Jewish population would be numerous and strong. A third possibility which has been suggested is Alexandria in Egypt. There was a large Jewish population there, and some strong affinities to Alexandrian type thinking and ideas are found in the gospel. This theory, however, has few proponents today.

Certainty in these matters is impossible, but a cautious solution can be postulated. It is possible that these writings originated in Palestine, possibly Syria, and they originated in and were circulated from a "Johannine School" which was related to the Apostle John. The author simply remained anonymous, but relied heavily on the traditions supposedly connected with the apostle. This would explain the insistence on the eye witness reliability of the accounts. The gospel later became associated with Ephesus as the major center of Christianity in that general area and which possibly served as a central point for numerous New Testament writings. In this way the traditions about the gospel relating to the Apostle John and Ephesus are explained.

As for the date, it has been almost universally accepted that the Fourth Gospel was the latest of the gospels to be written. This was a part of the tradition and has stood the test of critical scrutiny. As to the exact date, one can only guess, but the usual designation is the last decade of the first century A.D. (ca. 90–100).

The purpose of writing for this literature is likewise uncertain. There appears to be at least two problems which are addressed both in the gospel and in the epistles. First, there is the gnostic tendency which would deny to Jesus real humanity. Both the gospel (1:14) and the epistles (1 John 1:1–4; 4:2) emphatically argue for the true humanity of Jesus. There was a "heresy" which was related to gnostic thought which arose about the end of the first century known as "Docetism." The term comes from the Greek word, "to seem," and it was argued that since God or deity could have nothing to do with matter or suffering or sinful human beings that Jesus, since he was of divine nature, only "seemed" to be human. There were various specific adaptations of this theme, but they all ultimately taught the same idea. This type of mind-set seems to be quite consciously attacked by the writer of these works, for the genuine humanity of Jesus was defended quite vigorously.

The second problem concerned that of the lifestyle expected of a Christian. While there were those who argued that Christians could not sin, there were others who argued that sin and human standards were no longers matters of concern for a Christian. The Christian was above the law. In these writings the two extremes of this ideology were put aside and a new term is used for the Christian life—eternal life. This term does not have to do with quantity of life but rather with quality of life. There is a new quality of life that is available to persons now; it is a quality of life that is different from the standards of the world, a life that is of such a nature that it is above the level of human existence. This life is characterized by love, genuine care and concern for one's brothers and sisters (cf. 1 John 4:7–21; John 13:34–35; 15:12ff.). The Christian fellowship is challenged to witness to the outside world, therefore, by the love which is practiced among the members.

1 John

Even though the general discussion of critical problems has been done, there are yet some specific questions which need to be addressed concerning the Johannine writings individually. Most scholars believe that the epistles and the gospel were written by the same person, whoever that may have been. There is a similarity of style and language which point toward that conclusion. Upon closer examination, however, one finds in spite of some similarities several significant differences. For example, in 1 John the eschatology seems to be primarily futuristic whereas in the gospel the eschatological outlook has been significantly altered, emphasizing the present almost to the exclusion of the future. Further, the term, "Paraclete," is applied to Jesus in the epistle whereas in the gospel it refers to the Spirit to be sent upon Jesus' departure. In the epistle "light" is related to God, whereas in the gospel the term relates to Jesus. In the epistle much is made of the death of Jesus being an expiation (1:7; 2:2; 4:10), but the gospel interprets Jesus' death as the unleashing of a tremendous power for transformation and life. There are other differences, but these will suffice to make the point. Even though the style and language are similar so as to suggest a common origin, the theology is so dissimilar as to argue against a common authorship *per se*. It is, therefore, probable that this letter (and the two others) were written by a person other than the author of the Fourth Gospel even though they shared a common tradition and originated from the same "school."

The purpose of the writing of the epistles was to combat a gnostic type teaching that denied Jesus had come in the flesh and also argued for a lifestyle that was alien to the Christian tradition. The place of writing and the destination are probably the same, either the churches around Ephesus or the Christians in Alexandria or, more likely, the churches in an area of Syria.

1 John is not really a letter, but it is neither a general tract addressed to all Christendom as some have argued. The author has a specific audience in mind and seems to assume certain common understandings and experiences which they have shared (cf. 1:1--4; 2:1ff.; 2:18ff.; 3:1ff., etc). He wrote to the people as one who has some authority over them and yet who was one of them. His tone of tenderness and rebuke reminds one of a loving parent who really cares about the well-being of the children.

1 John: Outline

The issues that are addressed in this short writing seem to be the problem of the denial of Jesus' true humanity and the problem of ethical behavior. Both of these themes are inter-twined throughout the writings in typical Johannine style. That style is characterized by an issue or problem being raised, spoken to, dropped, and later discussed again. Sometimes this occurred in several contexts in the writing.

The first problem is that of the reality of Jesus' humanity. Almost immediately the reality of the humanity of God's Son is affirmed with an obvious attempt to claim eyewitness support (1:1–4). Further, the false teachers who denied that Jesus had really come in the flesh and that he was truly one with the Father are called "antichrists" (2:18–27). It is interesting that these epistles are the only writings in the New Testament where the term "antichrist" appears; and it does not refer to one person or being but to any and all who deny the reality of the humanity of Jesus and his unique relationship both to the world and to God (cf. also 4:1ff.).

The second problem appears to be a bit more complex, but it basically revolved around ethical behavior. There were, obviously, those who were claiming that, once a person became a Christian, that person could no longer sin. The idea had two possible interpretations: one, that the person actually could not commit an act of sin; or secondly, that the ordinary laws of morals and ethical behavior were transcended for the Christian. To the first of these the author says a resounding NO! As long as the Christian is in this world, given its nature and order, there is no way that a person can escape committing acts of sin (1:8–10). But the Christian need not despair; God will forgive these sins through Christ.

It is also true that becoming a Christian gives a person a new kind of life, eternal life, which is above the level of life in this world. It is a different quality of life that is described as a union between God and the believer where the believer "abides" or "remains" with God in a long term transforming relationship. This is described in 3:6, "no one who abides in him sins; no one who sins has either seen him or knows him." Upon first reading this appears to be contradictory to the comment in 1:8ff. But the difference lies in the fact that the author is speaking to specific acts of sin in 1:8ff., whereas in 3:6ff. he is speaking about a lifestyle that is characterized by continual and habitual sinning. The world as it is structured forces a person to commit acts of sin (which can be forgiven), but the new life with God frees one from constant and continuous enslavement to sin. The Christian, therefore, is a person whose life is basically and primarily characterized by righteousness, not sin. Therefore the Christian is under even greater obligations than other people; thus the author dealt with the second part of the false teaching.

This new life is also characterized by love, specifically love for others within the fellowship of the new community committed to Christ. There is a new commandment for such people, to "love one another" (3:23). This love by its very nature will cast away one of humanity's worst enemies–fear (4:18). Fear is, in reality, the opposite of love, for fear causes hate, jealousy, pettiness, envy, greed, and the like. And the Christian can love, because the Christian has already experienced God's love. In this epistle Christians do have responsibilities for the world, but their primary responsibility is to love each other within the fellowship of the new community of life.

2 John

This second letter is addressed to the "Elect Lady," the church, to warn again against false teachers who deny the importance and the reality of the Son.

2 John: Outline

I. Salutation vv. 1–3
II. Exhortation to Beware of False Teachers vv. 4–11
III. Concluding Remarks vv. 12–13

This is as close to a "pure" letter as there is in the New Testament (cf. also 3 John). The warning is given to the people not to be misled by those who deny the Christ, i.e., deny the reality of his humanity. The author indicates that there is more to be said, but he will say it in person (v. 12).

3 John

This letter is addressed to a specific person, Gaius, who is probably a leader of some sort in the church where he is. In this instance there is a certain person, Diotrephes, who is ambitious and who is trying to undermine the authority of the "elder."

3 John: Outline

I. Salutation v. 1
II. Thanksgiving vv. 2–8
III. Warning Against Diotrephes vv. 9–12
IV. Concluding Remarks vv. 13–15

This letter praises Gaius, who has by his life testified to the truth and has assisted many persons within the church and some without (vv. 2–8). The author has warnings about Diotrephes whose ambition is such that he can tolerate no persons around him who disagree with him (vv. 9–10).

As with 2 John, the writer wished to say more but decides that it was best to speak in person.

The Gospel of John

Most of the major critical problems connected with the Fourth Gospel have already been discussed. The primary issue for consideration here is the question as to why John (the author will be designated "John" without specificity as to his identity) wrote the gospel. And further, why did he write it as he did, since it is so very different from the Synoptics?

In all probability the book was written more precisely to a specific problem or problems in the churches of the area in which it originated. It has already been seen that these problems concerned a docetic interpretation of Jesus and the emphasis upon a lifestyle that was alien to the traditions of the church. That much seems to be clear because the gospel as it is written speaks quite directly to those issues.

But why another gospel? Would not a letter or a general homily have sufficed for such a purpose? In all probability, if those were the only factors involved, a letter or a general homily would have been sufficient. There seems to have been, however, some other factors which were also involved. One of these factors may well have been to preserve those traditions about Jesus that had come to these people and had been treasured and developed by them. These traditions, for whatever reason, seem to have been in some way connected with the Apostle John. It would have been unthinkable to allow these traditions to be lost. They were, therefore, used in the composition of this gospel as a means of preserving these particular traditions as well as speaking to the immediate problems at hand.

The methodology used by the author of this work is intriguing, to say the least. The gospel appears to have been consciously written on two levels: (1) a literalistic or materialistic level on which the people in the gospel understood the acts and teachings of Jesus and, (2) a higher or spiritual level at which Jesus intended his followers to understand. To illustrate, the reader finds that the gospel is filled with episodes in which an incident or a teaching could be interpreted quite literally (and was), but the author points the reader beyond that level to the higher level of understanding. To accomplish this motif almost everyone in the Fourth Gospel except Jesus appears to be an absolute numbskull. Even the most obvious points are taken quite literally so that the higher understanding can be made clear in a discourse like teaching given by Jesus. For example, in the Nicodemus story Jesus says to Nicodemus, "You must be born *añothen.*" The word *añothen* in the Greek can mean either "from above" or "again." In this setting Nicodemus understood the story quite literally, almost crudely! But this gave Jesus the opportunity to give a discourse on what it means to be born "from above," born of the Spirit. Another aspect of this same motif can be seen in that the miracles in this gospel are called "signs," and as signs they point beyond themselves as merely "mighty works" to deeper levels of spiritual truth and understanding.

There is, moreover, another theme which runs through the book and permeates the narrative. It is closely linked to the "two levels" motif; it is that the author appeals to the readers to have faith that is not based on external proofs. Throughout the ministry of Jesus as it is depicted in this book, there are numerous "signs" which could be used as a basis for faith on the part of those who saw the "signs" performed. But the author appeals beyond the "sign" for a faith that is *not* based on any external "proofs." Real faith is a new relationship with God made possible through the One God has sent, Jesus the Son. This relationship issues for the believer in what the gospel writer calls "eternal life." This life is not a quantitative matter of life extended *ad infinitum* but rather a qualitative mode of life which transcends the lifestyle and values of this world. Eternal life in John's gospel is a different quality of life given to those who are committed to the Son, and this new life is available to all who will receive it. It is also a *present* possession, something that begins now and continues and which transcends this life and this world because it belongs to the world of God.

When one approaches the portrait of Jesus painted by the Fourth Evangelist, it becomes obvious almost immediately that the Jesus of this gospel and the Jesus of the Synoptic portrait are very different. In the Synoptics Jesus is protrayed as uniquely Son of God, but he is a human being with human emotions and limitations. In the Fourth Gospel even though his humanity is strongly defended, however, the emphasis is upon Jesus' divinity, his origin with God; the Jesus of this gospel has no human needs and shows no human emotions (except perhaps anger). He resists and rejects all attempts to force his hand with the recurring comment, "My hour has not yet come." And when the hour does come, it is Jesus himself who determines that it has. In a sense, the Jesus of this gospel is quite like an actor who is both the director and the star in a movie. Jesus directs the scenes and controls the events even down to the moment of his death!

There are many other differences between the Synoptics and John. In the Synoptics Jesus' ministry lasts only about 6-12 months, is centered primarily in Galilee, and one trip is made to Jerusalem at the conclusion of his life. In John the ministry is at least two to three years (perhaps even three to four), is centered primarily in Jerusalem, with Jesus making frequent visits to that city during the course of his ministry. In the Synoptics Jesus teaches by means of parables and short wisdom sayings, but in the Fourth Gospel he teaches in long involved discourses. In the Synoptics the key to the teaching was the theme, the Kingdom of God, but in John the term Kingdom of God is mentioned very infrequently, the key theme being "eternal life." In the Synoptics the miracles of Jesus were called "mighty works" and witnessed to the idea that the Kingdom of God was present in the life and ministry of Jesus; in John's gospel the miracles are called "signs" and point to theological truths and religious teachings which are part of the "other" level of existence emphasized in this presentation of Jesus and his significance. In the Synoptics exorcism of demons is the most frequent mighty work; in John's gospel there is not a single exorcism. These are the major differences between the protrait of Jesus and his ministry as given in the Synoptics and John. There are numerous other differences at specific points, such as the date of the crucifixion. The Synoptics have Jesus eating the meal with his disciples on Thursday evening, which is the Passover, and Jesus is crucified on the Passover itself. John has Jesus eat a meal on Thursday evening with his disciples, but it is the day *before* the Passover here, and Jesus is crucified at the same time the Passover lambs are being slain. There are quite a few of these differences, some of which will be pointed out in the discussion of the content of the gospel.

This leads to two much debated points connected with the study of this gospel. Did John know the Synoptic gospels? And did John use sources in the composition of his work; and if so, what kind of sources were they? Tremendous controversy still revolves around these points among New Testament scholars; some argue that John used the Synoptics or at least Mark and/or Luke, while others say that John may have been aware of the Synoptic traditions but did not know or use the gospels. Some have postulated sources utilized by the author, such as a "sign" source; and others argue that no such sources existed. There are those who postulate a redactor or redactors who worked on the materials over a period of time, even to the point of speculating about how many stages were involved in getting the book to its present form.

While certainty is not to be found and unanimity among scholars is even less likely in the discussion of these problems, several matters seem to be clear. Even though John may not have known the Synoptic gospels, he certainly was aware of the traditions from which the Synoptics developed. There seems to be no doubt, however, that John basically used traditions that were known to him and which were different from the Synoptic traditions. Just how exact one can be in the isolating of specific sources which may have been used in the composition of this gospel is an open question. And the theories which attempt to explain the steps by which the gospel may have been constructed are quite speculative and incapable of proof.

Some of the answers to these and other questions could be perhaps solved if the real reasons for the writing of this work could be determined. It was already recognized in the early church that John's gospel was different. One theory, espoused by Clement of Alexandria, held that since the Snyoptics portrayed Jesus "historically," John decided to write a "spiritual gospel." Just how that may be interpreted, however, may differ from person to person.

That the gospel is the product of a mind and tradition which had meditated deeply and conscientiously on the underlying meaning of all that Jesus was and continued to be for the church is clear. Perhaps that is all that can be said with any degree of finality about this protrait of Jesus. The most obvious point is that this interpretation of the Christ is simply brilliant.

John: Outline

The Gospel of John begins with a prologue which in essence summarizes the Johannine portrait of Jesus. It is set down as a hymn to the *Logos* (the Greek for "Word"). In earlier times the prologue was relegated to the realm of an afterthought or even a later introduction to the book which really had no connection with the gospel *per se.* It is obvious, however, that the prologue is truly the vehicle which sets the stage for the remainder of the gospel and, in fact, summarizes the Johnnine Christ.

The term *Logos* was well-known in both Jewish and Hellenistic cultures. The creative word of God, the relationship of the creative word with the personification of wisdom, and other such identifications were all part of the Jewish background. In the Hellenistic world also the term was used by several religious or religio-philosophical groups, most especially the Stoics. Scholars have labored long and hard to determine exactly what kind of background ought to be presupposed in attempting to interpret the idea in John's gospel, but it seems best to understand simply that the term was known in both cultures and that John probably used the term because it was familiar. And he gave whatever meaning to the term that he wished to convey rather than allowing the other motifs to determine his meaning. To determine what John meant, one must examine John's own presentation.

If one carefully reads the prologue, it becomes very clear that the two basic elements in the *Logos* idea of John are the creative activity and the revelatory activity of this figure. The two terms that are most prominent here and in the gospel are that Jesus as the *Logos* of God come to earth gives Life and Light. It is only through the *Logos* that life came into the world (1:3), and it is only through the *Logos* that real life can be given now in this world order (cf. 3:16, 6:49ff., and many others). Further, the second function of the *Logos* is to reveal the very nature of God to the world, not simply to show what God is like but to demonstrate what human beings are in their present situation and therefore to challenge them to accept the new life offered through the *Logos.*

While the author was very careful to relate the *Logos* to God from the very beginning, he is just as emphatic in emphasizing that the human Jesus *is* the *Logos.* It is interesting to note that once the author stated that the *"Logos* became flesh" (1:14) he never used the term again. From this point on he designates Jesus as the Son and Messiah sent to give light and life to the world. And the terms used in 1:14–18 (grace and truth) which Jesus brings to the world are in the Old Testament terms that were used exclusively as attributes of God. Jesus, therefore, was God incarnate in a human being to demonstrate to the world what God is like (1:18).

After the prologue the ministry of Jesus begins as in the Synoptics with a brief statement about John the Baptizer. In John's gospel, however, Jesus is not baptized, even though that occurrence seems to be presupposed (1:32–33). After this brief introduction Jesus calls the disciples, some of whom had been disciples of John, and they recognize immediately that he is the Messiah (1:41, 49).

The "Book of Signs" begins in earnest with two episodes, one of which is peculiar to John's gospel and the second which is a Synoptic story retold and replaced in this gospel. The first is the famous story of the wedding at Cana where Jesus changed water into wine. This was a stupendous feat, but the meaning of the story is quite different from a superficial and literalistic interpretation. The key here is that the water, used by the Jews for ritual and ceremonial cleansing symbolic of their religious heritage, is transformed into the best wine. In the Graeco-Roman world and in Jewish thought water and wine were both symbols for life. The point of this story is obviously that Jesus, as the *Logos,* is indeed the dispenser of new life, transforming even the good life, up till now dispensed through Judaism, into something much better. As good as Judaism had been, something better had now come. The first act of the Messiah-Logos was to demonstrate that he could give the best and most potent life.

The second episode, the account of the cleansing of the Temple, is placed at the beginning of Jesus' ministry in this gospel. In the Synoptics Jesus only visited Jerusalem once; therefore, the story could only be related there. In John's gospel Jesus went to Jerusalem on numerous occasions, but John places this incident in the first visit. The story is reinterpreted here, for in the Synoptics the idea seems to be a portrayal of the Messiah come to the Temple to begin the process of God's judgment in accordance with the Old Testament Scriptures (cf. Malachi 3:1ff.). In this gospel the incident is only an introduction to a much deeper and more meaningful religious teaching.

The point of the matter centers in Jesus' saying to the Jews, "Destroy this temple, and in three days I will raise it up" (2:19). They understood the saying quite literally (as almost all do in this gospel), but Jesus was speaking about a new center of worship, i.e., his own resurrected body which would not be restricted by time or space or geographical locale. The center of the old order was the Temple in Jerusalem; the center for the new order would be in the resurrected body of Jesus himself. It is interesting that the author included the comment that the disciples did not understand this saying until after the resurrection!

In chapter three the well-known story of Jesus and Nicodemus is recounted where Nicodemus totally misunderstood Jesus so that Jesus could give a long discourse on what it means to be born of the Spirit. Chapter four takes place in Samaria where Jesus offers the Samaritan woman "living water" which, if she would drink, would enable her never to thirst again. The woman understood very literalistically again (4:11, 15) which directed the discussion toward what true worship is and where it is enacted. The episode in chapter five revolves around the identity of the real, authentic ("true") Son of God, and chapter six uses the traditional story of the feeding of the multitude as the occasion for Jesus to announce that he is the living bread, and only he can give real life. This again is the use of a Synoptic story with a different emphasis and meaning in this gospel.

In chapter seven the scene is that of the Jewish feast of Booths (Tabernacles) which commemorates the time of the wilderness wandering. During this occasion there are two very important rituals which are preformed, one a pouring out of water to recall how Yahweh gave the people of Israel water in the desert, and the other a period of darkness followed by the lighting of candles to commemorate the pillar of fire which accompanied them on the journey. Against this background Jesus goes to the feast and announces, "If any one thirst, let him come to me and drink" (7:37), and "I am the light of the world; he who follows me will not walk in darkness, but will have the light of life" (8:12). The reader cannot help but be struck with the twin themes of the gospel again, life and light, creation and revelation, and how Jesus transcends the old religious traditions of Judaism.

Immediately following the discourse and the ensuing discussion about Jesus being the light of the world, John introduces a story peculiar to his gospel–the healing of a man born blind. The "light of the world" gives sight to a man blind from birth, but that is not really the crux of the story. The man who was healed does not really "see" until he learns who the Son of Man is and commits his life to that Son of Man (9:35–38). Again the physical and material are important, but there is something which transcends that level of being and understanding.

The Book of Signs is now rushing towards its dramatic climax. In chapter ten Jesus gives a discourse on being the good shepherd who cares for the sheep, knows the sheep by name, and lays down his life for the sheep. In chapter eleven he does just that. His friend Lazarus has become ill, but Jesus lingered where he was for two days. He returned then to bring Lazarus back from his "sleep" which the disciples again interpreted literally (11:11–15). The story has in a sense two climaxes: one, Jesus' statement to Martha in which it becomes very clear that real, authentic life is not bounded by materialistic restraints and restrictions (11:25–26); and second, the actual raising of Lazarus and the subsequent response of the people.

One of the most interesting aspects of this story concerns the emotions of Jesus as he saw the reaction of the people and the sisters to Lazarus' death. The translations are usually misleading here, for verse 33 literally reads in the Greek, " . . . he snorted like a horse in anger, and he shook himself up!" In other words Jesus was angry, not overwhelmed with compassion or grief. The people standing around again misunderstood by saying, "See how he loved him!" (11:36). The point that John seems to be attempting to project to the readers is that there is a more important life to be concerned about than simply physical existence. For these people to stand in the very presence of the One who could dispense real life and to weep over the loss of physical existence and not be able to understand that there was something far more important than that in this world was the epitome of the lack of human understanding about spiritual matters. It is not the quantity of life that is important but the quality. "I am the resurrection and the life; he who believes in me, though he die, yet shall he live, and whoever lives and believes in me shall never die." (11:25–26).

To drive home the point that physical wonders do not form the basis of faith, John related the response to this stupendous sign. Some did believe, but many did not and told the religious leaders what had occurred. At this point the religious leaders made the decision that Jesus must die.

It is in chapter twelve that Jesus decided that the "hour has come." Up till this time he has constantly had to restrain and silence others who wanted him to do something dramatic. But on each occasion he told them that his hour had not yet come. Now it has. There is no Gethsemene in John's gospel, the closest parallel being Jesus' comment in 12:27. "Now is my soul troubled. And what shall I say? 'Father, save me from this hour' ? No, for this purpose I have come to this hour. Father, glorify thy name." The dramatic incident is about ready to become reality, but it will be death on a cross not a glorious display of power and might.

The next major portion of the gospel is centered in the discourses Jesus has with his disciples at the time of the last meal they eat together. In John's gospel this is not Passover but the day before the Passover. In these chapters (13–16) there are several themes that are intertwined throughout the discussion which Jesus has with his disciples. The new commandment to love one another, the emphasis upon the Paraclete (John's term for the Spirit) which will come when Jesus leaves them, the intimate relationship that exists between the believer and Jesus, and the enmity of the world towards those who are allied to the Christ are all discussed in these discourses.

Most of these themes are self-evident upon reading the text, but there is a subheading of one, the intimate relationship between the believer and the Christ, which speaks to a new understanding of eschatology. This point is very important because many commentators feel that John has reinterpreted the eschatology of the early church from an externalistic, apocalyptic, materialistic understanding to an internalistic, spiritualistic, individualistic viewpoint. It is true that in John's gospel the emphasis is upon the present time for the possession of the new life, but there are a few instances where the older ideas have been retained (at least on the surface); cf. 5:28f.

One of the most usually cited references when arguing that John has changed the earlier eschatology of the church is the passage in 14:1ff. This is usually interpreted to mean that the "coming" of Jesus is now seen as his "coming" to a believer at the time of death. And the emphasis on the idea of the Christian suffering persecution in this world and being sustained by the Spirit is interpreted as the author's understanding that Christians must look for the long-range purpose in such activity. This would indicate that the idea of an imminent Parousia has been given up (cf. especially 15:18ff.; 16:1ff.; 16:33). The tone of the discourses does seem to point in that direction.

Even more pointed is the famous prayer of Jesus related in chapter 17. In numerous verses the long-range development of the church and the individual is emphasized (cf. 17:11; 17:20ff.), and in this prayer a definition of eternal life is given. "And this is eternal life, that they know [i.e., experience in daily living, make a commitment to, or covenant with] thee the only true God, and Jesus Christ whom thou has sent." (17:3)

The time has now come for the Passion narrative; and as with the remainder of this gospel Jesus directs the scenario. When the soldiers come to arrest Jesus, he asks them whom they are seeking. They tell him, "Jesus of Nazareth." When Jesus replies, "I am he," they fall to the ground! Only when Jesus allows them to take him are they able to do what they are sent out to do. The incidents in John's Passion narrative are quite similar to those of the Synoptics, but there are some Johannine emphases present. For example, Pilate does not understand what "truth" has to do with this trial (18:38), interpreting Jesus' comment literally instead of understanding the real meaning.

It is interesting that in John's version of the trial Pilate has Jesus scourged in an attempt to satisfy the mob. In the Synoptics the scourging is part of the sentence of death, but here the beating has a different meaning. It is perhaps John's way of further placing "the Jews" in a very bad light. The intensity of this feeling in this gospel must reflect some very severe conflicts with a Jewish community or communities in the area to which the gospel was directed.

Some incidents peculiar to John's Passion narrative include the fact that Jesus was slain at the time when the Passover lambs were being slain, the direction of Jesus to the "beloved disciple" to care for Jesus' mother, and the incident about the spear being thrust into Jesus' side. The outcome was the same. An innocent man was cruelly executed as a criminal, died quickly, and was placed in a nearby tomb. When Jesus died, he said, "It [his work] has been brought to completion" (19:30, paraphrase), and he even sent his spirit away at the moment of his death (19:30). In this gospel the cross is the throne for the *Logos*.

The resurrection appearances differ in each gospel. John's accounts are quite in keeping with his usual emphases. When Mary recognized Jesus in the garden, she was told not to cling to the body she can see or touch. It is only the resurrected body of the *Logos* that is to form the basis of faith. Jesus then appeared to his disciples and gave them the gift of the Spirit on the same day of his resurrection (cf. Luke–Acts).

The climax of the gospel comes in the scene with Thomas who was absent when the first appearance was made. Jesus appeared and told Thomas to put his finger and hand into the wounds; and Thomas confessed, "My Lord and My God!" Many feel that this is the great confession, i.e., Jesus as Lord and God, toward which John has been moving, but this recognition has already been made from the very first of the gospel. The real climax comes in reality in the next verse; this is the important challenge that John has been attempting to set before his readers and hearers. "Have you believed because you have seen me? Blessed are those who have not seen and yet believe." (20:29) The appeal for faith that is not based upon external signs comes to full force at this point. Real faith cannot be based on external signs but must rest upon a personal relationship with and commitment to the One who gives real life, eternal life, the life that transcends the values and traditions of this world. It is the kind of life that even physical death cannot extinguish.

The conclusion of the book then comes quickly in 20:30–31, and John gives the reason for his writing:

> Now Jesus did many other signs in the presence of the disciples, which are not written in this book; but these are written that you may believe that Jesus is the Christ, the Son of God, and that believing you may have life in his name.

It is almost universally agreed that chapter 21 is a later addition to the original work. The purpose in the addition to the book is at least in part to verify that the tradition upon which the gospel rested was that of an eyewitness (21:24). And further there is the attempt to explain why "that disciple," in all probability John, had died. There was a tradition in the early church that held that John would live until the Parousia. Obviously, he had not, and the comment which is given here is that Jesus did not really say that he *would* remain till he came but only, "If it is my will that he remain until I come, . . ." 21:21–23).

In spite of all the critical problems connected with the Fourth Gospel, it remains as one of the greatest interpretations and understandings of Jesus and his real significance recorded in the entire New Testament.

Suggestions for Further Study

The Johannine Epistles

Rudolf Bultmann. *The Johannine Epistles.* Translated by R. P. O'Hara. Philadelphia: Fortress Press, 1973. Hermeneia.

C. H. Dodd. *The Johannine Epistles.* New York: Harper & Row, 1946. The Moffatt New Testament Commentary.

James L. Houlden. *A Commentary on the Johannine Epistles.* London: A. & C. Black, 1973.

Robert Law. *The Tests of Life: A Study of the First Epistle of St. John.* Edinburgh: T. & T. Clark, 1909.

The Gospel of John
C. K. Barrett. *The Gospel According to St. John.* Second edition. Philadelphia: Westminster Press, 1978.

Raymond E. Brown. *The Gospel According to John: Introduction, Translation and Notes.* Garden City, New York: Doubleday & Co., 1966 and 1970. 2 vols. Anchor Bible.

Rudolf Bultmann. *The Gospel of John: A Commentary.* Translated by G. R. Beasley-Murray. Philadelphia: Westminster Press, 1971.

J. C. Fenton. *The Gospel According to John.* Oxford: Clarendon Press, 1970. New Clarendon Bible.

R. H. Lightfoot. *St. John's Gospel: A Commentary.* Edited by C. F. Evans. Oxford: Clarendon Press, 1956.

J. L. Martyn. *History and Theology in the Fourth Gospel.* New York: Harper & Row, 1968.

Leon Morris. *The Gospel According to St. John.* Grand Rapids, Michigan: Wm. B. Eerdmans Publishing Co., 1971.

J. N. Sanders. *A Commentary on the Gospel According to St. John.* Edited and completed by B. A. Mastin. New York: Harper & Row, 1968.

D. M. Smith. *John.* Philadelphia: Fortress Press, 1976. Proclamation Commentaries.

Conclusion

The fundamental purpose of this book has been to introduce the uninitiated student to the books of the New Testament in their historical setting and to demonstrate how scholarly critical procedures can assist in interpreting the content of these books. Many more problems, theories, and methods could have been discussed but have been omitted not because they are unimportant but because they were beyond the realm of the task which we set for ourselves.

There was, for example, no attempt to deal with the problems of inspiration or authority or the concept of revelation. That is perhaps best left to the theologian! What was basically aimed at here was involving the student with the meaning of the content of the New Testament writings. With the background offered here the student can certainly begin a pilgrimage of investigation into many other aspects of New Testament study which may lead in literally hundreds of directions. And that pilgrimage can certainly be challenging as well as both fascinating and rewarding.

Perhaps two points should be presented briefly for the benefit of the reader before concluding this work. First of all, there is the question concerning the problem of the New Testament *canon* (the list of which books were ultimately considered authoritative). Just how did the early church come to decide upon these twenty-seven documents as being authoritative and normative for their religious faith and practice?

It is, of course, only reasonable to understand that we cannot recover all of the thinking and history which finally produced the canon as we have it. But we can at least in a general way understand the history of the development.

First of all, it must be understood that each of the New Testament writings had a separate and unique origin and history. These pieces of literature were designed specifically for settings and contexts which had particular and peculiar needs which the documents attempted to meet. (We have already investigated that part of the matter!) One must not be misled into thinking that these documents were the only documents produced by the early Christian community. Much literature was being written and circulated, most of which did not ultimately become a part of the New Testament canon.

These writings then originally circulated individually and were preserved quite likely by individual churches. In all probability the first New Testament documents to be collected together were the Pauline letters. Exactly when this took place is simply not known, but in all likelihood it happened sometime late in the first century A.D. Then somewhat later the four gospels were collected together. After that a third collection probably came into existence which contained Acts and the Catholic Epistles, and at times Revelation.

By the end of the second century A.D. most of the writings which were later to be formally accepted as canonical were basically used and considered to be authoritative by the majority of the Christian churches. Certain of the writings had some difficulty, however, in being accepted by all geographical areas of the church specifically Hebrews, 2 Peter, James, Jude, 2, 3 John, and Revelation. In fact, through the years various "canons" were drawn up partly in response to the practical needs of the developing church and partly in response to "heretical" persons or groups who used certain writings in ways thought to be detrimental to the life and purity of the Christian faith.

Finally, in 367 A.D. a church leader at Alexandria named Athanasias wrote a letter setting out the twenty-seven books which he thought were authoritative. By the end of that century the church at large had generally accepted these books as authoritative for the Christian faith. Exactly why these books were finally selected may not ever be known, humanly speaking, but these twenty-seven were the writings which were believed both in terms of authorship (apostolic or closely related to apostles) and in terms of direction and guidance in spiritual matters and Christian lifestyle to be normative for the religion of the followers of Jesus, whom they believed to be uniquely Son of God.

The second point which deserves to be emphasized concerns the centrality of the idea of resurrection for understanding the essence of New Testament religion. This discussion must begin, naturally, with the resurrection of Jesus. Even though it has already been emphasized that the resurrection by itself should not be interpreted as *proof* that the church's interpretation of Jesus was correct, nevertheless this event lay at the heart of the early church's proclamation about Jesus and his significance. It is *the* event without which the Christian church and the New Testament would never have come into being.

The first question that comes to our minds when we hear about the resurrection concerns what "really happened" in this event. And much time and effort have been expended through the years in attempts to sort out what really happened. But the honest truth is that no one really knows the answer to that question. There were no eyewitnesses to the resurrection *per se*. And the New Testament writings themselves do not give us a consistent picture of the events surrounding that occurrence. In fact, it is very difficult to find consistency among the stories and accounts which relate to the resurrection event!

The earliest reaction on the part of Jesus' disciples and followers to the resurrection, according to the stories, seems to have been bewilderment. The disciples of Jesus even failed to recognize him; and when they did, they were afraid and did not believe. It was because of the report of the women (according to all four gospels) about the empty tomb that the disciples were alerted to the fact that something curious had transpired. The women had found the tomb empty. Some scholars have held that the report about the empty tomb was a later invention by the church to explain (or to help in explaining) the resurrection appearances. But the stories about the empty tomb seem to be authentic and part of the earlier strata of tradition. In the church the empty tomb was a puzzlement; it did not explain the resurrection. Rather it was the resurrection that explained the empty tomb!

If one examines the resurrection stories and traditions carefully, one can detect certain tendencies at work in the transmission of the material relating to that event. For example, there is the obvious attempt to push the report of the women into the background since women were not allowed in those days to give testimony. Further, there is the attempt to make Peter the central character in the traditions concerning the resurrection (from the human perspective). Other motifs may also be detected and/or conjectured.

The tendency, however, on the part of modern thinkers to emphasize only the sheer historicality of "what really happened," or to analyze the factors at work in the transmission of the material, causes many to miss the very point which the early church emphasized. These people did not understand exactly what had happened or how it had happened. But the important point for them was that God had done a mighty thing. This involved not simply the raising of someone who had died, but more importantly it actualized for them the triumph of life over death. God can and had and would *overcome* death! This was a theological interpretation which affirmed that God's kingdom and justice and righteousness and mercy are the only things in this world that are of ultimate significance and importance. The power of sin, so fearful and horrible for the world in general and human beings in particular, had been broken. The resurrection was the affirmation that life is the natural order in this world, not death; that good is the lasting and ultimately triumphant entity in creation, not evil; that God is in control of his universe, not Satan.

God had triumphed over the worst that the sinful and demonic forces of this world could impose on his messenger. It was the nature and the character of that messenger that caused the early church leaders to affirm that Jesus was uniquely God's Son. It was not simply the resurrection by itself, but *who* had been raised that was of significance to them. The resurrection was important and meaningful because of what Jesus had done, had said, what he was as a Person living in this world, and what the consequences of the resurrection event were. Jesus had been a Person totally devoted and dedicated to God; he had a quality of life and experience of

God that no one else had ever had. Yet he said that this new life and new relationship with God was available to all people. This new life is different; it is lasting. And this was demonstrated dramatically and convincingly by the resurrection of Jesus. His resurrection was unique; but it pointed, beyond the shadow of a doubt to these people, to the fact that physical death no longer was to be feared by those who knew God intimately. The quality of life that was created by this new relationship with God could never be snuffed out by sin or evil or even death. The new relationship established between God and human beings could not be eradicated or abruptly halted by anything in all creation—not even physical death.

The death that is to be feared is, in reality, the "second death" (as the author of Revelation called it). This is the death that is of ultimate significance because the situation which it depicts is that of human beings irrevocably cut off from the source of real life, namely God. These early Christians did not understand all the mysteries involved in these matters, but they trusted God and really believed that there was a better way for people to live, a way freed from sin, hate, fear, lust, greed, war, and all those things that cause human misery. These things are not God's will for the world. Life, peace, health, happiness, care and concern for all of God's people and creatures, love, hope, all of which stem from faith (i.e., trust in God), these are the things God wants for his creatures. The basic message which they proclaimed to the world, then, was the message of the meaning of the resurrection; it was the message about *new life.*

People may argue over theological niceties and orthodox doctrines, but what really mattered to the early Christians was the quality of one's life which could be transformed through a new relationship with God. This is what the resurrection meant to these people. To argue over the exact details of what happened is to miss the point. Even though they were confused and troubled and baffled by what had transpired among them, they did not miss the essential point.

The Easter faith proclaimed by the early Christians, and for which many of them literally gave their lives, affirmed that God not human beings as they are apart from God, righteousness not sin, justice not injustice, love not fear and hate, are the true realities in this world. This proclamation sharply differentiated between those who chose to live out an empty and false existence, chained to this world order and its value system, and those who chose to share in the fullness of the true existence now made available through Jesus, the Messiah of God.

They believed that ultimately all people devote and dedicate their lives to something; they urged all people, therefore, to devote and dedicate their lives as living sacrifices to the God revealed in Jesus. To them it was only from such a sacrifice that there could be resurrection to real life.

The resurrection then is central to New Testament theology, for that concept emphasizes that there is a new order of life now available to all. The "proof" for the early Christians revolved around Jesus of Nazareth and the *totality and quality* of his life which was affirmed by God through his resurrection. That same power of God is available to all who will accept it.

So they believed; so they proclaimed; and so they wrote. The New Testament documents were truly written from faith for faith.

Suggestions for Further Study

Books on Canon **Kurt Aland.** *The Problem of the New Testament Canon.* London: A. R. Mowbray, 1962.

B. M. Metzger. *The Text of the New Testament: Its Transmission, Corruption and Restoration.* New York: Oxford University Press, 1964.

C. F. D. Moule. *The Birth of the New Testament.* Second edition. London: Black, 1966.

Alexander Souter. *The Textual Canon of the New Testament.* Second edition. Revised by C. S. C. Williams. London: Gerald Ducksworth, 1965.
Books on the New Testament Apocrypha
E. Hennecke. *New Testament Apocrypha.* Edited by W. Schneemelcher. Translated by R. McL. Wilson. 2 vols. Philadelphia: Westminster Press, 1963.

M. R. James, editor. *The Apocryphal New Testament.* Oxford: Clarendon Press, 1924. An older but very useful work.

For books dealing with the resurrection, see the bibliographical listing at the conclusion of Chapter III, p. 84.

Bibliography

In order to study the New Testament in depth, certain resources are available and are listed below for further investigation. Note that these are sources to be consulted in addition to the works cited at the conclusion of each chapter in this book.

General Works

Bible Atlases:

Oxford Bible Atlas. H. G. May, ed. New York: Oxford University Press, 1962.

The Westminster Historical Atlas to the Bible. Revised edition. G. E. Wright and F. V. Filson, editors. Philadelphia: Westminster Press, 1956.

Bible Dictionaries:

Dictionary of the Bible. James Hastings, editor. Revised edition by F. C. Grant and H. H. Rowley. New York: Charles Scribner's Sons, 1963.

Interpreter's Dictionary of the Bible. G. A. Buttrick et al., editors. 4 volumes. New York: Abingdon Press, 1962. *Supplementary Volume,* 1976.

One-Volume Bible Commentaries:

Interpreters One Volume Commentary on the Bible. Charles M. Laymon, ed. Nashville: Abingdon Press, 1971.

The Jerome Biblical Commentary. R. E. Brown, J. A. Fitzmyer, and R. E. Murphy, editors. Englewood Cliffs, New Jersey: Prentice-Hall Inc., 1968.

Peake's Commentary on the Bible. Revised edition. M. Black and H. H. Rowley, editors. New York: Thomas Nelson & Sons, 1962.

Books that survey the history of New Testament scholarship:

R. H. Fuller. *The New Testament in Current Study.* New York: Charles Scribner's Sons, 1962.

A. M. Hunter. *Interpreting the New Testament: 1900 –1950.* Philadelphia: Westminster Press, 1951.

W. G. Kümmel. *The New Testament: The History of the Investigation of Its Problems.* Translated by S. Maclean Gilmour and H. C. Kee. Nashville: Abingdon Press, 1972.

Stephen Neill. *The Interpretation of the New Testament: 1861 –1961.* London: Oxford University Press, 1964.

New Testament Introductions

W. D. Davies. *Invitation to the New Testament: A Guide to Its Main Witnesses.* Garden City, New York: Doubleday & Co., 1966.

Donald Juel with J. S. Ackerman and T. S. Warshaw. *An Introduction to New Testament Literature.* Nashville: Abingdon Press, 1978. An attempt to deal with the New Testament as literature, but it is basically limited to the gospels.

H. C. Kee, F. W. Young, and K. Froehlich. *Understanding the New Testament.* Third edition. Englewood Cliffs, New Jersey: Prentice-Hall Inc., 1973.

N. Perrin. *The New Testament: An Introduction.* New York: Harcourt, Brace, Jovanovich, 1974.

James L. Price. *Interpreting the New Testament.* Second edition. New York: Holt, Rinehart, and Winston, Inc., 1971.

J. A. T. Robinson. *Redating the New Testament.* Philadelphia: Westminster Press, 1976.

Samuel Sandmel. *A Jewish Understanding of the New Testament.* New York: University Publishers Inc., 1956. A Jewish perspective.

E. F. Scott. *The Literature of the New Testament.* New York: Columbia University Press, 1932.

R. Spivey and D. M. Smith. *Anatomy of the New Testament.* Second edition. New York: Macmillan Co., 1974.

Two New Testament introductions that are excellent but quite detailed:
W. G. Kümmel. *Introduction to the New Testament.* Revised edition. Translated by H. C. Kee. Nashville: Abingdon Press, 1975.

A. Robert and A. Feuillet. *Introduction to the New Testament.* Translated by P. W. Skehan et al. New York: Desclee, 1965. A Roman Catholic viewpoint.

Books on New Testament Theology

Rudolf Bultmann. *Theology of the New Testament.* 2 vols. Translated by K. Grobel. New York: Charles Scribner's Sons, 1951 –1955.

Hans Conzelmann. *An Outline of the Theology of the New Testament.* Translated by John Bowden. New York: Harper & Row, 1969.

J. Jeremias. *New Testament Theology: The Proclamation of Jesus.* Vol. I. Translated by John Bowden. New York: Charles Scribner's Sons, 1971.

W. G. Kümmel. *The Theology of the New Testament According to Its Major Witnesses: Jesus-Paul-John.* Translated by J. E. Steely. Nashville: Abingdon Press, 1973.

G. E. Ladd. *A Theology of the New Testament.* Grand Rapids, Michigan: Wm. B. Eerdmans Publishing Co., 1974.

Books on Christology:
Oscar Cullmann. *The Christology of the New Testament.* Translated by S. C. Guthrie and C. A. M. Hall. Revised edition. Philadelphia: Westminster Press, 1964.

R. H. Fuller. *The Foundations of New Testament Christology.* New York: Charles Scribner's Sons, 1965.

Series commentaries that are valuable for New Testament study, especially helpful for beginners:
Layman's Bible Commentary. Published by John Knox Press.

The Cambridge Bible Commentary on the New English Bible. Published by Cambridge University Press.

There are numerous intermediate type series that are helpful:
The New Century Bible Series is probably the best and most up-to-date. Published in England by Oliphants and distributed in this country by the Attic Press of Greenwood, S. C.

The New Clarendon Bible Series. Published by the Clarendon Press in Great Britain.

The Harper New Testament Commentary Series. Published by Harper & Row and by A. & C. Black in Great Britain. The volumes in this series are very good.

The Anchor Bible. Published by Doubleday & Co. This series has a few excellent volumes but the series suffers overall from too many volumes presenting highly "unusual" theses.

The New International Commentary on the New Testament. Published by

Wm. B. Eerdmans Publishing Co. This is an excellent series overall and represents the viewpoint of evangelical scholarship.

The Moffatt New Testament Commentaries. Published by Harper & Row in the U.S.A. This is an older series but certain volumes are still quite useful.

Proclamation Commentaries. Published by Fortress Press. This series is designed primarily for pastors. It does not contain a verse by verse commentary but rather topical discussions of the books and recent research.

More difficult series usually requiring some knowledge of Greek:

The International Critical Commentary. Published by T. & T. Clark. This series is somewhat old now but some of the critical scholarship included in the volumes is still quite relevant.

Hermeneia. Published by Fortress Press. An up-to-date and high powered commentary series. The volumes thus far have been of excellent quality.

Glossary

APOCALYPTIC. A type of literary genre and theological ideology current in the time of Jesus. The literature appeared in times of persecution to encourage faithfulness on the part of the persecuted. The thought pattern emphasized the dualistic conflict between the forces of good and the forces of evil. The present age of persecution was dominated by evil, but God would intervene, destroy the persecutor and establish a new age. The literature itself was characterized by elaborate symbolism and imagery.

APOCRYPHA. Literally "hidden" books. The term refers to those books which were also in use at the time of the finalization of the canons of the Old Testament and the New Testament but which were not accepted as part of the authoritative Scriptures. The Old Testament Apocrypha is even more specialized in meaning, referring to those books not accepted into the Jewish canon but found in the Greek versions of the Old Testament.

CANON. Literally a "reed," standard of measure. This term refers to the body of literature accepted as "standard," or authoritative, for a group of believers.

ESCHATOLOGY. This term refers to a "study of the end." It is loosely defined and used by New Testament scholars, some interpreting eschatology as referring only to the end of the world, or the return of Jesus, or the like, while others give a much broader interpretation to the word indicating something of ultimate significance. In the New Testament period many writings referred to the "end," but exactly what each author meant by the "end" has to be determined by a careful study of the writing itself.

FORM-CRITICISM. A methodological discipline used by biblical scholars which concentrates on the oral preservation and transmission of the traditions connected with a group. This methodology is especially useful in studying certain traditions related to the life and teachings of Jesus.

GERMARA. Interpretation of the Mishnah, codified about 500 A.D. The combination of the Mishnah and the Gemara comprises that great body of Jewish literature known as the Talmud.

KERYGMA. The "proclamation" of the early church basically related to the Person and work of Jesus. This proclamation contains the basic religious ideas of the church and was designed to convince the hearer of the truth of these ideas.

MACCABEAN. The era in Jewish history which began with the rebellion of the Jews against the proscription of their religion by Antiochus IV in 168/7 B.C. This fight for independence ultimately was successful in removing the religious ban and won a measure of independence for the Jewish people until the Romans moved into the area ca. 63 B.C.

MIDRASH. A type of scriptural interpretation practiced by the Rabbis during the New Testament era and beyond. It consisted basically in a verse by verse commentary on the books of the Torah.

MISHNAH. Oral interpretation of the Torah current during the New Testament period among the Rabbis. These traditions were codified ca. 200 A.D. and arranged topically in six tractates. As mentioned already the Mishnah coupled with the Gemara comprises the Talmud, the "learning" of the Jewish people.

PAROUSIA. A Greek word that literally means "coming" or "presence." The idea was prevalent in the early church that Jesus would return *soon* to consummate the Kingdom. This belief in Jesus' early return is called the Parousia.

PSEUDEPIGRAPHA. The technical term used to designate the body of literature not accepted as part of the Old Testament canon but which is additional to the books known as the Apocrypha.

REDACTION-CRITICISM. A methodological discipline used by biblical scholars which concentrates on the individual books as wholistic entities. The basic idea is that the author or final redactor of the finished document had certain emphases, motifs, and points to make which caused him to write, structure, and edit the book in such a way as to present his interpretation in the finished product.

SEPTUAGINT. The Greek translation of the Hebrew Old Testament. This project began in the third to second century B.C. in order to make the Jewish scriptures available to Jewish people scattered throughout the Roman Empire who no longer spoke or understood Hebrew. The symbol commonly used to designate this work is LXX, since seventy (or seventy-two) persons were supposed to have been involved in the project.

SYNOPTIC PROBLEM. The name given to the problem of the relationship between Mark, Matthew, and Luke. Why are these three so similar, and why are they also so different?

YAHWEH. The name of God used by the Hebrew people, especially in the earlier Old Testament period. By the New Testament period, however, this name was not used but had been basically replaced by the broader terms "God" and "Lord."